全球减贫与发展经验分享系列

The Sharing Series on Global Poverty
Reduction and Development Experience

非洲减贫与发展年度报告 2024

中国国际减贫中心　编著

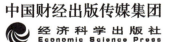

中国财经出版传媒集团

经济科学出版社
Economic Science Press

·北 京·

图书在版编目（CIP）数据

非洲减贫与发展年度报告2024：中文，英文 / 中国
国际减贫中心编著. --北京：经济科学出版社，2024.
7. --ISBN 978-7-5218-6006-1

Ⅰ. F125.4；F140.54

中国国家版本馆CIP数据核字第2024RU0461号

责任编辑：吴　敏
责任校对：易　超
责任印制：张佳裕

非洲减贫与发展年度报告2024

FEIZHOU JIANPIN YU FAZHAN NIANDU BAOGAO 2024

中国国际减贫中心　编著

经济科学出版社出版、发行　新华书店经销

社址：北京市海淀区阜成路甲28号　邮编：100142

总编部电话：010-88191217　发行部电话：010-88191522

网址：www.esp.com.cn

电子邮箱：esp@esp.com.cn

天猫网店：经济科学出版社旗舰店

网址：http：//jjkxcbs.tmall.com

北京季蜂印刷有限公司印装

710×1000　16开　18.25印张　370000字

2024年7月第1版　2024年7月第1次印刷

ISBN 978-7-5218-6006-1　定价：82.00元

《非洲减贫与发展年度报告 2024》
课 题 组

课题组组长　唐丽霞　　刘俊文

课题组成员　李小云　　刘懿锋　　方永新　　周紫升　　骆嫣妮

　　　　　　　　席振华　　宫雅琪　　徐丽萍　　贺胜年　　刘欢欢

　　　　　　　　姚　远　　赵文杰　　刘浩然　　袁柏冰

　　　　　　　　Abdoul Razak Toure　　Aghaton Elias Madonda

　　　　　　　　Zikusooka Harriet Sarah　　Osman Tarawalie

　　　　　　　　Baxter Bwalya Musonda

消除贫困是人类梦寐以求的理想，人类发展史就是与贫困不懈斗争的历史。中国拥有 14 亿人口，是世界上最大的发展中国家，基础差、底子薄，发展不平衡，长期饱受贫困问题困扰。消除贫困、改善民生、实现共同富裕是社会主义的本质要求，是中国共产党的重要使命。为兑现这一庄严政治承诺，100多年来，中国共产党团结带领中国人民，以坚定不移、顽强不屈的信念和意志与贫困进行了长期艰苦卓绝的斗争。改革开放以来，中国实施了大规模、有计划、有组织的扶贫开发，着力解放和发展社会生产力，着力保障和改善民生，取得了前所未有的伟大成就。党的十八大以来，以习近平同志为核心的党中央把脱贫攻坚摆在治国理政的突出位置，习近平总书记亲自谋划、亲自挂帅、亲自督战，推动实施精准扶贫精准脱贫基本方略，动员全党全国全社会力量，打赢了人类历史上规模空前、力度最大、惠及人口最多的脱贫攻坚战。

脱贫攻坚战的全面胜利，离不开有为政府和有效市场的有机结合。八年间，以习近平同志为核心的党中央加强对脱贫攻坚的集中统一领导，发挥中国特色社会主义制度能够集中力量办大事的政治优势，把减贫摆在治国理政的突出位置，为脱贫攻坚提供了坚强政治和组织保证。广泛动员市场、社会力量积极参与，实施"万企帮万村"等行动，鼓励民营企业和社会组织、公民个人参与脱贫攻坚，促进资金、人才、技术等要素向贫困地区集聚。截至 2020 年底，现行标准下 9899 万农村贫困人口全部脱贫，832 个贫困县全部摘帽，12.8 万个贫困村全部出列，区域性整体贫困得到解决，完成了消除绝对贫困的艰巨任务，建成了世界上规模最大的教育体系、社会保障体系、医疗卫生体系，实现了快速发展与大规模减贫同步、经济转型与消除绝对贫困同步。

一直以来，中国始终是世界减贫事业的积极倡导者、有力推动者和重要贡献者。按照世界银行国际贫困标准，改革开放以来，中国减贫人口占同期全球减贫人口 70% 以上，占同期东亚和太平洋地区减贫人口的 80%。占世界人口近五分之一的中国全面消除绝对贫困，提前 10 年实现联合国 2030 年可持续发展议程的减贫目标，不仅是中华民族发展史上具有里程碑意义的大事件，也是人类减贫史乃至人类发展史上的大事件，为全球减贫事业发展和人类发展进步作出了重大贡献。

中国立足自身国情，把握减贫规律，走出了一条中国特色减贫道路，形成了中国特色反贫困理论，创造了减贫治理的中国样本。坚持以人民为中心的发展思想，坚定不移走共同富裕道路，是扶贫减贫的根本动力。坚持把减贫摆在治国理政突出位置，从党的领袖到广大党员干部，目标一致、上下同心，加强顶层设计和战略规划，广泛动员各方力量积极参与，完善脱贫攻坚制度体系，保持政策连续性稳定性。坚持用发展的办法消除贫困，发展是解决包括贫困问题在内的中国所有问题的关键，是创造幸福生活最稳定的途径。坚持立足实际推进减贫进程，因时因势因地制宜，不断调整创新减贫的策略方略和政策工具，提高贫困治理效能，精准扶贫方略是打赢脱贫攻坚战的制胜法宝，开发式扶贫方针是中国特色减贫道路的鲜明特征。坚持发挥贫困群众主体作用，调动广大贫困群众积极性、主动性、创造性，激发脱贫内生动力，使贫困群众不仅成为减贫的受益者，也成为发展的贡献者。

脱贫攻坚战取得全面胜利后，中国政府设立了5年过渡期，着力巩固拓展脱贫攻坚成果，全面推进乡村振兴。按照党的二十大部署，在以中国式现代化全面推进中华民族伟大复兴的新征程上，中国正全面推进乡村振兴，建设宜居宜业和美乡村，向着实现人的全面发展和全体人民共同富裕的更高目标不断迈进。中国巩固拓展脱贫成果和乡村振兴的探索和实践，将继续为人类减贫和乡村发展提供新的中国经验和智慧，为推动构建没有贫困的人类命运共同体贡献中国力量。

面对国际形势新动向新特征，习近平总书记提出"一带一路"倡议、全球发展倡议等全球共同行动，将减贫作为重点合作领域，致力于推动构建没有贫困、共同发展的人类命运共同体。加强国际减贫与乡村发展经验分享，助力全球减贫与发展进程，业已成为全球广泛共识。为此，自2019年起，中国国际减贫中心与比尔及梅琳达·盖茨基金会联合实施国际合作项目，始终坚持站在未来的角度、政策的高度精心谋划项目选题，引领国内外减贫与乡村发展前沿热点和研究走向。始终坚持将中国减贫与乡村发展经验与国际接轨，通过国际话语体系阐释中国减贫与乡村振兴道路，推动中国减贫与乡村发展经验的国际化传播，至今已实施了30余个研究项目，形成了一批形式多样、影响广泛的研究成果，部分成果已在相关国际交流活动中发布。

为落实全球发展倡议，进一步促进全球减贫与乡村发展交流合作，中国国际减贫中心精心梳理研究成果，推出四个系列丛书，包括"全球减贫与发展经验分享系列""中国减贫与发展经验国际分享系列""国际乡村发展经验分享系列"和"中国乡村振兴经验分享系列"。

"全球减贫与发展经验分享系列" 旨在跟踪全球减贫进展，分析全球减贫与发展趋势，总结分享各国减贫经验，为推动联合国2030年可持续发展议程、参与全球贫困治理提供知识产品。该系列主要包括"国际减贫年度报告""国际减贫理论与前沿问题"等全球性减贫知识产品，以及覆盖非洲、东盟、南亚、拉丁美洲及加勒比地区等区域性减贫知识产品。

"中国减贫与发展经验国际分享系列" 旨在讲好中国减贫故事，向国际社会分享中国减贫经验，为广大发展中国家实现减贫与发展提供切实可行的经验。该系列聚焦中国精准扶贫、脱贫攻坚和巩固拓展脱贫攻坚成果的经验做法，基于国际视角梳理形成中国减贫经验分享的知识产品。

"国际乡村发展经验分享系列" 聚焦国际乡村发展历程、政策和实践，比较中外乡村发展经验和做法，为全球乡村发展事业提供交流互鉴的知识产品。该系列主要包括"国际乡村振兴年度报告""乡村治理国际经验比较分析报告""县域城乡融合发展与乡村振兴"等研究成果。

"中国乡村振兴经验分享系列" 聚焦讲好中国乡村振兴故事，及时总结乡村振兴经验、做法和典型案例，为国内外政策制定者和研究者提供参考。该系列主要围绕乡村发展、乡村规划、共同富裕等议题，梳理总结有关政策、经验和实践，基于国际视角开发编写典型案例等。

最后，感谢所有为系列图书顺利付梓付出辛勤汗水的相关项目组、出版社和编辑人员，以及关心和支持中国国际减贫中心的政府机构、高校和科研院所、社会组织和各界朋友。系列书籍得到了比尔及梅琳达·盖茨基金会的慷慨资助以及盖茨基金会北京代表处的悉心指导和帮助，在此表示衷心感谢！

全球减贫与乡村发展是动态的、不断变化的，书中难免有挂一漏万之处，敬请读者指正！

刘俊文

中国国际减贫中心主任

2024 年 1 月

贫困是当今世界面临的全球性挑战。作为贫困发生率最高的大洲，非洲是全球减贫与发展的重点关注区域。21世纪以来，尽管非洲国家经济呈现出快速增长的态势，但仍不能掩盖其区域发展不均衡的事实。一方面，非洲国家的多维贫困问题不断升级，疫情对健康、教育和生活水平方面的挑战十分严峻，改善居民生活状况迫在眉睫。另一方面，非洲国家的粮食安全和营养状况不断恶化，包括自然灾害、疾病、地区冲突和经济困境在内的多重危机导致粮食不安全问题不断加剧。截至2022年，非洲国家的食物不足率和粮食不安全率分别高达19.7%和60.9%，均是全球平均水平的两倍多。更令人担忧的是，在预期寿命、生育率、婴儿死亡率等基本健康状况指标方面，非洲国家仍然远远落后于全球平均水平。

非洲的贫困问题是宏观经济困境、粮食危机、气候变化、地区冲突以及恶劣的自然条件等多种因素共同驱动的结果。其一，缓慢的经济增长难以驱动减贫发展。面对较低的人口城镇化率和较大的人口增长压力，大部分非洲国家人均国民收入仍处于极低水平，加上沉重的债务负担以及低水平的对外投资，导致非洲经济增长动力不强，缓慢的经济增长难以发挥其减贫效益。其二，由于非洲农业生产环境脆弱、粮食生产能力低和农业要素投入不足等，造成非洲主要粮食作物产量不足，粮食安全形势恶化。同时，脆弱的粮食供应体系以及对主要粮食进口的高度依赖，增加了粮食市场的脆弱性以及粮食获得的不稳定性风险。其三，由于应急能力不足和策略不完善，非洲国家难以有效应对全球气候变化带来的冲击，尤其是大范围的干旱及洪水等极端气候对非洲地区的农业生产、粮食安全、基础设施等造成灾难性损害。其四，地区冲突和国际不安全局势造成难民增多，不仅扰乱了经济生产活动和市场，而且阻碍了农村社会发展，加剧了非洲国家的贫困。其五，非洲国家发展的基础条件薄弱，电力、通信、互联网以及基础设施等严重滞后，而较低的人口素质以及不充分的就业状况也在很大程度上阻碍了非洲地区的减贫进程。

　　非洲国家将消除贫困作为经济社会发展的重要议题，并在强化自主发展能力方面做出了诸多努力。在政治方面，非洲国家强化政治民主建设和经济体制改革，提出非洲复兴计划。非洲联盟（简称"非盟"）也提出了"非洲互查机制"来推动成员国的发展。在经济方面，非洲国家领导人制定了"非洲发展新伙伴计划"（NEPAD），并获得了西方国家的支持。非盟制定了《2050年非洲海洋整体战略》，发展蓝色经济。非洲国家因地制宜制定金融战略，推动当地经济发展并为贫困家庭提供资金支持。在区域合作方面，西非国家经济共同体、东非共同体以及南部非洲发展共同体在基础设施、金融、教育、健康、安全等广泛领域推动减贫事业发展。以上减贫实践取得了一定的成效，但是依然存在很多不足：从非洲内部角度看，国家财政能力低下，减贫战略和政策的执行效果差；从非洲对外角度看，非洲国家对国际社会的援助和资金依赖程度较高，外债负担较为沉重。更重要的是，西方援助的附加条件削弱了非洲国家制定减贫战略的自主权，制约了国家治理能力的提升。

　　长期以来，国际社会持续开展对非洲国家的大规模援助。从传统援助主体对非援助来看，发达国家忽视了非洲自身发展需求，援助的领域与非洲所希望的有出入。一方面，西方发展援助较为重视对社会发展领域的支持，缺少对欠发达国家的大型公共基础设施建设和工业发展等的支持；另一方面，对非援助通常以提供软件能力建设为主，较少采取直接提供生产资料援助的方式。这不仅未能促进当地的发展，而且使非洲国家成为对援助依赖程度最高的地区，且由于各种附加条件，非洲国家获得发展援助的成本越来越高。从新兴经济体对非援助来看，中国、印度、巴西等国从传统受援国转型为新兴援助国，成为国际对非援助的重要补充力量。新兴经济体重点对地理区位邻近、社会经济发展相似、资源条件丰富、文化传统相近的非洲地区提供援助，援助资金规模不断增加。此外，新兴经济体依托三方合作机制和峰会外交向非洲提供多层次、多领域、多形式的援助内容，主要以基础设施援助、技术援助、人道主义援助为主。

　　聚焦中国对非援助实践，从合作的基础来看，中国在减贫方面取得了巨大的成就，这些成就根植于长期减贫实践，其中包括宏观经济增长与专项扶贫相辅相成的实践模式。中国的减贫政策具有长期性、连续性和阶段性，同时采用了普惠型与瞄准型政策工具，探索了独特的社会参与扶贫机制，为中非减贫合作提供了坚实的基础。从合作的政策框架来看，主要包含两项内容：一是全球发展合作目标，其中最重要的是联合国可持续发展框架，中国政府将其作为指导国内自身发展和国际发展合作的普遍性政策框架和目标导向；二是中非之间达成的合作战略和框架，包括中非合作论坛及后续行动计划、减贫合作纲要文件等。当前，中非减贫合作主要在中非合作论坛框架下展开，经历了"达成共识—经验分享与机制化—深化合作"三个阶段。从合作的方式来看，合作与交流机制更加成熟，合作内容和形式更加丰富，从减贫经验交流不断拓展到具体的、多领域的合作项目。

鉴于此，未来中非减贫合作应在《中非合作2035年愿景》的指导下，以支持非洲培育内生增长力量为重点，重点关注以下几个方面：第一，持续深化中非减贫合作；第二，积极支持非洲国家减贫和发展能力建设；第三，加强"小而美"的减贫项目合作；第四，继续开展各种形式的减贫交流活动。

目录

Contents

第一章
引　言

一、研究背景与研究意义

（一）研究背景

　　贫困是当今世界面临的全球性挑战，作为贫困发生率最高的大洲，非洲是全球减贫与发展的重点关注地区，消除贫困是非洲国家乃至国际层面的重要议题。在过去数年，新冠疫情、极端气候事件以及经济冲击等增加了整个非洲大陆的社会脆弱性。许多非洲国家同时存在收入过低、严重缺粮、严重债务危机等问题。非洲极端贫困发生率以及极端贫困人口显著上升，减少多维贫困方面的进展倒退，弱势群体和农村地区多维贫困问题尤为突出。联合国开发计划署（UNDP）2023年发布的《全球多维贫困指数》报告显示，大约5.8亿贫困人口生活在撒哈拉以南非洲，诸如南苏丹、赤道几内亚等非洲国家的极端贫困人口比例高于70%。与贫困问题相伴生的是粮食安全和饥饿问题，《2022年世界粮食安全和营养状况》报告显示，2021年1/3的世界饥饿人口（约2.8亿人）生活在非洲，预计到2030年，非洲的食物不足人口将从近2.8亿人增加到超过3.1亿人；非洲地区极端贫困人口将占世界总量的86%，非洲仍将是世界极端贫困人口最集中、贫困发生率最高的地区。加快推动非洲减贫进程是实现联合国2030年可持续发展首要目标"在全世界消除一切形式的贫困"的重要挑战。

　　从国际援助角度来看，对非减贫援助虽然获得广泛关注，但也因非洲减贫进程缓慢而受到质疑。一方面，国际社会对非援助资金主要流向撒哈拉以南非洲，强调良治、促进本土能力建设、加强科技创新、增进就业等项目，对消除贫困、促进可持续发展具有重要意义。例如，在联合国机构的协助和支持下，非洲国家签署《联合国可持续发展合作框架》战略文件，确定了在联合国机构协助下非洲国家减贫和发展的短期目标。另一方面，非洲作为接受国际发展援助总量最大的地区，其经济增长和减贫未有明显的进展，更有学者提出非洲国家长期处于"援助陷阱"之中的观点。非洲大陆尤其是撒哈拉以南非洲正成为世界贫困中心。**此外，国际对非援助的趋势也在不断发生变化。**随着新兴经济体日益积极地向非洲提供援助，中国、印度、巴西等新兴经济体开始成为提供国际发展援助的主力军。与传统的"援助国—受援国"主从关系不同，新兴援助国将自己视为非洲国家的发展伙伴，而非援助国，新发展援助是基于经验共享和知识共同创造的平行过程。新兴经济体在国际对非援助领域的迅猛崛起具有不容忽视的意义，并对以西方传统援助理念为中心的"援助—受援"范式提出了挑战。

从非洲本土减贫战略来看，**以非洲联盟（简称"非盟"）《2063年议程》为导向，非洲国家制定和实施国家减贫和发展战略，但由于国家自主性程度低、国家财政能力不足，导致部分减贫政策难以有效落实。**许多非洲国家制定了相应的国家发展战略和减贫计划以促进增长和减少贫困，如乌干达的"消除贫困行动计划"（PEAP）、刚果（布）的"减贫与增长战略（2022—2026）"等。根据非盟《2063年议程》，非洲国家先后启动非洲大陆自贸区建设、可持续农业创新数字村庄倡议（DVI）等多个项目，以加快基础设施建设。非盟专门制定了一项全面减贫计划——"非洲发展新伙伴计划"，试图通过刺激包容性经济增长、实施经济和体制改革、推动小额信贷机构相关项目、改善营销系统等多种方式，鼓励私营部门投资和促进经济增长，减少非洲大陆的贫困，促进可持续发展。然而，非洲大陆内部经济发展不足、财政能力有限，对国际社会的援助和投资依赖性较强，减贫策略和政策执行效果差。此外，沉重的债务负担以及援助的附加条件限制不断削弱非洲国家制定减贫战略的自主权，制约了其国家治理能力的提升，陷入"有政策没有行动"的困境。

值得关注的是，**减贫是中非合作的重要领域，并在中非合作论坛的框架下取得了显著成效。**自改革开放以来，中国在减贫方面取得了显著成效，并致力于为全球减贫与发展贡献中国力量，尤其是对贫困问题最严重的非洲国家。中非合作论坛是中非合作的重要机制化框架和交流平台，在该框架下中非减贫合作经历了共识达成、经验交流以及实质合作三个阶段的发展。随着中非减贫与发展合作的深入，逐步建立以中非合作论坛为总体框架的政府间、社会间多层次减贫与乡村发展对话机制，减贫合作领域从减贫经验交流拓展到基础设施建设、人力资源培训、农业合作、债务减免等多个领域，减贫合作的关注焦点也从"减贫合作"拓展到"减贫与乡村发展"。当前，中非减贫合作已从经验分享迈向经验转移，更加关注中国减贫经验在非洲国家的适用性和可推广性。未来，中非合作将根据《中非合作2035年愿景》确定的目标任务，继续以支持非洲培育内生增长能力为重点，以促进中非合作转型升级、提质增效为主线，巩固传统合作，开辟新兴领域，创新合作模式，推动中非共建"一带一路"高质量发展。

疫情后面临非洲贫困程度日益加深的现状，需要进一步梳理非洲贫困的基本状况，分析非洲发展落后的主要原因，并在国际发展的视角下系统整理与分析国际社会对非援助的主体、规模、特点，阐明非洲本土宏观战略和政策演变、减贫议题及其实施效果等重点内容，以便进一步优化和完善中国对非减贫合作策略，更好分享中国巩固拓展脱贫攻坚成果以及推进乡村振兴战略的有益经验，持续推动中非减贫合作在全球变局中稳步发展，有效应对全球性减贫发展问题。

（二）研究意义

通过梳理非洲贫困现状、减贫进展、国际对非援助以及中国对非援助的总体信息与关键案例，一是及时了解并更新非洲国家减贫的需求、基本理念、宏观战略和主要政策等方面的演变及未来发展方向；二是呈现和分析国际对非援助的基本合作情况、关注领域以及援助实践中面临的问题；三是明确中国开展对非国际减贫援助的基本架构和援助特点，为深化中非减贫与发展合作伙伴关系提供必要支撑，把握中非合作的机遇和挑战，为中非开展务实合作提供指导，制定符合双方利益和需求的合作方案，推进"一带一路"建设和新型南南合作发展。

总体而言，梳理和总结非洲减贫与发展的最新进展、对非国际发展合作项目的成效，有助于增进国际发展合作机构对非洲贫困现状和减贫需求的了解，为国际社会制定更有效、可持续的对非援助政策和项目提供依据和指导，促进非洲减贫与发展。同时，非洲是中国共建"一带一路"倡议和推进南南合作的重要合作伙伴，本研究可以帮助中国更好地开展国际减贫合作，总结与传播中国减贫经验和模式，为推动全球减贫治理贡献中国方案和中国智慧，提升中国在国际减贫领域的影响力，助力构建人类命运共同体。

二、研究目标与方法

（一）研究目标

本书主要从三个层次对非洲减贫与发展进行研究。第一，结合宏观政策文件、统计数据、学术研究成果等内容，分析梳理当前非洲尤其是撒哈拉以南非洲地区减贫的基本情况；第二，通过对相关文献和重要案例的梳理，总结国际社会对非援助的主要进展，分析西方发达国家、新兴经济体对非国际援助的做法、特点及其减贫效应，并对不足之处进行剖析；第三，结合中国脱贫攻坚与乡村振兴的有益经验，思考中国与非洲减贫合作的重点与优势，在全球发展倡议与中非合作论坛框架下，擘画中非减贫合作前景与策略。

（二）研究方法

为实现上述研究目标，本书主要采用文献资料分析法、案例研究法、预测分析法等方法，并有效运用相关数据以充分展示非洲减贫发展现状。一是通过文献资料，进行宏观分析。通过文献资料的搜集与整理，对非洲减贫进程、非洲减贫议题相关的数据、理论、主要关注点等内容进行梳理，深入刻画非洲减贫图景，为非洲贫困现状及其驱动因素提供重要依据。同时，结合对国际组织数据、非洲本土减贫报告等系列数据、公报等的分析和整理，阐明现阶段对非国际援助的体系框架、整体脉络、具体项目，分析相关的国际标准、战略合作与协定、评价体系、减贫成效与不足等（见表1-1）。二是通过典型案例，进行中、微观分析。研究充分利用非洲留学生资源，关注撒哈拉以南非洲的减贫实践，梳理重要的减贫议题、项目及进展，观察内源式减贫策略与外部援助的适应性，并进行比较分析，塑造案例分析的可及空间。三是通过数据总结，进行预判分析。结合国际社会对非减贫援助与非洲本土减贫进展的分析，以及全球减贫发展形势和整体背景，采取预测分析法，总结中国对非减贫援助的主要经验与贡献，提出未来发展趋势等，为更好地开展对非减贫援助提供参考。

表1-1　　　　　　研究主要参考的国际报告资料

类型	来源	名称/网站
联合国系统	联合国（UN）	The Sustainable Development Goals Report 2022
		2022 Global Multidimensional Poverty Index（MPI）
		OPHI and UNDP Regional MPI Brief Sub-Saharan Africa：An Age Group Analysis of the 2021 Global MPI
		The State of Food and Agriculture 2019：Moving Forward on Food Loss and Waste Reduction
		Climate Change and Poverty in Africa：Challenges and Initiatives
		2023 Global Report on Food Crises
		How the United Nations System Supports Ambitious Action on Climate Change

续表

类型	来源	名称/网站
联合国系统	联合国人道主义事务协调办公室（OCHA）	Southern Africa Humanitarian Snapshot
		South Sudan Humanitarian Needs Overview 2022
		West and Central Africa：Weekly Regional Humanitarian Snapshot
	世界粮食计划署（WFP）	An Analysis of the Impacts of Ongoing Drought across Eastern Horn of Africa
		2022：A Year of Unprecedented Hunger
	世界气象组织（WMO）	State of the Climate in Africa 2021
		State of Climate Services Report：Water
	联合国粮食及农业组织（FAO）	Annual Review 2021
		Statistical Yearbook：World Food and agriculture 2022
	联合国开发计划署（UNDP）	Measuring the Multiple Dimensions of Poverty in Africa
		Human Development Report 2021-22 Uncertain Times, Unsettled Lives：Shaping our Future in a Transforming World
	联合国儿童基金会（UNICEF）	The Climate Crisis Climate Change Impacts，Trends and Vulnerabilities of Children in Sub-Saharan Africa
	国际移民组织（IOM）	Mozambique Cyclone Eloise Response Plan
金融机构	世界银行（WB）	Africa's Pulse：An Analysis of Issues Shaping Africa's Economic Future
		Poverty and Climate Change Reducing the Vulnerability of the Poor through Adaptation
		Macro Poverty Outlook Country-by-country Analysis and Projections for the Developing World
		Climate Change Complicates Efforts to End Poverty
		Revised Estimates of the Impact of Climate Change on Extreme Poverty by 2030
	国际货币基金组织（IMF）	Africa Regional Economic Outlook 2023
		Climate Change and Chronic Food Insecurity in Sub-Saharan Africa

续表

类型	来源	名称/网站
专业性组织	政府间气候变化专门委员会（IPCC）	Climate Change 2022, Impacts, Adaptation and Vulnerability, Summary for Policymakers
	国际粮食政策研究所（IFPRI）	2023 Global Food Policy Report: Rethinking Food Crisis Responses
其他组织	红十字会与红新月会国际联合会（IFRC）	Emergency Appeal, Algeria, Forest Fires
	国家国际发展合作署（CIDCA）	中非合作论坛—沙姆沙伊赫行动计划
		中非合作论坛—约翰内斯堡行动计划（2016—2018年）
		中非合作论坛—北京行动计划（2019—2021年）
		中非合作论坛—达喀尔行动计划（2022—2024）
		《中非合作2035年愿景》
	非洲发展银行（African Development Bank）	African Economic Outlook 2023: Mobilizing Private Sector Financing for Climate and Green Growth in Africa
数据库	世界银行数据库（World Bank Open Data）	https://data.worldbank.org.cn/
	联合国数据库（UNCTAD）	https://unctad.org/statistics
	经济合作与发展组织数据库（OECD Statistics）	https://stats.oecd.org/Index.aspx?DataSetCode=TABLE5A#
	联合国粮食及农业组织数据库（FAOSTAT）	https://www.fao.org/faostat/zh/#data/FS
其他	Devex	Devex Emerging Donors Report

资料来源：根据相关参考资料整理所得。

第二章
疫情后非洲贫困状况

进入21世纪以来，非洲经历了相对快速且连续的增长，政治和宏观经济更趋稳定，非洲从"没有希望的大陆"转变为"充满希望的大陆""跃动的雄狮""世界经济增长中心"，一些乐观主义者宣称21世纪将是"非洲世纪"，认为非洲有望成为"明天的中国"或"新的印度"①②。尤其是，拥有超过10亿人口的撒哈拉以南非洲是一个多元化的地区，到2050年，该地区25岁以下人口将占到总人口的一半，充沛的人力资源和自然资源使其具备实现包容性增长和消除贫困的巨大潜力③。凭借世界上最大的自由贸易区和12亿人口的广大市场，非洲大陆正在创造一条利用其资源和人口潜力的新发展道路。然而，非洲整体的经济发展繁荣并不能掩盖非洲国家所面临的发展困境，非洲仍是社会经济转型最缓慢的地区，也是全球减贫发展的重点区域。此外，非洲各国以及不同产业部门间增长的异质性导致了非洲与其他地区、非洲各区域以及不同国家之间的减贫与发展呈现出巨大差别。

虽然非洲是全球贫困问题最严重的区域，疫情、气候变化等对非洲经济社会发展带来严重冲击，但随着后疫情时代的到来，非洲国家积极出台各种政策措施，寻求国际合作机会，致力于社会经济发展。疫情后，非洲大陆经济开始出现恢复性增长，社会经济发展总体向好。本章试图结合联合国系统、世界银行、国际粮食政策研究所等国际机构的相关数据资料，围绕衡量减贫发展的核心指标对非洲国家极端贫困发生率、多维贫困水平、饥饿指数、粮食安全和营

---

① 非洲——"绝望的大陆"or"崛起的新星"？参见 https：//www.focac.org/chn/zfgx/jmhz/t1486100.htm（访问日期：2023年6月1日）。

② Ewout Frankema，Marlous van Waijenburg. Africa rising? A historical perspective［J］. African Affairs，2018，117（469）：543 - 568.

③ 根据世界银行网站资料整理。

养状况、收入不平等程度以及人类发展水平等方面展开具体分析，以此廓清非洲整体落后但区域和国别层面差异化的减贫与发展现状，并对疫情后非洲贫困现状作出整体判断。

一、非洲经济变化

非洲经济逐步复苏，部分国家经济增长率恢复甚至高于疫情前水平。从表2-1可知，根据国际货币基金组织（IMF）的数据，疫情之前，非洲大陆经济增速达到2.99%，略高于2.84%的世界平均水平，远高于拉丁美洲和加勒比地区（0.17%）。2020年，受疫情影响，除东部非洲外，非洲大陆普遍出现经济负增长，整体经济增速为-1.74%，但仍高于世界平均水平（-2.85%）以及拉丁美洲和加勒比地区（-6.78%）。2021年以来，非洲大陆经济复苏，每个区域的经济都呈现出中速增长态势，尤其是进入2022年后，非洲经济增速达到3.78%，高于世界平均水平，也高于疫情前2019年的水平（2.99%），除南部非洲外的各区域的经济增速均高于世界平均水平，但强劲程度仍弱于世界平均水平。

表2-1　　　　2015~2022年非洲不同区域的经济增速　　　单位：%

地区	2015年	2016年	2017年	2018年	2019年	2020年	2021年	2022年
南部非洲	1.45	0.58	1.31	1.43	0.27	-5.79	4.46	2.47
中部非洲	2.64	-0.28	1.26	2.24	2.88	-0.34	3.23	4.10
东部非洲（东非）	6.21	4.96	5.18	4.71	5.21	0.71	5.37	4.32
北部非洲（北非）	3.73	3.10	4.67	4.19	2.96	-1.77	5.36	4.06
西部非洲（西非）	3.15	0.78	2.87	3.22	3.72	-0.63	4.39	3.89
非洲	3.44	2.17	3.48	3.40	2.99	-1.74	4.85	3.78
拉丁美洲和加勒比地区	0.36	-0.61	1.35	1.20	0.17	-6.78	7.01	3.96
亚洲（不包括高收入国家）	6.32	6.82	6.28	6.08	4.96	-0.59	7.34	4.42
世界	3.48	3.28	3.75	3.64	2.84	-2.85	6.28	3.46

资料来源：IMF，World Economic Outlook Database，April 2023.

2020年，受疫情影响，非洲国家普遍出现了经济负增长。从表2-2可知，根据经济合作与发展组织的相关数据，2020年有34个非洲国家的经济增长率为负，一些国家经济失速情况比较严重，如毛里求斯、纳米比亚、利比亚、津巴布韦、安哥拉和佛得角等；2021年，只有两个非洲国家的GDP增长率为负，分别为乍得和赤道几内亚；2022年，同样只有两个非洲国家的GDP增长率为负值，分别为苏丹和利比亚，其主要原因在于地区冲突对经济增长的冲击。

表2-2　　　　　　　　2019~2022年非洲国家GDP增长率　　　　单位：%

国家	2019年	2020年	2021年	2022年	国家	2019年	2020年	2021年	2022年
尼日尔	6.14	3.55	1.40	11.11	喀麦隆	3.42	0.54	3.65	3.38
佛得角	5.67	-14.78	7.00	10.50	尼日利亚	2.21	-1.79	3.65	3.25
塞舌尔	3.09	-7.72	7.91	8.84	加纳	6.51	0.51	5.36	3.22
毛里求斯	2.89	-14.60	3.50	8.30	津巴布韦	-6.12	-7.82	8.46	3.03
卢旺达	9.47	-3.36	10.87	6.76	阿尔及利亚	1.00	-5.10	3.40	2.93
科特迪瓦	8.31	1.70	7.00	6.70	加蓬	3.92	-1.86	1.48	2.85
刚果（金）	4.49	1.67	6.23	6.63	安哥拉	-0.70	-5.64	1.09	2.84
埃及	5.53	3.51	3.31	6.61	刚果（布）	1.03	-6.20	1.50	2.78
南苏丹	0.86	-6.49	5.33	6.55	塞拉利昂	5.25	-1.97	4.10	2.77
博茨瓦纳	3.03	-8.73	11.84	6.43	厄立特里亚	3.84	-0.53	2.89	2.62
埃塞俄比亚	9.04	6.06	6.27	6.36	突尼斯	1.59	-8.82	4.41	2.52
贝宁	6.87	3.85	7.16	6.02	吉布提	5.55	1.20	4.81	2.50
多哥	5.46	1.76	5.26	5.40	乍得	3.42	-2.14	-1.10	2.49
肯尼亚	5.11	-0.25	7.52	5.37	布基纳法索	5.69	1.93	6.90	2.47
毛里塔尼亚	5.43	-0.94	2.45	4.96	科摩罗	1.76	-0.20	2.11	2.43
乌干达	7.78	-1.30	6.00	4.93	莱索托	-1.97	-3.90	2.10	2.09
利比里亚	-2.52	-2.97	5.01	4.81	南非	0.30	-6.34	4.91	2.04
塞内加尔	4.61	1.33	6.07	4.71	布隆迪	1.84	0.34	3.12	1.83
坦桑尼亚	6.99	4.82	4.95	4.69	索马里	2.70	-0.28	2.94	1.70
冈比亚	6.22	0.59	4.27	4.44	赤道几内亚	-5.48	-4.24	-3.19	1.57
几内亚	5.62	4.92	4.29	4.29	摩洛哥	2.89	-7.19	7.93	1.13
马达加斯加	4.41	-7.14	5.74	4.21	圣多美和普林西比	2.21	3.02	1.88	0.89
莫桑比克	2.31	-1.20	2.33	4.15	马拉维	5.45	0.91	4.57	0.80

续表

国家	2019年	2020年	2021年	2022年	国家	2019年	2020年	2021年	2022年
纳米比亚	−0.84	−8.04	2.66	3.84	斯威士兰	2.70	−1.56	7.88	0.47
马里	4.76	−1.24	3.05	3.70	中非共和国	2.97	0.96	0.98	0.38
几内亚比绍	4.50	1.50	6.40	3.50	苏丹	−2.50	−3.63	0.50	−2.50
赞比亚	1.44	−2.79	4.60	3.44	利比亚	−11.20	−29.46	28.33	−12.81

资料来源：根据经济合作与发展组织《2023年非洲发展动态：投资于可持续发展》的数据整理所得，参见 https：//www.oecd.org/dev/africa/development-dynamics/。

结合国际货币基金组织的经济增速预测，非洲国家的经济总量将全部恢复到2019年的水平，并实现较大幅度的增长。考察各国的经济体量可以发现，从2020年到2021年，低于2019年经济总量水平的非洲国家数量从28个减少到10个，到2022年，仅有五个国家的经济总量低于2019年水平，分别为刚果（布）、利比亚、毛里求斯、纳米比亚和斯威士兰。除利比亚以外，其他国家经济总量和2019年水平相差已经非常小（见表2-3）。

表2-3　　　　　　　　　2019~2022年非洲国家GDP　　　　单位：亿美元

国家	2019年	2020年	2021年	2022年	差值（2020-2019）	差值（2021-2019）	差值（2022-2019）
安哥拉	693.09	536.19	674.04	1214.17	−156.90	−19.05	521.08
布隆迪	25.77	26.50	27.80	38.94	0.73	2.03	13.17
贝宁	143.92	156.52	171.45	174.13	12.60	27.53	30.21
布基纳法索	161.78	179.34	197.38	195.68	17.56	35.60	33.90
博茨瓦纳	166.96	149.30	176.15	191.76	−17.66	9.19	24.80
中非共和国	22.21	23.27	25.16	24.62	1.06	2.95	2.41
科特迪瓦	585.39	613.49	700.43	700.46	28.10	115.04	115.07
喀麦隆	396.71	407.73	453.38	437.16	11.02	56.67	40.45
刚果（金）	517.76	487.17	553.51	628.59	−30.59	35.75	110.83
刚果（布）	127.50	104.83	133.66	125.30	−22.67	6.16	−2.20
科摩罗	11.95	12.25	12.96	12.33	0.30	1.01	0.38
佛得角	19.82	17.04	19.36	22.24	−2.78	−0.46	2.42

续表

国家	2019年	2020年	2021年	2022年	差值（2020-2019）	差值（2021-2019）	差值（2022-2019）
吉布提	30.89	31.81	34.83	36.46	0.92	3.94	5.57
阿尔及利亚	1717.67	1450.09	1630.44	1954.15	−267.58	−87.23	236.48
埃及	3030.81	3652.53	4041.43	4752.31	621.72	1010.62	1721.50
埃塞俄比亚	959.13	1076.58	1112.71	1203.69	117.45	153.58	244.56
加蓬	168.74	153.15	202.17	219.31	−15.59	33.43	50.57
加纳	683.38	700.43	775.94	728.39	17.05	92.56	45.01
几内亚	134.43	141.78	160.92	204.69	7.35	26.49	70.26
冈比亚	18.14	18.12	20.38	21.33	−0.02	2.24	3.19
几内亚比绍	14.40	14.32	16.39	17.05	−0.08	1.99	2.65
赤道几内亚	113.64	100.99	122.69	164.51	−12.65	9.05	50.87
肯尼亚	1003.80	1006.67	1103.47	1159.89	2.87	99.67	156.09
利比里亚	33.20	30.40	35.09	39.74	−2.80	1.89	6.54
利比亚	692.52	503.57	428.17	440.66	−188.95	−264.35	−251.86
莱索托	24.54	22.31	24.96	24.80	−2.23	0.42	0.26
摩洛哥	1289.20	1213.48	1428.66	1380.52	−75.72	139.46	91.32
马达加斯加	141.05	130.51	144.73	152.33	−10.54	3.68	11.28
马里	172.80	174.65	191.40	190.48	1.85	18.60	17.68
莫桑比克	153.90	140.29	157.77	179.40	−13.61	3.87	25.50
毛里塔尼亚	80.66	84.05	99.96	103.21	3.39	19.30	22.55
毛里求斯	144.36	114.01	115.29	127.72	−30.35	−29.07	−16.64
马拉维	110.25	121.82	126.27	125.12	11.57	16.02	14.87
纳米比亚	125.42	105.82	123.11	123.45	−19.60	−2.31	−1.97
尼日尔	129.16	137.44	149.15	152.22	8.28	19.99	23.06
尼日利亚	4481.20	4321.99	4408.34	4773.76	−159.21	−72.86	292.56
卢旺达	103.56	101.84	110.70	127.03	−1.72	7.14	23.47
苏丹	323.38	270.35	343.26	494.23	−53.03	19.88	170.85
塞内加尔	233.99	244.93	276.25	274.62	10.94	42.26	40.63
塞拉利昂	40.77	40.63	40.42	39.39	−0.14	−0.35	−1.38
索马里	64.85	68.83	76.28	81.58	3.98	11.43	16.73
圣多美和普林西比	4.27	4.73	5.27	5.52	0.46	1.00	1.25

续表

国家	2019年	2020年	2021年	2022年	差值（2020-2019）	差值（2021-2019）	差值（2022-2019）
斯威士兰	44.95	39.82	47.43	44.62	-5.13	2.48	-0.33
塞舌尔	16.84	12.61	14.54	19.26	-4.23	-2.30	2.42
乍得	113.15	107.15	117.80	119.09	-6.00	4.65	5.94
多哥	72.20	75.75	84.13	81.73	3.55	11.93	9.53
突尼斯	419.06	425.38	466.87	466.01	6.32	47.81	46.95
坦桑尼亚	611.37	624.10	678.41	770.63	12.73	67.04	159.26
乌干达	353.53	376.00	405.30	488.41	22.47	51.77	134.88
南非	3885.32	3376.20	4190.15	4057.05	-509.12	304.83	171.73
赞比亚	233.09	181.11	221.48	285.00	-51.98	-11.61	51.91
津巴布韦	218.32	215.10	283.71	330.20	-3.22	65.39	111.88

注：厄立特里亚、南苏丹无数据。

资料来源：根据《世界发展指标》（WDI）2023年5月10日更新数据整理所得，以2023年美元计。

二、非洲城镇化水平变化

整体来看，非洲城镇化水平和质量有所提升。进入21世纪以来，非洲国家城镇化率保持较为稳定的增长，从2000年的34.95%上升至2021年的43.99%，增幅超过9个百分点。在区域层面，南部非洲和北非地区城镇化率相对较高，城镇化速度较慢；中部非洲、西非和东非地区城镇化水平较低，但城镇化速度较快，是非洲推进城镇化发展的重点区域，尤其是东非地区，许多国家都处于快速推进城镇化阶段。

在国家层面，几乎所有非洲国家的城镇化率均有不同程度的增长，2021年有17个非洲国家城镇化率高于世界平均水平（56.47%）。但从增长速度来看，非洲城镇人口增长速度放缓，2021年城镇人口年增长率降至3.53%，仅比2000年高0.11%，部分国家（如津巴布韦、毛里求斯）甚至出现了逆城市化现象。参见表2-4和图2-1。

表2-4 　　　　2021年非洲国家城镇化水平及其增长率 　　　　单位：%

序号	国家	城镇化水平	城镇化增长率	序号	国家	城镇化水平	城镇化增长率
南部非洲（65.38%）				27	科特迪瓦	52.18	4.61
1	博茨瓦纳	71.56	5.34	28	贝宁	48.97	5.93
2	南非	67.85	3.84	29	塞内加尔	48.60	4.98
3	纳米比亚	53.01	10.52	30	马里	44.68	9.55
4	莱索托	29.48	7.92	31	几内亚比绍	44.62	4.90
5	斯威士兰	24.37	3.88	32	塞拉利昂	43.37	5.20
北部非洲（56.16%）				33	多哥	43.36	6.72
6	利比亚	80.99	1.83	34	几内亚	37.26	5.09
7	吉布提	78.22	0.89	35	布基纳法索	31.24	11.04
8	阿尔及利亚	74.26	3.92	36	尼日尔	16.75	2.83
9	突尼斯	69.89	2.26	东部非洲（29.77%）			
10	摩洛哥	64.07	4.41	37	塞舌尔	57.97	3.83
11	埃及	42.86	0.30	38	索马里	46.73	6.65
中部非洲（51.14%）				39	赞比亚	45.19	6.49
12	加蓬	90.42	2.10	40	厄立特里亚	41.99	8.13
13	圣多美和普林西比	75.07	5.60	41	毛里求斯	40.78	-0.33
14	赤道几内亚	73.56	3.41	42	马达加斯加	39.21	9.35
15	刚果	68.28	3.46	43	莫桑比克	37.63	7.74
16	安哥拉	67.46	5.16	44	坦桑尼亚	35.95	11.20
17	喀麦隆	58.15	5.38	45	苏丹	35.59	4.31
18	刚果民主共和国	46.24	6.76	46	津巴布韦	32.30	0.02
19	中非共和国	42.65	5.00	47	科摩罗	29.61	3.47
20	乍得	23.78	4.87	48	肯尼亚	28.49	9.15
西部非洲（48.30%）				49	乌干达	25.55	12.95
21	佛得角	67.10	3.58	50	埃塞俄比亚	22.17	11.62
22	冈比亚	63.22	5.51	51	南苏丹	20.51	7.45
23	加纳	57.99	5.91	52	马拉维	17.70	7.20
24	毛里塔尼亚	56.13	8.03	53	卢旺达	17.57	3.00
25	尼日利亚	52.75	8.35	54	布隆迪	14.06	13.48
26	利比里亚	52.57	4.61	撒哈拉以南非洲		43.99	5.61

资料来源：根据《世界发展指标》（WDI）2023年5月10日更新数据整理所得。

图2-1　2000~2021年非洲国家城镇化情况

资料来源：根据《世界发展指标》（WDI）2023年5月10日更新数据绘制。

三、非洲国家人类发展水平变化

　　人类发展指数是预期寿命指数、教育指数和国民总收入（GNI）指数的几何平均值，在国际上被用于考察不同国家的人类发展水平。人类发展指数为0~1，越接近1，表示人类发展水平越高。从表2-5可知，自2000年以来，撒哈拉以南非洲的人类发展指数逐渐上升，并在2019年达到0.552，为历史最高水平。根据联合国开发计划署发布的人类发展指数，2000~2021年非洲国家人类发展指数均有不同程度的增长，其中埃塞俄比亚的涨幅最大，从0.287上升至0.498，增长幅度超过73%；安哥拉、卢旺达、尼日尔、布基纳法索和塞拉利昂五个国家的增长幅度均超过50%。与2015年相比，2021年有32个非洲国家的人类发展水平排名有所提升，这说明非洲国家人类发展水平整体在提升。

　　从各个国家来看，截至2021年，非洲大陆有八个国家进入了高度人类发展水平（0.700~0.799），分别是毛里求斯、塞舌尔、阿尔及利亚、埃及、突尼斯、利比亚、南非和加蓬；有17个国家进入了中等人类发展水平（0.550~0.699）；同期，仍有28个国家处于低人类发展水平（低于0.550），其中人类发展指数低于0.500的有13个国家，低于0.400的有两个国家（最低的是南苏丹，为0.385）[①]。

---

　　① 根据联合国公布的数据整理所得，参见 https://hdr.undp.org/data-center/documentation-and-downloads（访问日期：2023年6月1日）。索马里无数据。

相比世界平均水平（0.732），2021年非洲仅有毛里求斯、塞舌尔和阿尔及利亚三个国家高于平均值，其余50个国家的人类发展水平均低于世界平均水平。

表2-5　　　　　　　　　非洲国家人类发展指数及其排名

国家	排名	1990年	2000年	2015年	2019年	2020年	2021年	2015~2021年排名变化	2000~2021年年增长率（%）
高人类发展水平（0.700~0.799）									
毛里求斯	63	0.626	0.681	0.795	0.817	0.804	0.802	2	17.77
塞舌尔	72	—	0.744	0.796	0.802	0.793	0.785	-8	5.51
阿尔及利亚	91	0.591	0.649	0.740	0.748	0.736	0.745	2	14.79
埃及	97	0.572	0.633	0.706	0.735	0.734	0.731	13	15.48
突尼斯	97	0.576	0.658	0.733	0.745	0.737	0.731	1	11.09
利比亚	104	0.666	0.712	0.699	0.722	0.703	0.718	10	0.84
南非	109	0.632	0.633	0.716	0.736	0.727	0.713	-4	12.64
加蓬	112	0.610	0.635	0.699	0.709	0.710	0.706	2	11.18
中等人类发展水平（0.550~0.699）									
博茨瓦纳	117	0.586	0.585	0.702	0.717	0.713	0.693	-6	18.46
摩洛哥	123	0.447	0.521	0.654	0.682	0.679	0.683	3	31.09
佛得角	128	—	0.569	0.663	0.676	0.662	0.662	-4	16.34
加纳	133	0.460	0.507	0.607	0.631	0.632	0.632	5	24.65
圣多美和普林西比	138	0.485	0.501	0.596	0.622	0.619	0.618	4	23.35
纳米比亚	139	0.579	0.546	0.628	0.639	0.633	0.615	-7	12.64
斯威士兰	144	0.545	0.471	0.575	0.615	0.610	0.597	4	26.75
赤道几内亚	145	—	0.512	0.603	0.605	0.599	0.596	-6	16.41
津巴布韦	146	0.509	0.452	0.582	0.601	0.600	0.593	-1	31.19
安哥拉	148	–	0.375	0.582	0.595	0.590	0.586	-3	56.27
喀麦隆	151	0.452	0.442	0.560	0.583	0.578	0.576	2	30.32
肯尼亚	152	0.474	0.481	0.561	0.581	0.578	0.575	0	19.54
刚果（布）	153	0.522	0.491	0.590	0.570	0.574	0.571	-9	16.29
赞比亚	154	0.412	0.418	0.562	0.575	0.570	0.565	-4	35.17
科摩罗	156	—	0.464	0.544	0.560	0.562	0.558	0	20.26
毛里塔尼亚	158	0.397	0.465	0.544	0.563	0.556	0.556	-2	19.57
科特迪瓦	159	0.427	0.457	0.513	0.550	0.551	0.550	8	20.35

续表

国家	排名	1990年	2000年	2015年	2019年	2020年	2021年	2015~2021年排名变化	2000~2021年年增长率（%）
低人类发展水平（低于0.550）									
坦桑尼亚	160	0.371	0.398	0.520	0.548	0.548	0.549	2	37.94
多哥	162	0.410	0.446	0.514	0.535	0.535	0.539	4	20.85
尼日利亚	163	—	—	0.516	0.538	0.535	0.535	1	—
卢旺达	165	0.319	0.340	0.515	0.534	0.532	0.534	0	57.06
贝宁	166	0.359	0.416	0.529	0.530	0.524	0.525	−6	26.20
乌干达	166	0.329	0.394	0.517	0.525	0.524	0.525	−3	33.25
莱索托	168	0.479	0.452	0.503	0.524	0.521	0.514	3	13.72
马拉维	169	0.303	0.374	0.491	0.519	0.516	0.512	4	36.90
塞内加尔	170	—	0.388	0.505	0.513	0.513	0.511	−1	31.70
吉布提	171	—	0.361	0.493	0.512	0.510	0.509	1	41.00
苏丹	172	0.336	0.424	0.508	0.514	0.510	0.508	−4	19.81
马达加斯加	173	—	0.443	0.504	0.510	0.501	0.501	−3	13.09
冈比亚	174	0.343	0.404	0.478	0.503	0.501	0.500	1	23.76
埃塞俄比亚	175	—	0.287	0.460	0.498	0.498	0.498	6	73.52
厄立特里亚	176	—	—	0.483	0.495	0.494	0.492	−2	—
几内亚比绍	177	—	—	0.472	0.490	0.483	0.483	2	—
利比里亚	178	—	0.438	0.473	0.484	0.480	0.481	0	9.82
刚果（金）	179	0.386	0.376	0.463	0.482	0.479	0.479	1	27.39
塞拉利昂	181	0.312	0.318	0.453	0.480	0.475	0.477	1	50.00
几内亚	182	0.269	0.345	0.440	0.467	0.466	0.465	1	34.78
布基纳法索	184	—	0.296	0.418	0.452	0.449	0.449	2	51.69
莫桑比克	185	0.238	0.303	0.440	0.456	0.453	0.446	−2	47.19
马里	186	0.237	0.317	0.416	0.433	0.427	0.428	1	35.02
布隆迪	187	0.290	0.297	0.428	0.431	0.426	0.426	−2	43.43
中非共和国	188	0.338	0.329	0.384	0.411	0.407	0.404	2	22.80
尼日尔	189	0.216	0.262	0.376	0.406	0.401	0.400	2	52.67
乍得	190	—	0.291	0.389	0.403	0.397	0.394	−1	35.40
南苏丹	191	—	—	0.412	0.393	0.386	0.385	−3	—
撒哈拉以南非洲	—	0.407	0.430	0.534	0.552	0.549	0.547	—	27.21

注：索马里无数据。

资料来源：根据联合国公布的数据整理所得，参见 https：//hdr.undp.org/data-center/documentation-and-downloads（访问日期：2023年6月1日）。

非洲人类发展水平的上升意味着该地区生活质量、预期寿命和教育水平等方面得到了一定提升，2020年撒哈拉以南非洲地区的出生时预期寿命上升到了63.5岁，平均受教育年限也逐渐上升至6年左右（见表2-6）。但相比于世界平均水平，非洲大陆除了北非地区的基本健康指标基本达到平均水平，其余四个次区域的出生时预期寿命、总生育率、婴儿死亡率以及五岁以下儿童死亡率等健康指标均存在不小的差距，非洲各国在未来的发展战略需要更加注重民生，提高福祉。

表2-6　　　　　　　　2020年非洲国家基本健康指标

地区	出生时预期寿命（岁）	出生时女性预期寿命（岁）	出生时男性预期寿命（岁）	总生育率（每名妇女的活产率）	婴儿死亡率（每1000名活产婴儿死亡人数）	五岁以下儿童死亡率（每1000名活产婴儿死亡人数）
南部非洲	61.9	64.9	58.8	3.7	40.0	54.6
中部非洲	60.9	63.1	59.0	4.9	46.5	66.6
东非	64.9	67.4	62.4	3.9	37.0	52.1
北非	71.9	74.4	69.7	2.9	20.4	25.4
西非	61.5	63.1	59.8	4.6	49.3	73.2
非洲	63.5	65.8	61.3	4.1	40.7	57.9
世界	71.7	74.5	69.1	2.6	19.9	26.5

资料来源：根据经济合作与发展组织《2023年非洲发展动态：投资于可持续发展》数据整理所得，参见https：//www.oecd.org/dev/africa/development-dynamics/。

四、非洲经济社会发展的优先问题

非洲地区的社会经济转型最为缓慢，是全球最不发达国家最集中的区域，减贫与发展面临严峻挑战。 截至2023年，非洲54个国家中，多数国家存在收入过低、严重缺粮、严重的债务危机等问题。按照联合国最新划分的全球46个最不发达国家[①]、联合国粮食及农业组织（以下简称"联合国粮农组织"）最新划分的全球51个低收入缺粮国家[②]，以及世界银行最新划分的全球39个重债穷

①　联合国最不发达国家名单，参见https://unctad.org/topic/least-developed-countries/list（访问日期：2023年6月3日）。
②　联合国粮农组织最新的低收入缺粮国家名单，参见https://www.fao.org/countryprofiles/lifdc/zh/（访问日期：2023年6月4日）。

国[①]，非洲有33个最不发达国家、36个低收入缺粮国家和33个重债穷国。

从最不发达国家、低收入缺粮国家和重债穷国三个维度来看，同时被划入这三个维度的非洲国家有28个，分别是贝宁、布基纳法索、布隆迪、中非共和国、乍得、科摩罗、刚果（金）、厄立特里亚、埃塞俄比亚、冈比亚、几内亚、几内亚比绍、利比里亚、马达加斯加、马拉维、马里、毛里塔尼亚、莫桑比克、尼日尔、卢旺达、圣多美和普林西比、塞内加尔、塞拉利昂、索马里、苏丹、多哥、乌干达、坦桑尼亚。这28个非洲国家贫困程度较深，在发展方面受到的约束条件较多，致贫因素也更为复杂。同时被划入重债穷国和低收入缺粮国家两个维度的有四个，分别是喀麦隆、刚果（布）、科特迪瓦和加纳；而同时被划入低收入缺粮国家和最不发达国家这两个维度的有两个国家，分别是南苏丹与莱索托（见图2-2）。这三个维度的分类从整体上反映出非洲国家经济社会发展严重滞后，非洲的减贫与发展面临严峻挑战。

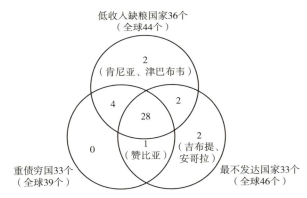

图 2-2　非洲国家贫困发展概况

资料来源：根据联合国、世界银行、联合国粮农组织公布的数据绘制。

（一）疫情后非洲的绝对贫困问题

现在乃至未来，撒哈拉以南非洲都是全球贫困人口最集中的地区。自1990年以来，非洲地区绝对贫困问题日益严峻，绝对贫困人口不减反增。从图2-3可知，按照世界银行每人每天2.15美元的贫困标准，撒哈拉以南非洲的绝对贫困人口从1990年的2.78亿人上升至2019年的3.97亿人，同比增长43%。同

---

① 世界银行重债穷国名单，参见https：//data.worldbank.org/indicator/SP.POP.GROW?locations=XE（访问日期：2023年6月3日）。

一期间，全球绝对贫困人口大幅下降，从1990年的20.11亿人下降至2019年的7.02亿人，降幅超过65%。从占比情况看，撒哈拉以南非洲绝对贫困人口占全球的比重从1990年的13.82%不断上升，2017年达到了52.24%，这意味着全球超过一半的绝对贫困人口集中在撒哈拉以南非洲，2019年这一占比上升至56.52%。从绝对贫困人口数量层面上看，撒哈拉以南非洲已日渐成为全球贫困人口最集中的地区。目前全球仍有10%的人口处于极端贫困[①]，其中世界极端贫困人口最集中、贫困发生率最高的是撒哈拉以南非洲[②]。截至2020年上半年，受新冠疫情影响，撒哈拉以南非洲的极端贫困人口上升至4.49亿人，极端贫困发生率为40.17%[③]。根据世界银行的预计，到2030年，撒哈拉以南非洲的极端贫困人口将不会明显下降，具体而言，到2025年，撒哈拉以南非洲极端贫困人口将达到4.31亿人，占全球的83.37%；到2035年，撒哈拉以南非洲极端贫困人口将达到4.16亿人，占全球的86.85%（见表2-7）。这也意味着从现在到未来近20年，贫困问题仍然是撒哈拉以南非洲面临的严峻挑战。

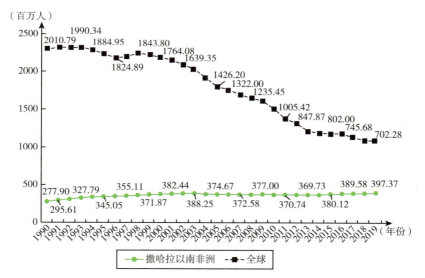

图 2-3　1990~2019年2.15美元标准下撒哈拉以南非洲贫困人口

资料来源：根据世界银行公布的数据整理并绘制，参见https：//pip.worldbank.org/home（访问日期：2023年6月1日）。

---

① 王瑜.继续向贫困宣战：世界仍有10%人口生活在极端贫困中［J］.中国纪检监察，2020（20）：19-20.

② 安春英.全球贫困治理中的非洲减贫国际合作［J］.当代世界，2019（10）：23-28.

③ 博鳌亚洲论坛. 亚洲减贫报告2020［EB/OL］. http：//www.boaoforum.org.

表2-7 　　　　　　　　世界及不同地区极端贫困人口数量变化 　　　单位：百万人

地区	1990年	1999年	2005年	2015年	2018年	2025年	2030年
东亚和太平洋地区	987.1	695.9	361.6	47.2	34.0	7.0	3.0
欧洲和中亚	13.3	36.7	22.9	7.1	5.0	3.0	2.0
拉丁美洲和加勒比地区	62.6	69.7	54.9	25.9	26.0	22.0	19.0
西亚和北非	14.2	10.6	9.4	18.6	25.0	26.0	26.0
南亚	535.9	534.4	510.4	216.4	121.0	20.0	5.0
撒哈拉以南非洲	277.5（14.65%）	376.1（21.76%）	387.7（28.67%）	413.3（56.16%）	437.0（66.62%）	431.0（83.37%）	416.0（86.85%）
其他	4.3	5.0	5.3	7.3	8.0	8.0	8.0
世界	1894.8	1728.6	1352.2	735.9	656.0	517.0	479.0

注：1990~2018年为实际数，2025~2030年为预计数。括号内为撒哈拉以南非洲极端贫困人口占世界总量的比重。

资料来源：https：//www.worldbank.org/en/understanding-poverty。

按照世界银行每人每天2.15美元的贫困标准，2022年，在非洲14.25亿人口中，极端贫困人口有3.75亿人，极端贫困发生率为26.3%。在次区域层面，除北非地区，其余四个次区域极端贫困率均远高于世界平均水平，超过3/4的贫困人口集中在南部非洲、东非以及西非地区（见表2-8）。

表2-8 　　2022年世界及非洲各区域人口与2.15美元标准下的贫困情况

地区	人口（百万人）	贫困发生率（%）	贫困人口（百万人）
南部非洲	193.90	38.7	75.04
中部非洲	173.38	28.0	48.48
东非	415.98	28.8	119.65
北非	217.26	2.4	5.16
西非	424.34	22.1	93.84
非洲	1424.85	26.3	375.02
世界	—	10.0	—

资料来源：根据经济合作与发展组织《2023年非洲发展动态：投资于可持续发展》公布的数据整理所得。

　　具体到国家层面，45个有数据的非洲国家的总人口为12.1亿人，2.15美元标准下的极端贫困人口超过3.4亿人，总体极端贫困发生率为28.1%。从贫困人口数量来看，极端贫困人口数量排名前五的国家依次是尼日利亚、埃塞俄比亚、坦桑尼亚、莫桑比克和乌干达，这五个国家的极端贫困人口占非洲大陆极端贫困人口的50.43%。从贫困发生率来看，超过30%的有16个国家；超过70%的有一个国家，即马拉维；超过60%的有四个国家，分别为南苏丹、布隆迪、莫桑比克和赞比亚；超过50%的有两个国家，分别是卢旺达和尼日尔。这些国家是非洲贫困程度最为严重的国家（见表2-9和表2-10）。

表2-9　　2022年2.15美元标准下部分非洲国家的极端贫困人口

序号	国家	极端贫困人口（百万人）	占非洲总贫困人口的比例（%）
1	尼日利亚	67.53	19.86
2	埃塞俄比亚	33.31	9.80
3	坦桑尼亚	29.41	8.65
4	莫桑比克	21.30	6.26
5	乌干达	19.94	5.86
6	肯尼亚	15.88	4.67
7	马拉维	14.30	4.21
8	尼日尔	13.26	3.90
9	赞比亚	12.29	3.62
10	南非	12.28	3.61
11	安哥拉	11.07	3.26
12	加纳	8.44	2.48
13	布隆迪	8.39	2.47
14	南苏丹	7.34	2.16
15	喀麦隆	7.17	2.11

　　资料来源：根据经济合作与发展组织《2023年非洲发展动态：投资于可持续发展》公布的数据整理所得。

表 2-10　　2022年非洲45国的人口与2.15美元标准下的贫困发生率

国家	人口（百万人）	贫困发生率（%）	国家	人口（百万人）	贫困发生率（%）
安哥拉	35.59	31.1	苏丹	46.87	15.3
博茨瓦纳	2.63	15.4	坦桑尼亚	65.50	44.9
斯威士兰	1.20	36.1	乌干达	47.25	42.2
莱索托	2.31	32.4	埃及	110.99	1.5
马拉维	20.41	70.1	毛里塔尼亚	4.74	6.5
莫桑比克	32.97	64.6	摩洛哥	37.46	1.4
纳米比亚	2.57	15.6	突尼斯	12.36	0.1
南非	59.89	20.5	贝宁	13.35	19.9
赞比亚	20.02	61.4	布基纳法索	22.67	30.5
津巴布韦	16.32	39.8	佛得角	0.59	4.6
布隆迪	12.89	65.1	科特迪瓦	28.16	11.4
喀麦隆	27.91	25.7	冈比亚	2.71	17.2
乍得	17.72	30.9	加纳	33.48	25.2
加蓬	2.39	2.5	几内亚	13.86	13.8
圣多美和普林西比	0.23	15.6	几内亚比绍	2.11	21.7
科摩罗	0.84	18.6	利比里亚	5.30	27.6
吉布提	1.12	19.1	马里	22.59	14.8
埃塞俄比亚	123.38	27.0	尼日尔	26.21	50.6
肯尼亚	54.03	29.4	尼日利亚	218.54	30.9
毛里求斯	1.30	0.1	塞内加尔	17.32	9.3
卢旺达	13.78	52.0	塞拉利昂	8.61	26.1
塞舌尔	0.11	0.5	多哥	8.85	28.1
南苏丹	10.91	67.3	**非洲45国**	**1210.01**	**28.1**

注：中非共和国、刚果（布）、刚果（金）、赤道几内亚、厄立特里亚、马达加斯加、索马里、阿尔及利亚和利比亚这九个国家无数据。

资料来源：根据经济合作与发展组织《2023年非洲发展动态：投资于可持续发展》公布的数据整理所得。

（二）非洲多维贫困程度状况

非洲多维贫困程度在加深，疫情带来的负面影响仍持续存在。多维贫困指数（介于0~1）通过衡量健康、教育和生活水平三个维度遭受的剥夺情况，反映不同个体或家庭的贫困程度。按照联合国有关组织规定，多维贫困指数越接近0，表明贫困程度越低；数值越接近1，则表明贫困程度越深。《2022年全球多维贫困指数》表明，全球减少多维贫困的进展倒退了8~10年，且贫困程度较深、多维度贫困指数较高的国家倒退的情况更为严重。2022年，撒哈拉以南非洲多维贫困指数上升至0.286，贫困发生率达到了30.88%，均远高于世界其他地区（见表2–11）。撒哈拉以南非洲也是多维贫困人口最多的地区，2022年全球超过5.79亿多维贫困人口生活在撒哈拉以南非洲[①]，占全球人口的48%，比2021年增加了5个百分点。**非洲多维贫困人口的构成和分布也较为集中，弱势群体和农村地区多维贫困问题尤为突出。**2021年，撒哈拉以南非洲儿童多维贫困发生率为59%，成年人多维贫困发生率则为47%[②]。此外，撒哈拉以南非洲农村地区70%的人口（4.57亿人）属于多维贫困人口，城市地区的这一比例为26%（9900万人）。

表2–11　　　　　　　2022年全球不同地区多维贫困状况

地区	多维贫困指数	极端贫困发生率（%）
东亚和太平洋地区	0.022	1.00
欧洲和中亚	0.004	0.07
拉丁美洲和加勒比地区	0.027	1.56
南亚	0.091	6.92
撒哈拉以南非洲	0.286	30.88

资料来源：根据联合国粮农组织公布的数据整理所得，参见https：//www.fao.org/faostat/zh/#data/FS。

较低的生活水平是造成非洲多维贫困问题的决定性因素，其次是教育，最后才是健康。2022年，在撒哈拉以南非洲，生活水平是导致多维贫困最重要的因素，贡献度达到了48.58%，比南亚地区高了10个百分点（见表2–12）。同期，世界其他地区生活水平的贡献度不超过40%。

---

①　数据来源于《2022年全球多维贫困指数》，参见https：//hdr.undp.org/content/2022-global-multidimensional-poverty-index-mpi#/indicies/MPI（访问日期：2023年6月1日）。

②　《牛津贫困与人类发展倡议和联合国开发计划署区域多维贫困简报 撒哈拉以南非洲：2021年全球多维贫困的年龄组分析》，参见https：//ophi.org.uk/wp-content/uploads/OPHI_and_UNDP_RMPIB_2022_SSA%E2%80%93Age%E2%80%93Group.pdf。

表 2-12　　　　　　　　2022 年全球不同地区多维贫困贡献度

地区	多维贫困贡献度（%）		
	健康	教育	生活水平
东亚和太平洋地区	27.92	35.24	36.84
欧洲和中亚	53.25	24.57	22.18
拉丁美洲和加勒比地区	39.77	24.91	35.32
南亚	27.97	33.69	38.34
撒哈拉以南非洲	21.90	29.52	48.58

资料来源：根据联合国粮农组织公布的数据整理所得，参见 https：//www.fao.org/faostat/zh/#data/FS。

　　根据各国的多维贫困数贡献度数据，48 个非洲国家中有 37 个国家多维贫困的主要影响因素是生活水平，10 个国家多维贫困的主要影响因素是教育，只有塞舌尔一国的主要影响因素是健康。通过绘制散点图可以进一步发现，当多维贫困指数低于 0.3 时，健康对贫困指数的贡献率较高；当多维贫困指数高于 0.3 时，生活水平是多维贫困指数的决定性因素，此时健康对贫困指数的影响较低；当多维贫困指数介于 0.3~0.35 时，教育是多维贫困的决定性因素（见图 2-4）。这表明，多数非洲国家的基本生活保障不足，多维贫困程度深。

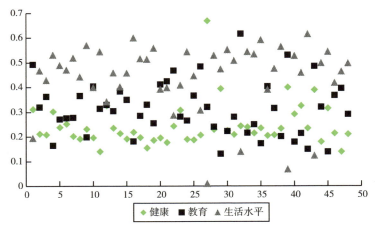

图 2-4　健康、教育和生活水平对多维贫困的贡献度散点图

注：佛得角、吉布提、厄立特里亚、赤道几内亚、毛里求斯、索马里无数据。

资料来源：根据《2022 年全球多维贫困指数》的数据整理并绘制。

生活水平低也直接反映在农村人口的消费习惯上，笔者在马拉维乡村调研时就发现了当地农民普遍的小包装或零星购买的"量入为出"生活逻辑。

案例2-1 马拉维农民的消费行为

笔者在非洲农村调研的时候，经常看到村里简陋的小卖部将食用油分装成10毫升左右进行销售；沿途叫卖的小商贩总是将花生米或腰果分装成大约只有几十克进行售卖；在一些国家，电话充值卡面值很多都是1美元……全部都是很小很小的包装，几乎看不到国内产品促销时普遍采用的加量减价的方式。这让人无法理解，因为小包装和零星购买从整体价格上来说一定是比一次性购买要贵很多。直到有一次笔者在坦桑尼亚的一个村庄调研时才恍然大悟。在Rudawe村，有一个非常简陋的房子，摆着一张简单的长条桌，房子墙角三块砖垒砌的灶台上煮着茶水，一位非洲妇女坐在地上制作一种叫Chapati（一种薄饼）的小吃，时不时会有村民来这里买薄饼或喝茶。笔者很奇怪，这里的农民收入都非常低，为什么不在家里自己做早饭，而要来买早点，自己做不是更便宜更合算吗？笔者问这位非洲妇女，"你一天能卖多少张薄饼？每一张成本是多少呢？"她告诉笔者，在当地市场买一袋25公斤的面粉需要3万先令，这25公斤面粉可以制作375张薄饼，每张薄饼卖200先令，五天要用一袋面粉；一般顾客会在店里吃，还会要一杯茶，这样一个套餐就是400先令。粗略计算后可以发现，如果农民自己买面粉做薄饼只需要80先令，但为什么本来就没有什么钱的农民会天天来买200先令一张的薄饼呢？这时刚好一名妇女来买薄饼，笔者就问她为什么不自己买面粉做。她回答说，"我没有购买一整袋面粉的预算，那需要3万先令，是一大笔钱。我帮别人除草、收玉米、干农活，每天只有3000先令的收入。而我一家全天的花销都得靠这3000先令，所以我只有每天购买几张薄饼的预算，那就天天来这了。"原来这些超小包装的商品实际上是为了满足当地人在有限的消费能力下的基本生活需求。虽然收入很低，但是他们也希望能够用一下手机，于是买1美元的电话卡充值，满足自己的需要；或是希望可以吃一点零食，花很少的钱，就可以吃到自己想吃的食物。他们在精心计算中量入为出，用自己的逻辑将生活过得更有滋味。

不同国家间多维贫困指数也存在较大差异。按照联合国的统计数据，2022年非洲48个有数据的国家中有15个国家多维贫困指数高于0.3，有12个国家低于0.1（见图2-5）。

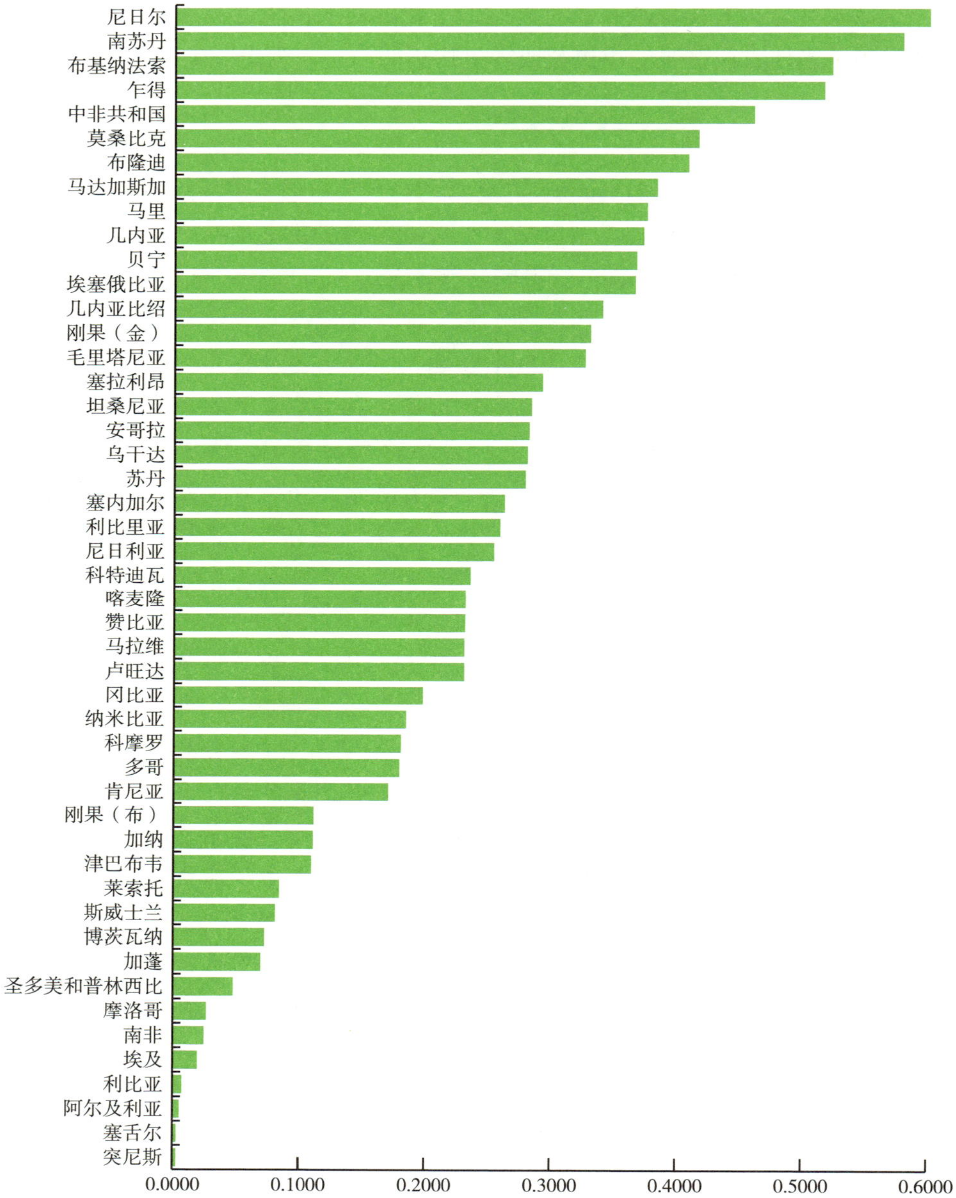

图2-5　2022年非洲48国多维贫困指数

注：佛得角、吉布提、厄立特里亚、赤道几内亚、毛里求斯、索马里无数据。
资料来源：根据《2022年全球多维贫困指数》的数据整理并绘制。

（三）非洲粮食安全与营养健康形势

非洲中度或严重粮食不安全率以及粮食不安全人口持续上升。近年来，多重危机冲突、自然灾害、疾病和经济冲击增加了整个非洲大陆的粮食安全风险，2021年非洲约有2.82亿人（占总人口的20%）面临粮食不安全和营养不良问题[1]。2022年，非洲地区粮食不足发生率、中度或重度粮食不安全率以及严重粮食不安全率仍居高不下，分别为19.7%、60.9%和24%，远高于世界其他地区，是世界平均水平的两倍以上（见表2-13）。

表2-13　　　　　　　2022年世界及不同地区粮食安全状况　　　　　单位：%

地区	粮食不足发生率	中度或重度粮食不安全率	严重粮食不安全率
欧洲	<2.5	8.2	1.9
拉丁美洲和加勒比地区	6.5	37.5	12.6
南亚	15.6	40.3	19.4
大洋洲	7.0	13.0	3.4
非洲	19.7	60.9	24.0
撒哈拉以南非洲	22.1	66.6	26.3
世界	9.2	29.6	11.3

资料来源：根据联合国粮农组织公布的数据整理所得，参见https://www.fao.org/faostat/zh/#data/FS。

疫情加剧了非洲的粮食不安全，尤其是撒哈拉以南非洲。从图2-6可知，2010年以来，撒哈拉以南非洲的食物不足发生率呈显著上升趋势，2019年该地区的粮食不足发生率达到20.1%，超过2.14亿人面临食物不足。疫情后，该地区的粮食安全问题愈发严峻，2022年该地区粮食不足发生率上升至22.1%，近2.5亿人面临粮食不足。同时，该地区的中度或重度粮食不安全率和严重粮食不安全率均处于全球最高水平，分别达到66.6%和26.3%。

---

[1]　国际粮食政策研究所，《2023全球粮食政策报告》，参见https://ebrary.ifpri.org/digital/collection/p15738coll2/id/136641（访问日期：2023年6月1日）。

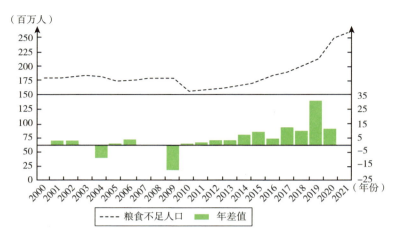

图2-6 2000~2021年撒哈拉以南非洲粮食不足人口

资料来源：根据联合国粮农组织公布的数据整理并绘制，参见https：//www.fao.org/faostat/zh/#data/FS。

在次区域层面，粮食不安全问题最突出的是中非，其次是东非，这两个区域的粮食不足发生率是世界平均水平的三倍，中度或重度粮食不安全率分别为69.2%和78.4%，是粮食不安全的重灾区（见表2-14）。

表2-14　　　　　　　　2022年非洲不同区域粮食安全状况　　　　　　　　单位：%

地区	粮食不足发生率	中度或重度粮食不安全率	严重粮食不安全率
东非	28.5	69.2	27.7
中部非洲	29.1	78.4	39.1
北非	7.5	32.4	12.0
南部非洲	11.1	25.9	12.5
西非	14.6	66.4	22.0
非洲	19.7	60.9	24.0

资料来源：根据联合国粮农组织公布的数据整理所得，参见https：//www.fao.org/faostat/zh/#data/FS。

非洲的粮食不安全人口也在持续增加。2021年，非洲约有1.163亿人处于中度或严重粮食不安全状态[1]，相较2019年增加了2550万人，严重粮食不安全

———————
[1]　国际粮食政策研究所，《2023全球粮食政策报告》，参见https：//ebrary.ifpri.org/digital/collection/p15738coll2/id/136641（访问日期：2023年6月1日）。

人口增加了1300多万人。具体来看，在绝对人数方面，刚果（金）的粮食安全问题最为严峻，超过2730万人处于中度或重度粮食不安全状态，埃塞俄比（2360万人）、尼日利亚（1945万人）和苏丹（1170万人）的粮食不安全人口也均超过千万。在增长情况方面，2021~2022年有三个非洲国家严重粮食不安全人口增长超过50万人：尼日利亚（增加了90万人）、索马里（增加了90万人）、肯尼亚（增加了80万人）。此外，在《2022年全球粮食危机报告》统计时间段内，七个国家或地区有超过37.6万人处于饥荒，其中索马里21.4万人（占57%）、南苏丹8.7万人（占23%），布基纳法索和尼日利亚处于饥荒的人口也分别达到了1.8万人和3000人（见图2-7）。由此可见，在这些国家，饥饿和粮食不安全对生命安全造成直接威胁。非洲持续增长的中度或重度粮食不安全率和粮食不安全的人口，使实现"到2030年消除饥饿"的目标变得更具挑战性。

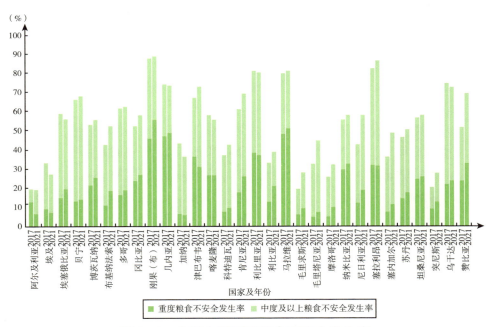

图2-7　非洲主要国家粮食不安全发生率

资料来源：根据联合国粮农组织公布的数据整理并绘制，参见 https://www.fao.org/faostat/zh/#data/FS（访问日期：2023年6月1日）。

高度依赖粮食进口已经严重威胁非洲地区的粮食安全。 非洲各国的粮食自给率普遍较低，粮食进口依赖程度高。受到非洲之角地区常年干旱的持续影响，非洲国家粮食内部供给持续下降，非洲各国粮食的对外依存度大幅上升，进口粮食所占比重不断上升。从表2-15可知，2020年，非洲有26个国家粮食进口占总进口的比重达20%以上。其中，六个国家超过30%，分别为塞舌尔、刚果（布）、圣多美和普林西比、利比里亚、尼日尔和吉布提；四个国家超过40%，分别是科摩罗、南苏丹、几内亚比绍和布隆迪。此外，索马里的粮食供应问题最为严峻，异常的气候状况和粮食不安全极大地影响了索马里国民的基本生计，其境内的粮食供应严重依赖援助维持。在全球粮食价格上升、产量下降的趋势下，高度依赖粮食进口已经在很大程度上威胁到了非洲地区的粮食安全。

表2-15　　　　　　　　2020年非洲国家粮食进口情况

序号	国家	粮食进口占总进口的比重（%）	粮食净进口额（百万美元）	序号	国家	粮食进口占总进口的比重（%）	粮食净进口额（百万美元）
粮食进口占比10%以下（4个）				16	加蓬	16.11	535
1	南非	6.25	-4067	17	多哥	16.47	133
2	乍得	6.43	60	18	肯尼亚	16.59	-152
3	赞比亚	8.16	2	19	卢旺达	17.63	165
4	坦桑尼亚	9.35	-597	20	中非共和国	18.00	74
粮食进口占比10%~20%（24个）				21	津巴布韦	18.15	734
5	马拉维	10.23	17	22	斯威士兰	18.50	-225
6	布基纳法索	10.37	142	23	马达加斯加	18.51	-273
7	刚果（金）	10.61	595	24	安哥拉	18.73	1721
8	乌干达	10.62	-580	25	塞拉利昂	18.97	340
9	突尼斯	11.19	601	26	莫桑比克	19.43	889
10	纳米比亚	11.24	-149	27	尼日利亚	19.84	5785
11	埃塞俄比亚	11.51	-27	28	莱索托	19.86	289
12	博茨瓦纳	11.73	687	粮食进口占比20%~30%（15个）			
13	马里	12.41	422	29	赤道几内亚	20.02	257
14	摩洛哥	12.97	-293	30	利比亚	20.93	2857
15	厄立特里亚	13.37	130	31	埃及	21.79	8469

续表

序号	国家	粮食进口占总进口的比重(%)	粮食净进口额(百万美元)	序号	国家	粮食进口占总进口的比重(%)	粮食净进口额(百万美元)
32	加纳	21.93	-276	44	塞舌尔	30.28	-148
33	毛里求斯	22.37	393	45	刚果(布)	30.50	566
34	科特迪瓦	22.94	-4585	46	圣多美和普林西比	32.60	34
35	苏丹	23.02	1012	47	利比里亚	34.39	328
36	喀麦隆	23.11	183	48	尼日尔	36.28	686
37	塞内加尔	23.83	703	49	吉布提	37.75	949
38	阿尔及利亚	23.84	7973	粮食进口占比40%以上(4个)			
39	贝宁	24.39	709	50	科摩罗	41.77	104
40	几内亚	25.38	798	51	南苏丹	42.42	412
41	冈比亚	26.98	152	52	几内亚比绍	50.56	20
42	毛里塔尼亚	29.37	177	53	布隆迪	77.16	52
43	佛得角	29.86	170	其他			
粮食进口占比30%~40%(6个)				54	索马里	152.54	1533

注:根据联合国粮农组织公布的数据,2020年索马里粮食进口额达到1800万美元,而世界银行统计的2020年索马里进口总额为1180万美元,主要是由于索马里对国际粮食援助的高度依赖。

资料来源:根据联合国粮农组织《2022年世界粮食及农业统计年鉴》和世界银行公布的数据整理所得。

满足人口的粮食和营养需求以实现零饥饿是许多非洲国家消除贫困的基础性目标,然而非洲国家饥饿状况仍十分糟糕,饥饿问题亟待解决。根据国际粮食政策研究所(IFPRI)发布的2022年全球饥饿指数排名,非洲国家的排名普遍靠后。2022年有数据的49个非洲国家中,仅有突尼斯、阿尔及利亚和摩洛哥三个国家的饥饿指数低于10,其余46个国家饥饿指数均超过10,表明多数非洲国家处于严重饥饿状况。其中,有19个非洲国家的饥饿指数超过20,16个国家超过30,并有4个国家超过40,饥饿情况极度严峻(见表2-16)。

表2-16　　　　　　　　　　非洲国家饥饿指数全球排名及变化

排名	国家	2022年非洲国家GHI指数排名				2014~2022年GHI差值	2014~2022年GHI变化率（%）
		2000年	2007年	2014年	2022年		
26	突尼斯	10.3	7.6	6.7	6.1	-0.6	-9.0
32	阿尔及利亚	14.5	11.4	8.7	6.9	-1.8	-20.7
47	摩洛哥	15.8	12.4	9.6	9.2	-0.4	-4.2
54	佛得角	15.3	11.9	12.1	11.8	-0.3	-2.5
57	埃及	16.3	17.2	14.6	12.3	-2.3	-15.8
59	南非	18.1	17.2	12.7	12.9	0.2	1.6
62	毛里求斯	15.3	14.1	13.0	13.4	0.4	3.1
67	加纳	28.5	22.1	15.5	13.9	-1.6	-10.3
71	塞内加尔	34.2	22.8	17.6	15.6	-2.0	-11.4
73	斯威士兰	24.7	22.9	18.4	16.3	-2.1	-11.4
74	科特迪瓦	33.4	35.8	22.7	16.8	-5.9	-26.0
76	加蓬	20.9	20.3	16.5	17.2	0.7	4.2
78	纳米比亚	25.4	26.8	22.9	18.7	-4.2	-18.3
80	喀麦隆	35.8	29.9	21.4	18.9	-2.5	-11.7
86	博茨瓦纳	27.7	25.8	20.5	20.0	-0.5	-2.4
87	冈比亚	29.0	26.5	22.2	20.7	-1.5	-6.8
87	马拉维	43.3	32.5	24.1	20.7	-3.4	-14.1
87	毛里塔尼亚	31.8	28.3	26.3	20.7	-5.6	-21.3
90	吉布提	44.3	35.8	27.4	21.5	-5.9	-21.5
91	贝宁	33.8	26.9	23.2	21.7	-1.5	-6.5
92	多哥	39.3	30.2	26.1	22.8	-3.3	-12.6
93	马里	41.7	35.7	26.1	23.2	-2.9	-11.1
94	肯尼亚	36.6	31.1	21.6	23.5	1.9	8.8
95	坦桑尼亚	40.8	30.9	25.5	23.6	-1.9	-7.5
96	布基纳法索	44.9	34.5	26.5	24.5	-2.0	-7.5
98	安哥拉	64.9	44.7	26.2	25.9	-0.3	-1.1
101	科摩罗	39.5	31.7	29.1	26.9	-2.2	-7.6
102	卢旺达	49.9	35.9	29.5	27.2	-2.3	-7.8
103	尼日利亚	40.4	32.1	28.4	27.3	-1.1	-3.9

续表

排名	2022年非洲国家GHI指数排名					2014~2022年 GHI差值	2014~2022年 GHI变化率（%）
	国家	2000年	2007年	2014年	2022年		
104	埃塞俄比亚	53.6	42.6	27.4	27.6	0.2	0.7
105	刚果（布）	34.7	33.7	25.3	28.1	2.8	11.1
106	苏丹	—	—	29.3	28.8	-0.5	-1.7
108	赞比亚	53.3	46.0	35.2	29.3	-5.9	-16.8
111	几内亚比绍	37.7	31.0	30.2	30.8	0.6	2.0
112	塞拉利昂	57.5	51.1	33.1	31.5	-1.6	-4.8
113	莱索托	32.7	29.1	29.3	32.4	3.1	10.6
113	利比里亚	48.2	39.0	34.8	32.4	-2.4	-6.9
115	尼日尔	52.5	40.2	32.8	32.6	-0.2	-0.6
*	几内亚	—	—	—	20.0~34.9*		
*	莫桑比克	—	—	—	20.0~34.9*		
*	乌干达	—	—	—	20.0~34.9*		
*	津巴布韦	—	—	—	20.0~34.9*		
117	乍得	50.7	49.0	40.7	37.2	-3.5	-8.6
118	刚果（金）	48.0	43.2	38.7	37.8	-0.9	-2.3
119	马达加斯加	42.5	37.2	37.3	38.7	1.4	3.8
120	中非共和国	48.8	46.8	44.6	44.0	-0.6	-1.3
*	布隆迪	—	—	—	35.0~49.9*		
*	索马里	—	—	—	35.0~49.9*		
*	南苏丹	—	—	—	35.0~49.9*		

注：利比亚、厄立特里亚、塞舌尔、赤道几内亚和圣多美和普林西比五个国家无数据。

资料来源：根据全球饥饿指数整理所得，参见 https：//www.globalhungerindex.org/（访问日期：2023年6月1日）。

五、区域发展问题

区域发展不平衡问题依旧突出。以人均国民总收入（GNI）作为衡量标准，非洲54个国家中有46个处于中等偏下收入水平和低收入水平，有一半国家的人均GNI低于非洲地区平均值。从表2-17可知，不同国家之间存在明显的发展不平衡，不仅高收入国家与低收入国家之间相差巨大，如2021年人均GNI最高

值（塞舌尔，13822美元）是最低值（布隆迪，222美元）的62倍，而且同一
收入水平组别中依然存在相当大的差距，且收入越低的组别差距越大。非洲国
家尤其是撒哈拉以南非洲国家（人均GNI低于1600美元）的发展水平处于全球
最低水平，绝大多数中等收入国家和低收入国家深陷"低水平发展的陷阱"。

表2-17　　　　　　　　2021年非洲国家人均GNI　　单位：2021年现价美元

序号	国家	人均GNI	序号	国家	人均GNI	序号	国家	人均GNI
高收入（13205美元及以上）			18	加纳	2303	37	卢旺达	805
1	塞舌尔	13821	19	刚果（布）	2190	38	几内亚比绍	796
中等偏上收入（4256~13205美元）			20	毛里塔尼亚	2134	39	乌干达	765
2	毛里求斯	9241	21	肯尼亚	2050	40	冈比亚	752
3	加蓬	7283	22	尼日利亚	1986	41	苏丹	722
4	南非	6919	23	安哥拉	1799	42	乍得	662
5	博茨瓦纳	6435	24	津巴布韦	1730	43	利比里亚	634
6	利比亚	6409	25	喀麦隆	1629	44	马拉维	623
7	赤道几内亚	5596	26	塞内加尔	1602	45	尼日尔	601
8	纳米比亚	4772	27	科摩罗	1585	46	刚果（金）	542
中等偏下收入（1086~4255美元）			28	贝宁	1354	47	中非共和国	492
9	摩洛哥	3800	29	莱索托	1246	48	马达加斯加	490
10	突尼斯	3681	低收入（1085美元及以下）			49	莫桑比克	481
11	斯威士兰	3658	30	坦桑尼亚	1063	50	塞拉利昂	474
12	阿尔及利亚	3609	31	几内亚	1050	51	索马里	444
13	埃及	3585	32	赞比亚	1038	52	布隆迪	222
14	佛得角	3229	33	多哥	975	53	厄立特里亚	—
15	吉布提	3095	34	埃塞俄比亚	920	54	南苏丹	—
16	科特迪瓦	2472	35	布基纳法索	846			
17	圣多美和普林西比	2386	36	马里	833	撒哈拉以南非洲		1577

注：厄立特里亚和南苏丹无数据。
资料来源：根据《世界发展指标》（WDI）2023年5月10日更新数据整理所得。

非洲地区收入不平等问题突出。在分配方面，非洲地区、各次区域以及各
国内部的收入不平等现象非常严重。最新数据表明，非洲地区的基尼系数达到
0.416。除北非地区，其余四个次区域的基尼系数均高于世界平均水平，其中南

部非洲的基尼系数达到0.526（见表2-18）。

表2-18　　　　　　　　世界及各地区基尼系数

地区	基尼系数
南部非洲	0.526
中部非洲	0.403
东非	0.397
北非	0.342
西非	0.381
非洲	0.416
拉丁美洲和加勒比地区	0.455
亚洲	0.352
世界	0.371

资料来源：根据经济合作与发展组织《2023年非洲发展动态：投资于可持续发展》的数据整理所得，参见https：//www.oecd.org/dev/africa/development-dynamics/。

根据世界银行公布的数据，50个有数据的非洲国家中，仅有几内亚和阿尔及利亚两个国家的基尼系数低于0.3，其余48个国家都在0.3以上。其中，有26个国家在0.4以上，并有九个国家超过0.5（见表2-19）。由此可见，许多非洲国家内部收入不平等现象相当严重，分配不平等问题依然突出。这也进一步说明，尽管疫情前非洲国家的经济普遍得到了较快的增长，但在发展过程中绝大多数国家的极端贫困和不平等现象并没有得到显著改善，区域间、国家间的收入不平等程度依然很深。

表2-19　　　　　　　　非洲国家基尼系数

国家	统计年份	基尼系数	国家	统计年份	基尼系数
南非	2014	0.630	坦桑尼亚	2018	0.405
纳米比亚	2015	0.591	摩洛哥	2013	0.395
赞比亚	2015	0.571	冈比亚	2020	0.388
中非共和国	2008	0.562	布隆迪	2013	0.386
斯威士兰	2016	0.546	马拉维	2019	0.385
莫桑比克	2014	0.540	塞内加尔	2018	0.381
博茨瓦纳	2015	0.533	加蓬	2017	0.380

国家	统计年份	基尼系数	国家	统计年份	基尼系数
安哥拉	2018	0.513	贝宁	2018	0.378
津巴布韦	2019	0.503	乍得	2018	0.375
刚果（布）	2011	0.489	尼日尔	2018	0.373
布基纳法索	2018	0.473	科特迪瓦	2018	0.372
喀麦隆	2014	0.466	毛里求斯	2017	0.368
科摩罗	2014	0.453	马里	2018	0.361
莱索托	2017	0.449	塞拉利昂	2018	0.357
南苏丹	2016	0.441	利比里亚	2016	0.353
卢旺达	2016	0.437	尼日利亚	2018	0.351
加纳	2016	0.435	埃塞俄比亚	2015	0.350
乌干达	2019	0.427	几内亚比绍	2018	0.348
马达加斯加	2012	0.426	苏丹	2014	0.342
佛得角	2015	0.424	突尼斯	2015	0.328
多哥	2018	0.424	毛里塔尼亚	2014	0.326
刚果（金）	2012	0.421	塞舌尔	2018	0.321
吉布提	2017	0.416	埃及	2019	0.319
肯尼亚	2015	0.408	几内亚	2018	0.296
圣多美和普林西比	2017	0.407	阿尔及利亚	2011	0.276

注：厄立特里亚、赤道几内亚、利比亚、索马里无数据。
资料来源：根据《世界发展指标》（WDI）2023年5月10日更新数据整理所得。

六、小结

非洲是全球贫困问题最严重的地区，该地区最不发达国家、低收入缺粮国家以及重债穷国高度集中，尤其是撒哈拉以南非洲。近年来，非洲减贫工作进展缓慢，成效甚微，2020年极端贫困人口达到4.49亿人，极端贫困发生率高达40.17%，是世界上极端贫困人口最集中、贫困发生率最高的地区。按照世界银行2022年发布的每人每天2.15美元的贫困标准，非洲贫困人口达3.75亿人，贫困发生率达到了26.3%。非洲的多维贫困问题日益突出，特别是弱势群体和农村地区，疫情对健康、教育和生活水平带来的负面影响将长期存在，较低的生活水平是当前非洲各国亟须采取措施应对的关键问题。在整体层面上，2022年撒哈拉以南非洲的粮食不足发生率达到22.1%，粮食不足人口将近2.5亿人，粮食安全和营养形势倒退，加剧了非洲的粮食危机，各次区域中度或严重粮食不安全率以及粮食不安全人口持续上升；高度依赖粮食进口也对非洲地区的粮食安全造成严重威胁，截至2022年，非洲国家饥饿指数较高，粮食不足造成的饥饿问题仍是非洲面临的首要问题。此外，非洲分配方面的不平等程度也普遍较高，各次区域和各国内部的收入不平等现象非常严重。相对而言，非洲国家人类发展水平均有所上升，但在预期寿命、生育率、婴儿死亡率等基本健康状况指标方面还存在较大差距。

　　总体来看，超过一半的非洲国家同时存在收入过低、严重缺粮、严重债务危机等问题，减贫发展面临严峻挑战。整体上非洲仍处于低发展阶段，区域发展不平衡不充分问题日益突出，多维贫困方面的减贫进展受阻，各地区贫困状况不容乐观，特别是受到新冠疫情、全球气候变化等多重不利于发展的因素的叠加影响。要理解非洲国家所面临的发展困境以及非洲各国减贫发展表现出的极大差异，需要对造成非洲国家贫困的主要原因展开深入分析，以有效应对和推动非洲减贫发展。

第三章
非洲减贫进展缓慢的主要原因

　　自疫情暴发以来，持续的全球通货膨胀以及紧缩的货币政策导致非洲国家借贷成本上升，加上援助预算长期下降以及公共债务的利息负担加重，非洲地区不得不与日益加剧的宏观经济失衡作斗争。从2022年开始，非洲的公共债务和通货膨胀就处于数十年来的最高水平，大约一半的非洲国家出现了两位数的通货膨胀[①]，不断上涨的粮食和能源价格影响着非洲地区最脆弱的群体。世界银行的数据显示，疫情后撒哈拉以南非洲的整体经济复苏缓慢，经济增长率从2021年的4.1%下降到2022年的3.6%[②]。

　　非洲国家的贫困在很大程度上是由宏观经济条件、粮食危机、气候灾害（尤其是干旱及洪水）、地区冲突以及薄弱的发展条件等多种因素共同导致的，以上所有因素都影响着非洲国家的减贫进展。未来这些内外部因素将变得更加复杂，尤其是在减贫发展方面，越来越受到各种冲突的影响，特别是新冠疫情和地区冲突对社会经济带来的全球性冲击，在非洲各区域和国家层面产生了连锁反应。

一、宏观经济层面的原因

　　缓慢的经济增长难以驱动减贫发展。非洲整体经济增长相对稳定，但经济增速趋缓，不能有效促进减贫。长期以来，撒哈拉以南非洲的经济发展保持着较为稳定的增长，GDP从2000年的4230亿美元增长到2019年的18033亿美元[③]，在经历了2020年大幅下跌后，2021年上升至27161亿美元，2022年继续增

---

①　国际货币基金组织发布的《2023非洲区域经济展望》，参见https：//www.imf.org/en/publications/reo?sortby=Date&series=Sub-Saharan%20Africa（访问日期：2023年6月1日）。

②　参见https：//www.worldbank.org/en/region/afr（访问日期：2023年6月1日）。

③　根据世界银行公布的数据计算所得，以2023年现价美元计，参见https：//data.worldbank.org.cn/indicator/NY.GDP.MKTP.CD?locations=ZG（访问日期：2023年6月1日）。

长，达到29833亿美元[①]。但从增长速度来看，非洲经济增长速度趋缓。受到疫情影响，2020年非洲地区GDP增长率出现了近二十年来的首次负增长，从2019年的2.56%下降至-2.07%。2021~2022年非洲经济增长速度持续放缓，从4.1%下降至3.6%。全球经济持续低迷、经济增长下降且通货膨胀率高、全球和国内金融形势严峻，以及非洲债台高筑，这些因素综合导致了撒哈拉以南非洲经济增长下降。据估计，2024年和2025年的经济增长率将分别回升至3.7%和3.9%，这表明2023年的增长放缓应该会触底。然而，从中长期来看，非洲的增长条件不足以减少极端贫困和促进共同繁荣。

在较低的人口城镇化率、较快的人口增长压力下，缓慢的经济增长难以发挥其减贫效应。 非洲是全球人口城镇化率最低的地区，2021年撒哈拉以南非洲的城镇化率为43.99%，低于世界其他地区和平均水平（56.48%）。在较低的城镇化率的背景下，非洲人口逐年稳定增长，GDP增速却相对缓慢。从表3-1可知，2015~2022年，撒哈拉以南非洲的年均人口增速超过2.6%，而同期世界其他地区的人口增速明显下降，全球人口增速从1.19%下降至0.80%，撒哈拉以南非洲的人口增速是世界平均水平的3倍以上。而GDP方面的情况则相反，相较于世界其他地区，非洲的GDP增速相对缓慢，2015~2022年从2.87%震荡上升至3.57%，仅2022年的经济增速略高于世界平均水平。与人口和GDP紧密相关的人均GDP增长也极为缓慢，2016~2020年撒哈拉以南非洲的人均GDP连续五年负增长，2022年的增速仅为1%。人均GDP的缓慢增长充分反映出非洲的经济增速低于人口增速，GDP增长的效应在很大程度上被人口的快速增长所抵消，导致减贫进程难以加快。

表3-1　　　　　　　　全球不同地区的人口增速和经济增速　　　　单位：%

	区域	2015年	2016年	2017年	2018年	2019年	2020年	2021年	2022年
人口增速	东亚和太平洋地区	0.71	0.71	0.71	0.61	0.53	0.43	0.26	0.21
	拉丁美洲和加勒比地区	1.03	1.01	0.98	0.92	0.89	0.81	0.68	0.66
	南亚	1.23	1.21	1.22	1.19	1.14	1.12	1.03	0.92
	撒哈拉以南非洲	2.77	2.72	2.68	2.68	2.67	2.65	2.59	2.54
	全球	1.19	1.17	1.15	1.10	1.06	1.01	0.86	0.80

---

① 根据《2023年宏观贫困展望》中非洲各国的GDP数据计算所得，以2023年现价美元计。

续表

区域		2015年	2016年	2017年	2018年	2019年	2020年	2021年	2022年
GDP增速	东亚和太平洋地区	4.72	4.67	5.05	4.76	3.96	−0.12	6.10	2.85
	拉丁美洲和加勒比地区	0.52	−0.16	1.88	1.62	0.74	−6.45	6.73	3.75
	南亚	7.34	7.68	6.53	6.33	3.94	−4.66	8.27	6.47
	撒哈拉以南非洲	2.87	1.27	2.44	2.65	2.59	−2.00	4.17	3.57
	全球	3.08	2.81	3.39	3.29	2.59	−3.07	6.02	3.08
人均GDP增速	东亚和太平洋地区	3.97	3.94	4.31	4.12	3.41	−0.54	5.82	2.63
	拉丁美洲和加勒比地区	−0.51	−1.16	0.89	0.70	−0.15	−7.20	6.01	3.07
	南亚	6.04	6.39	5.25	5.09	2.76	−5.72	7.16	5.50
	撒哈拉以南非洲	0.10	−1.41	−0.23	−0.03	−0.07	−4.54	1.54	1.00
	全球	1.87	1.62	2.22	2.16	1.52	−4.04	5.12	2.26

资料来源：根据世界银行公布的数据整理所得。

沉重的债务负担以及低水平的对外投资也导致非洲经济增长动力不强。在债务方面，自世纪之交以来的一系列境外冲击使非洲债务水平迅速上升，制约了非洲的增长潜力。2000~2022年，非洲的公共债务从4130亿美元攀升至1.8万亿美元，处于十多年来的最高水平（见图3-1）。尤其是在2010~2022年，非洲的公共债务增加了183%，几乎是GDP增长率的4倍。许多非洲国家的债务占GDP的比例极高，2022年有24个国家的债务水平超过了GDP的60%（见图3-2）。国际货币基金组织的数据显示，非洲的公共债务相对集中，2022年埃及、南非、尼日利亚、阿尔及利亚以及摩洛哥五个国家的公共债务达到了1087亿美元，占非洲债务的60%。相较于其他发展中国家，非洲国家降低债务水平的速度较慢，而债务的快速上升阻碍了经济增长，并限制其应对未来危机或为发展进行投资的能力。

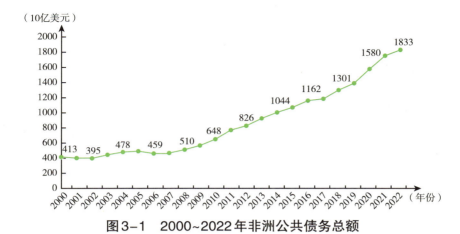

图3-1　2000~2022年非洲公共债务总额

注：数字代表以当前美元为单位的名义价值。公共债务是指一般政府内债和外债。一般政府由中央、州和地方政府以及这些单位控制的社会保障基金组成。

资料来源：根据国际货币基金组织《世界经济展望（2023年4月）》的数据计算并绘制。

图3-2　债务水平较高的国家数量（公共债务超过GDP的60%）

资料来源：联合国全球危机应对小组，根据国际货币基金组织《世界经济展望（2023年4月）》的数据计算并绘制。

在引进外资方面，非洲人均以及区域层面获得对外投资（FDI）的水平低，难以拉动经济增长。在区域层面，非洲是全球获得对外投资金额最少的地区，且所占比重呈下降趋势。2015~2022年，撒哈拉以南非洲获得的对外投资占全球的比重从1.61%下降至0.39%（见表3-2），是全球唯一一个获得对外投资额度占比下降的地区。在人均层面，2015年撒哈拉以南非洲人均获得的对外投资为44.04美元，是世界平均水平的12%；到2022年，撒哈拉以南非洲人均获得的对外投资下降至5.91美元，仅为世界平均水平的2.6%，是全球降幅最大的区域（见表3–3）。

表3–2　　2015~2022年全球部分区域获得的FDI占全球FDI的比重　单位：%

地区	2015年	2016年	2017年	2018年	2019年	2020年	2021年	2022年
东亚和太平洋地区	22.35	19.41	25.5	63.55	31.20	46.06	38.49	35.21
拉丁美洲和加勒比地区	11.66	8.08	9.27	22.22	11.58	11.60	9.88	11.74
南亚	1.80	1.87	2.11	5.16	3.33	5.40	2.39	2.93
撒哈拉以南非洲	1.61	1.12	1.27	3.08	1.61	1.86	3.52	0.39

资料来源：根据世界银行的数据整理所得。

表3–3　　　2015~2022年全球部分区域人均获得的FDI　单位：美元/人

地区	2015年	2016年	2017年	2018年	2019年	2020年	2021年	2022年
东亚和太平洋地区	269.05	229.02	240.63	255.86	225.44	249.02	340.64	271.43
拉丁美洲和加勒比地区	518.46	350.74	320.69	327.55	305.29	227.88	316.53	326.13
南亚	28.00	28.34	25.47	26.44	30.45	36.63	26.32	27.93
撒哈拉以南非洲	44.03	29.53	26.10	26.62	24.47	20.67	62.59	5.91
全球	373.05	363.83	289.47	123.04	219.7	163.41	265.93	230.30

资料来源：根据世界银行的数据整理所得。

二、产业结构层面的原因

非洲农业生产长期保持低水平，增加了粮食安全的脆弱性。世界银行的预测模型显示，按照既有的经济增长趋势，到2030年撒哈拉以南非洲的贫困人口将达到全球贫困人口总量的87%。按照当前饥饿人口增加的趋势，到2030年，非洲将成为长期饥饿人口最多的地区。由于农业生产环境脆弱、农业要素投入不足，非洲农业生产水平低，粮食产量难以满足基本生存需求，这使2030年实现零饥饿目标更具不确定性。

（一）农业生产环境

非洲农业生产环境脆弱，气候灾害和社会暴力冲突频发，加大了粮食生产的难度。一方面，由于非洲大陆独特的地理区位，农业生态环境极为脆弱，易遭受极端天气引发的旱涝等各类气象灾害的侵袭，导致粮食大面积歉收、农作物减产。例如，2019年3月和4月，飓风"伊代"和"肯尼斯"袭击南部非洲的莫桑比克、津巴布韦、马拉维等国，大量即将收获的农作物及有限的农业基础设施遭到严重破坏。此外，病虫害的侵袭也令非洲国家深受其害，2020年初，非洲之角国家遭受了严重的蝗灾，使东非八国约500万人面临粮食危机。另一方面，各类暴力冲突恶化了农业生产环境。非洲部分国家和地区是全球战乱频繁、政局不稳定的高风险地区，即使在新冠疫情笼罩下的2020年和2021年，非洲的恐袭事件依然有增无减，使该地区农业生产因战乱而难以为继。

（二）粮食生产能力

长期以来，农业发展水平增长缓慢是非洲面临粮食安全和饥饿问题的重要原因。世界银行的数据显示，1978年，撒哈拉以南非洲国家的谷物单产为1031.64公斤/公顷；到2021年，提高到1588.77公斤/公顷，在过去40多年里作物单产仅仅增加了54%（见表3-4）。同期，世界谷物单产从2198.13公斤/公顷提高到4153.72公斤/公顷，增加了88.97%，而非洲谷物单产水平不到世界平均水平的40%。

非洲主要粮食作物平均产量均低于世界平均水平。薯类和玉米（非洲最主要的粮食作物）的平均产量不及世界平均产量的40%，分别为3030公斤/公顷和2276公斤/公顷；稻谷的平均产量不及世界平均产量的50%，为2276公斤/公顷；小麦的平均产量和木薯的平均产量也不高，是世界平均产量的67.27%和80.50%，分别为2349公斤/公顷和8546公斤/公顷（见表3-5）。

表 3-4 世界及撒哈拉以南非洲的谷物单产水平 单位：公斤/公顷

地区	1978 年	1980 年	2012 年	2013 年	2014 年	2015 年
世界	2198.13	2175.11	3615.04	3817.84	3890.07	3926.47
撒哈拉以南非洲	1031.64（46.93%）	1064.54（48.94%）	1410.22（39.01%）	1325.25（34.71%）	1435.87（36.91%）	1437.31（36.61%）
地区	2016 年	2017 年	2018 年	2019 年	2020 年	2021 年
世界	4011.04	4073.45	4029.56	4125.45	4116.43	4153.72
撒哈拉以南非洲	1402.19（34.96%）	1518.13（37.27%）	1525.19（37.85%）	1521.67（36.88%）	1605.74（39.01%）	1588.77（38.25%）

注：括号内为撒哈拉以南非洲谷物单产水平占世界水平的比重。
资料来源：根据世界银行的数据整理所得。

表 3-5 世界及非洲主要粮食作物的平均产量及占比

地区	木薯	玉米	稻谷	小麦	薯类（Yams）
世界（公斤/公顷）	10616	5878	4764	3492	8651
非洲（公斤/公顷）	8546（80.50%）	2276（38.72%）	2276（47.77%）	2349（67.27%）	3030（35.02%）

注：括号内为非洲主要粮食作物的平均产量占世界产量的比重。
资料来源：根据世界银行的数据整理所得。

　　随着非洲人口规模的持续扩大，粮食消费需求呈刚性增长，非洲粮食供需矛盾愈发突出。非洲地区人口增长率长期居高不下，每年约为 2.5%（世界年均增长率不及 1%）[①]，导致粮食消费需求呈刚性增长态势，给粮食系统和经济带来了额外的压力。此外，非洲国家粮食生产存在良种、农化产品和农机设备使用率低、缺乏田间管理能力等诸多问题，粮食生产水平落后，粮食供应量的增长难以满足国内消费需求的增长。其直接结果是，人口规模的持续扩大对冲了粮食供应量改善的正效应。从粮食供求关系看，2010~2021 年，大米、小麦、玉米三大主粮需求缺口从 5801 万吨增加到 8223.7 万吨，2021 年主粮缺口占主粮总消费量的 35.6%，表明非洲国家粮食自我保障能力较弱，粮食安全水平较低。

---

① 国际粮食政策研究所，《2023 全球粮食政策报告》，参见 https：//ebrary.ifpri.org/digital/collection/p15738coll2/id/136641（访问日期：2023 年 6 月 1 日）。

三、粮食供应体系层面的原因

非洲粮食产业体系韧性弱，抗风险能力低。粮食产业体系韧性包括粮食可供性、粮食可获性、粮食利用率、粮食市场稳定性等多个维度，其中粮食获取的稳定性和可持续性颇为重要。非洲主粮自给率低，2021年北非地区的大米、小麦、玉米三大主粮的自给率为34.1%，撒哈拉以南非洲为76.1%，均低于联合国85%的安全标准（见表3-6）。而且大部分非洲国家粮食体制不甚健全，粮食储备能力建设不足。2021年，撒哈拉以南非洲大米和小麦的库存消费比分别为9.8%和11.8%，均远低于联合国粮农组织的安全标准（17%~18%）[1]。此外，根据非盟的相关数据，撒哈拉以南非洲每年粮食损失约占总产量的13%，其中粮食储存、运输和加工包装三个环节的粮食损耗率分别高达59%、19%和18%[2]。由此可见，非洲粮食可获得性不高、利用率低以及粮食供给的不稳定抑制了非洲国家抵御各类风险和应对突发事件的能力，导致非洲地区粮食安全体系脆弱性上升。

表3-6	撒哈拉以南非洲的粮食自给率				单位：%
品类	平均水平			增长率	
	2010~2012年	2020~2022年	2032年	2013~2022年	2023~2032年
谷物	83.5	81.9	77.6	0.09	−0.24
肉类	87.4	83.4	77.5	−0.71	−0.47
糖料	73.7	64.3	53.1	−0.61	−1.10
食用油	58.6	58.5	49.7	1.21	−1.46

资料来源：根据世界银行的数据整理所得。

此外，联合国粮农组织2023年2月发布的粮食价格监测和分析公报显示，87.8%的中等偏下收入国家、93%的中等偏上收入国家以及其他许多国家正在经历两位数的通货膨胀。受此影响最大的国家位于非洲、北美、拉丁美洲、南亚、欧洲和中亚。根据发布的粮食价格通货膨胀数据，撒哈拉以南非洲国家中，津巴布韦位居第一[3]（见表3-7）。

---

① 参见美国农业部海外统计局（USDA Foreign Agricultural Service）网站：https：//apps.fas.usda.gov/psdonline/app/index。

② FAO，The State of Food and Agriculture 2019：Moving forward on Food Loss and Waste Reduction，https：//www.fao.org/3/ca6030en/ca6030en.pdf。

③ 参见https：//www.gafs.info/home/。

表3-7　　　　　　　粮食价格通货膨胀排名前十的国家　　　　　　单位：%

国家	名义粮食通货膨胀	实际粮食通货膨胀
津巴布韦	264	41
委内瑞拉	158	26
黎巴嫩	143	22
阿根廷	98	21
土耳其	70	18
苏里南	61	17
加纳	61	15
斯里兰卡	60	13
卢旺达	57	13
老挝	49	13

资料来源：https：//www.gafs.info/home/。

四、气候变化层面的原因

气候变化是非洲贫困的关键原因之一。气候变化导致灾害高发并引发了一系列冲击，这增加了气候多变性和极端情况带来的压力，不仅破坏整个非洲大陆的粮食稳定性，威胁非洲消除饥饿的能力，而且加剧了非洲的极端贫困。根据世界气象组织的数据，非洲因气候变化而陷入贫困的人口为3200万人~1.32亿人，到2030年，仅气候变化就可能使1亿人陷入贫困[1]。在脆弱国家和低收入国家，特别是撒哈拉以南非洲国家，穷人和边缘群体受到的冲击最大。大约60%的非洲人口缺乏预警系统来应对极端天气和气候变化[2]，各类异常气候状况及其带来的负面影响都将持续并愈发严重。

（一）气候变化对农业的影响

气候变化冲击导致非洲农业生产率大幅下降。温度上升及其导致的海平面上升等问题对非洲的农业、工业生产造成了直接冲击。一方面，气温上升将对非洲的农业生产力、农业用地、农业产量产生负面影响，从而恶化非洲的饥饿和贫困问题。在非洲各个次区域，气温都呈上升趋势，而整个非洲地区气温长期异常偏高，极端高温天气天数也呈上升趋势（见图3-3和图3-4）。长期持续的气候变暖和气温异常导致非洲农业生产能力大幅下降。自1961年以来，气温

[1]　参见世界银行气候变化集团和全球减灾和恢复基金发布的《到2030年气候变化对极端贫困影响的评估修订》。
[2]　参见世界气象组织发布的《非洲气候状况2021》。

上升导致非洲农业生产能力下降了34%，是世界农业生产能力下降最严重的地区。这一趋势将持续，从而不断增加非洲的粮食不安全和营养不良风险。据世界气象组织统计，气候变化将导致非洲国家的雨养作物产量减少50%，撒哈拉以南非洲的作物产量也将减少约20%。

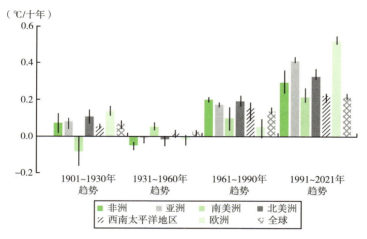

图3-3　非洲各次区域的平均温度趋势

资料来源：英国气象局。

图3-4　1979~2021年非洲年度极端高温天气情况

资料来源：非洲气象应用促进发展中心（ACMAD），基于ERA5。

另一方面，随着气温上升，非洲各地的相对海平面上升可能会继续，这将增加低洼地带和大多数沙质海岸沿海地区洪水发生的频率和严重程度。低洼沿海地区也将不得不应对海平面上升和气候变化造成的土地面积不断减少、农业用地盐碱化、鱼类种群减少和洄游等问题。到2050年，撒哈拉以南非洲国家与海平面上升相关的损失可能达到GDP的2%~4%[①]。

（二）极端气候事件对粮食生产和基础设施的影响

极端气候事件不断增加粮食不安全程度，并对基础设施造成严重破坏。长期干旱是非洲面临的主要极端气候事件之一。当前，1/3的非洲人口生活在干旱易发地区，绝大部分集中在萨赫勒地区、非洲之角附近地区和南部非洲地区[②]，同时，全球1/3的干旱发生在撒哈拉以南非洲，长期干旱导致该地区面临长期粮食贫困。极端天气事件可以显著提高粮食安全风险，特别是对于农业生产力已经不到全球平均水平一半的国家[③]。干旱会对农业和畜牧业生产的多样性产生负面影响，撒哈拉以南非洲的许多国家将不得不面对半干旱气候。2021年，东非地区气候持续恶化，赤道和南部非洲地区经历了过去40年来最严重的干旱，特别是马达加斯加南部地区遭受了至少持续两年的严重干旱[④]。在过去的50年里，与干旱相关的灾害已经夺走了50多万人的生命，并导致非洲的经济损失超过700亿美元[⑤]。联合国政府间气候变化专门委员会（IPCC）估计，到2080年，非洲干旱和半干旱地区将增加5%~8%，非洲之角地区的干旱更加普遍，由此带来的粮食生产性短缺也将更加严重。

非洲由于应急能力不足、措施不完善，热带气旋及大范围洪水等极端气候导致的问题难以有效解决。例如，2021年南部非洲再次遭受热带气旋"埃洛伊丝"袭击，莫桑比克和马达加斯加等国超过46.7万人受到波及[⑥]，特别是莫桑比克，60多个重新安置地点、8700多个避难所被破坏[⑦]，超过4.3万人在国内流离失所，3.45万人被疏散。此外，大范围的洪水对非洲许多国家造成了广泛影响，比如南苏丹连续三年发生极端洪灾，至少83.5万人受到影响[⑧]；在尼日尔，暴雨及其导致的洪水影响了约23万人，超过1.2万所房屋被摧毁，近6000公顷

---

① 参见世界气象组织发布的《非洲气候状况2021》。
② 参见联合国区域发展中心分布的《非洲的气候变化和贫困：挑战和倡议》。
③ 参见Fuglie et al.（2020）；Ritchie（2022）。
④ 参见世界气象组织发布的《非洲气候状况2021》。
⑤ WMO, State of Climate Services report: Water. World Meteorological Organization, 2021, WMO-No.1278.
⑥ OCHA, 2021, Southern Africa Humanitarian Snapshot.
⑦ IOM, 2021, Mozambique Cyclone Eloise Response Plan.
⑧ OCHA, 2022, South Sudan Humanitarian Needs Overview 2022.

可耕地被淹没，超过1万头牲畜丢失[1]；在刚果（金）坦噶尼喀省，一系列洪水影响了28万多人（占总人口的8%以上），造成16人死亡，2.6万多所房屋受损，116所学校、50个医疗中心受损，5000公顷的农作物被毁[2]。

（三）水资源缺乏的影响

非洲面临严重的水资源压力和气候变化压力，包括降水和气温的变化，这导致水资源的可用性显著下降。缺水是全世界贫困人口面临的一个主要问题，据IPCC估计，高水资源压力将影响非洲约2.5亿人[3]。在快速增长的非洲经济体中，维持人口增长的淡水供应需求不断增加，农业和工业部门的用水需求也在不断增加，而更频繁的干旱和高温给本已稀缺的水资源带来额外压力。2021年，整个非洲有66个地区、超过320万人缺少水资源。特别是索马里，大约90%的地区水资源获取受限，南部和中部地区最为突出，水资源极度缺乏[4]，许多井、井洞和伯卡德[5]干涸。2021年，马达加斯加南部也出现了河流干涸，导致水价飙升。截至2021年底，马达加斯加南部超过70%的人无法获得基本饮用水，该地区50%的人口迫切需要水、环境卫生和个人卫生援助[6]。

五、地区安全稳定层面的原因

地区冲突和不安全局势及其导致的大量难民扰乱了经济生产活动和市场，损害了农村生计和基础设施，加剧了非洲国家的贫困问题。局部战争冲突和不安全局势是导致境内难民处于极端贫困状态的主要原因。自2020年以来，中西非七国三年九次政变，极大地加剧了各国的贫困程度，如马里、布基纳法索、苏丹和乍得，政变当期极端贫困人口超千万（见表3-8）。旷日持久的冲突和不安全局势扰乱了这些国家的经济生产活动和市场，损害了农村生计和基础设施，而援助不及时和不充分，难以缓解和改善这些地区的贫困问题。此外，资源竞争也是地区冲突的重要原因，如喀麦隆西北和西南地区由于资源竞争而产生的冲突同样严重扰乱了农业、畜牧业、市场和贸易的发展，对农村贫困人口带来更严重的影响。

---

[1] CHA, 2021, West and Central Africa: Weekly Regional Humanitarian Snapshot.

[2] 参见https：//reliefweb.int/sites/reliefweb.int/files/resources/20210705_rdc_tanganyika_inondations.pdf.

[3] IPCC，2022，Climate Change 2022，Impacts，Adaptation and Vulnerability，Summary for Policymakers.

[4] FAO/SWALIM, 2021, Somalia Drought Update.

[5] 伯卡德（berkad）是在雨季收集水的蓄水池，以备旱季使用。

[6] 参见世界气象组织发布的《非洲气候状况2021》。

表3-8　近三年中西非七国政变时间及其2.15美元标准下的贫困状况

国家	政变时间	当期贫困人口（万人）		2022年贫困发生率（%）	
加蓬	2023年8月	—	—	2.5	8.1
马里	2020年8月	—	—	14.8	47.5
	2021年5月	348.21	1062.15		
布基纳法索	2022年1月、9月	691.14	1355.67	30.5	59.8
尼日尔	2023年7月	—	—	50.6	80.1
几内亚	2021年9月	204.3	687.32	13.8	46.6
苏丹	2021年10月	1397.2	3086.62	15.3	49.7
乍得	2021年4月	623.63	1185.42	30.9	64.6

资料来源：根据经济合作与发展组织《2023年非洲发展动态：投资于可持续发展》的数据以及相关非洲国家政变资讯报道整理所得。

地区冲突和不安全局势下，非洲各国境内和跨境流离失所问题日益突出，社会不稳定性不断增加。就撒哈拉以南非洲而言，区域难民数量自2010年起快速攀升，截至2021年，难民数达到有统计数据以来的最高水平（706万人）（见图3-5）。除难民以外，非洲各国尤其是粮食危机严重的国家，其被迫流离失所者，包括寻求庇护者、国内流离失所者、遣返者等需要国际保护的人口也在迅速增加。

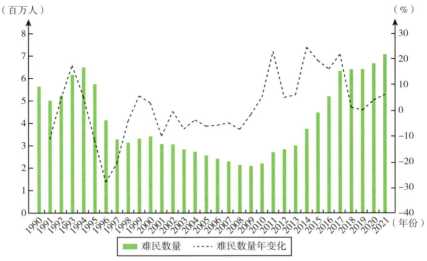

图3-5　撒哈拉以南非洲难民数量及变化趋势

资料来源：根据《世界发展指标》（WDI）2023年5月10日更新数据整理并绘制。

　　具体到次区域层面，根据《2023全球粮食政策报告》，东非地区的社会不稳定性最高，八个粮食危机国家约有1627万被迫流离失所者、1170万国内流离失所者，且集中在苏丹（371万人）、索马里（297万人）、埃塞俄比亚（273万人）、南苏丹（223万人）、马拉维（95万人）等国。其次是中部非洲和南部非洲地区。由于刚果（金）和莫桑比克的冲突以及中非共和国的政治暴力，两个区域超过830万人被迫流离失所，其中刚果（金）的社会不稳定形势最为严峻，国内流离失所人口达到570万人，难民超过52万人。西非地区的流离失所危机同样日益严重，六个粮食危机国家有723万国内流离失所者。其中，尼日利亚2022年底国内流离失所者达到356万人，布基纳法索和喀麦隆的国内流离失所者分别高达188万人和101万人。由于资金严重短缺，粮食配给及营地和定居点的其他基本服务削减，被迫流离失所者的贫困程度与非洲地区的社会不稳定性不断上升。

六、基础设施条件层面的原因

　　非洲发展的基础条件仍然十分薄弱，电力、互联网以及基础交通等设施严重滞后，已经成为制约经济增长的"瓶颈"。电力、互联网以及基础交通是衡量发展的重要指标，虽然近年来撒哈拉以南非洲国家基础设施建设方面有所改善，但是基础设施薄弱仍然是制约其经济发展和减贫进展的重要原因。

　　在用电方面，2021年全球只有不到10%的人口为无电人口，但在撒哈拉以南非洲，这一比例将近50%，可见目前全球无电人口主要集中在撒哈拉以南非洲国家（见表3-9）。2022年非洲用电人口比例仅为56%，城市地区的这一比例较高，达到了82%，但农村地区这一比例远不及城市地区的一半，仅为36%（见表3-10）。区域间、国家间的城乡差异也十分突出，在有数据的54个国家中，47个国家的农村地区用电人口比例低于世界平均水平（82%），其中14个国家的比例低于10%，八个国家的比例低于20%，15个国家的比例低于40%（见表3-11）。在许多非洲国家，即便是能够用电的地方，也由于电量供应不稳定、电力设施老化等原因，供电的稳定性和可靠性都相对比较低。由于没有或者基本电力供应不完善，大部分非洲国家的工业化进展非常缓慢，尤其是农村地区。

表 3-9　　　2012~2021 年世界及撒哈拉以南非洲用电人口比例　　单位：%

地区	2012年	2013年	2014年	2015年	2016年	2017年	2018年	2019年	2020年	2021年
撒哈拉以南非洲	36.69	37.92	38.26	39.11	43.73	43.68	46.34	47.13	48.48	50.58
世界	85.06	85.82	86.31	87.03	88.19	89.02	89.89	90.19	90.48	91.41

资料来源：根据世界银行的数据整理所得。

表 3-10　　　　　2022 年世界及非洲各区域城乡用电人口比例　　单位：%

地区	总用电人口比例	城市用电人口比例	农村用电人口比例
南部非洲	54	81	27
中部非洲	28	56	5
东非	49	80	37
北非	98	99	97
西非	53	84	26
非洲	56	82	36
世界	90	97	82

资料来源：根据经济合作与发展组织《2023 年非洲发展动态：投资于可持续发展》的数据整理所得，参见 https：//www.oecd.org/dev/africa/development-dynamics/。

表 3-11　　　　　　2022 年非洲各国城乡用电人口比例　　单位：%

序号	国家	用电人口比例	城市用电人口比例	农村用电人口比例	序号	国家	用电人口比例	城市用电人口比例	农村用电人口比例
农村用电人口占比 10% 以下（14个）					10	南苏丹	7	14	6
1	布基纳法索	19	62	0	11	马拉维	15	54	7
2	赤道几内亚	67	91	1	12	安哥拉	52	74	7
3	刚果（金）	19	41	1	13	利比亚	70	85	8
4	乍得	11	41	2	14	利比里亚	28	45	8
5	中非共和国	15	34	2	农村用电人口占比 10%~20%（8个）				
6	布隆迪	12	64	3	15	马达加斯加	34	70	11
7	毛里塔尼亚	51	88	4	16	尼日尔	19	48	13
8	莫桑比克	31	75	4	17	赞比亚	45	82	14
9	塞拉利昂	26	55	5	18	刚果（布）	50	66	15

续表

序号	国家	用电人口比例	城市用电人口比例	农村用电人口比例	序号	国家	用电人口比例	城市用电人口比例	农村用电人口比例
19	几内亚比绍	33	56	15	38	埃塞俄比亚	51	93	39
20	马里	51	94	16	农村用电人口占比 40%~80%（8个）				
21	贝宁	41	66	18	39	苏丹	55	82	41
22	几内亚	45	88	19	40	科特迪瓦	70	94	43
农村用电人口占比 20%~40%（16个）					41	塞内加尔	70	95	47
23	坦桑尼亚	40	73	22	42	肯尼亚	71	94	63
24	多哥	54	94	24	43	圣多美和普林西比	77	78	71
25	尼日利亚	55	84	25	44	加纳	86	95	74
26	吉布提	62	72	25	45	南非	84	89	75
27	喀麦隆	65	94	25	46	斯威士兰	80	92	76
28	博茨瓦纳	72	91	26	农村用电人口占比 80%以上（8个）				
29	加蓬	92	99	28	47	科摩罗	87	100	81
30	冈比亚	62	81	32	48	佛得角	94	94	94
31	索马里	50	70	32	49	阿尔及利亚	100	100	100
32	乌干达	42	70	33	50	毛里求斯	100	99	100
33	莱索托	47	78	35	51	塞舌尔	100	100	100
34	纳米比亚	56	75	36	52	摩洛哥	100	100	100
35	津巴布韦	53	86	37	53	埃及	100	100	100
36	卢旺达	47	86	38	54	突尼斯	100	100	100
37	厄立特里亚	54	76	39					

资料来源：根据经济合作与发展组织《2023年非洲发展动态：投资于可持续发展》的数据整理所得，参见 https://www.oecd.org/dev/africa/development-dynamics/。

在使用互联网方面，非洲互联网可使用率低，这也使非洲国家难以有效利用互联网平台和技术来创造经济和社会效益，无法享受到互联网经济的红利。随着互联网时代的不断发展，移动互联网改变了经济发展模式，成为当前参与经济和社会发展的重要平台。但从全球层面来看，2019年非洲可使用互联网的人口比例仅为33.2%，远低于世界平均水平（53.6%），尤其是中非和东非地区，可使用互联网人口比例分别为18.8%和17.2%（见表3-12）。有七个国家可使用互联网人口比例低于10%，分别是布基纳法索、厄立特里亚、乍得、中非共和国、乌干达、南苏丹以及布隆迪。这意味着非洲还没有参与到全球数字化的潮流中，该地区数字化发展缓慢，没有享受到数字化经济发展的红利。

表3-12　　　2019年世界及非洲各区域使用互联网人口的比例　　单位：%

地区	可使用互联网人口比例
南部非洲	38.2
中部非洲	18.8
东非	17.2
北非	62.7
西非	36.3
非洲	33.2
世界	53.6

资料来源：根据经济合作与发展组织《2023年非洲发展动态：投资于可持续发展》的数据整理所得，参见 https：//www.oecd.org/dev/africa/development-dynamics/。

在交通基础设施方面，非洲缺乏覆盖整个大陆的完整交通体系，主要以公路运输为主，且运输成本高。承担85%货物运输的非洲公路总里程为264万公里，道路密度仅为拉丁美洲的1/2，亚洲的1/3。许多非洲国家道路网建设不完善，城乡之间几乎没有直通的公路。例如，马拉维总体铺装道路占比仅为26.36%（见表3-13），主要公路的铺装还未能实现全覆盖，地区道路几乎没有铺装。非洲的铁路普及率也很低，铁路总里程9万公里，占全球6%，且26%与邻国不通，国家间及区域间铁路网没有形成，如中非共和国、索马里等15个国家还没有铁路，许多国家的铁路总里数少（见表3-14）。此外，非洲的航空及海运也严重滞后，整个非洲没有一个大港口，机场也多为非民用且航线少。各类基础交通的不完善导致非洲地区运输成本极高，如从蒙巴萨陆运一个集装箱到乌干达，费用高达三四千美元，而从中国航运一个集装箱到蒙巴萨的费用仅1000多美元。

表3-13　　　　　　　　　　　马拉维道路网

道路级别	铺装道路（公里）	未铺装道路（公里）	合计（公里）	各级铺装道路占总道路的比重（%）
主要公路	2809	548	3357	83.68
二级公路	442	2683	3125	14.14
三级公路	44	4077	4121	1.07
地区道路	8	3492	3500	0.22
城市道路	770	578	1348	57.12
合计	4073	11378	15451	26.36

资料来源：根据马拉维道路管理局（2011）公布的数据整理所得。

表3-14　　　　　2022年部分非洲国家铁路总里程　　　　单位：公里

国家	铁路总公里数	国家	铁路总公里数
布基纳法索	518	马达加斯加	673
阿尔及利亚	4000.5	毛里塔尼亚	728
博茨瓦纳	886	刚果（金）	3684
科特迪瓦	639	津巴布韦	3120
喀麦隆	884	突尼斯	1777
赞比亚	1248	摩洛哥	2295
加蓬	648	苏丹	2747
南非	20953		

资料来源：根据世界银行的数据整理所得。

七、劳动力就业层面的原因

就业不充分、就业农业化和非正式化限制了收入增长。就业不充分是非洲贫困的根本原因。由于总体经济发展水平不高，非洲劳动力的失业率较高，这是当前撒哈拉以南非洲面临的重要挑战，也是其极端贫困人口大量存在的主要原因。按照国际劳工组织较为宽松的统计数据，撒哈拉以南非洲失业率呈现出上升的趋势，尤其是新冠疫情以来，劳动力就业形势更加严峻，2020年撒哈拉以南非洲失业率达到12.65%，2021年和2022年仍然超过12%，是全球平均水平的2倍以上（见表3-15）。此外，撒哈拉以南非洲就业人口中大部分是非正式就业和农业就业，就业极其不稳定。

表3-15　　　2012~2022年世界及撒哈拉以南非洲的失业率　　　单位：%

地区	2012年	2013年	2014年	2015年	2016年	2017年	2018年	2019年	2020年	2021年	2022年
撒哈拉以南非洲	11.49	11.12	11.19	11.28	11.29	11.30	11.30	11.57	12.65	12.42	12.35
世界	6.14	6.12	5.98	6.01	6.00	5.87	5.70	5.54	6.90	6.20	5.77

资料来源：根据世界银行的数据整理所得。

根据世界银行的相关数据，虽然撒哈拉以南非洲就业人口中农业从业人员所占比重有所下降，但下降速度非常缓慢。2000年，农业从业人员所占比重为61.91%，2021年这一比重下降至51.57%，仅下降了10个百分点，而当前农业从业人员比重的世界平均水平为26.42%（见表3-16）。由此可见，促进非洲非农产业的发展，创造更多的非农就业机会是未来非洲减贫的重要路径。

表3-16　　　　2000~2021年世界及撒哈拉以南非洲
农业从业人员占总就业的比重　　　单位：%

地区	2000年	2001年	2002年	2003年	2004年	2005年	2006年	2007年	2008年	2009年	2010年
撒哈拉以南非洲	61.91	61.67	61.35	60.99	60.55	60.27	59.60	58.90	58.35	57.82	57.04
世界平均	39.73	39.34	39.02	38.52	37.36	36.43	35.38	34.44	33.88	33.38	32.74

地区	2011年	2012年	2013年	2014年	2015年	2016年	2017年	2018年	2019年	2020年	2021年
撒哈拉以南非洲	56.24	55.58	55.32	54.21	53.39	53.10	52.61	52.02	51.58	51.96	51.57
世界平均	31.80	30.93	30.07	29.15	28.53	28.01	27.50	26.87	26.39	26.95	26.42

资料来源：根据世界银行的数据整理所得。

在非洲，就业的另一个典型特征是非正式就业比重高。在许多非洲国家，80%~90%的就业人口属于非正式就业，如马里、科特迪瓦和塞内加尔的非正式就业比重均超过90%，分别为93%、91.7%、90.2%；津巴布韦、卢旺达、赞比亚和莱索托非正式就业比重超过80%，分别是88.2%、87.8%、84.8%、80.9%。非正式就业包括家庭佣工、街头小贩、垃圾收集者和小贩等，非正式就业者没有雇主的正式合同或社会保障，因此一旦遇到风险或者紧急情况，非正式就业人员非常容易失业。例如，新冠疫情期间，尼日利亚有500万人失业，刚果（金）有200万人失业；2020年上半年，埃塞俄比亚仅园艺工人就有15万人失业。

非洲正式就业比重低主要有两个原因。一是非洲地区高技能型劳动力短缺。二是第二产业、第三产业发展落后，无法提供充分的就业机会。

这两个问题在笔者的实地调研过程中十分突出。

笔者曾经在马拉维调研了一些中资企业，企业负责人都表示在非洲本土雇用低技能工人比较容易，雇用成本也比较低，但是雇用技术工人就非常难。一家酒店管理企业的负责人表示，只能通过支付高于本地平均工资水平的工资才能留住有技能的熟练员工，如当地酒店业当时最低工资标准是每个月15000克瓦查，而该企业支付给当地员工的工资平均为每月60000克瓦查。笔者调研时也对当地员工进行了访谈，当地员工普遍表示该酒店支付的高工资是他们长期留在这家酒店工作的主要原因。另外一家建筑企业负责人也表示，在当地很容易找到小工，小工的工资为每天700克瓦查左右，但是如果雇用当地的技术工人，如各种机械的操作人员、驾驶员等，则每天需要支付1500克瓦查，并且还要支付专门的出差补贴。

　　笔者在马拉维调研时，入住酒店的两名门童是当地一所科技大学计算机和通信技术专业毕业的毕业生，因毕业半年都没有找到专业对口的工作，于是就到这个酒店来当门童，为旅客提供引导服务。他们在这家酒店工作已经两年了，每个月工资为40000克瓦查，这两年他们也一直在寻找和专业相关的工作，但没有找到。

　　由于就业机会少，农业生产水平低，为了满足基本生存需求，在农村经营非农小商业的人员较多，这导致了村内小商业的高度竞争，每个经营者只能维持最低的利润水平。例如，笔者在坦桑尼亚农村调研发现，以第三产业为主的、规模较小的商业形式是当地农户维持生计的重要策略。笔者在非洲实地调研中发现，坦桑尼亚的Wasmba村仅有100多户居民，但分布着超过20家小型商店，这种低成本和低回报的商业业态是当地非常普遍的非正式经济的存在方式。

八、公共服务供给层面的原因

非洲公共服务供给不足，阻碍了非洲地区的减贫发展。

　　清洁饮水是公共卫生和健康的重要前提。中国在脱贫攻坚阶段，专门将解决贫困人口的饮用水作为消除贫困的重要指标。国际社会也非常关注非洲的饮水安全问题，开展了很多有关饮水条件改善的援助项目。但从目前的情况来看，撒哈拉以南非洲人口在饮水安全方面进展相对缓慢，到2020年，撒哈拉以南非洲（包括城市人口在内）能够享受到基本饮水条件的人口比重仅为64.41%（见表3-17），远低于世界平均水平，且农村人口能够享受到基本饮水条件的比重更低。

表3-17　　　　2012~2020年世界及撒哈拉以南非洲有基本
饮水条件的人口比重　　　　　　　单位：%

地区	2012年	2013年	2014年	2015年	2016年	2017年	2018年	2019年	2020年
撒哈拉以南非洲	56.48	57.51	58.55	59.60	60.62	61.63	62.60	63.57	64.41
世界	76.69	77.33	77.97	78.61	79.23	79.87	80.48	81.09	81.67

资料来源：根据世界银行的数据整理所得。

在教育方面，非洲中等教育的入学率仍较低，大量的非洲劳动力缺乏很好的技能。虽然教育，尤其是基础教育，一直是国际社会援助非洲的重点领域，非洲的基础教育条件也得到了明显改善，初等教育入学率基本达到100%，但是非洲人口素质的整体提升仍然面临诸多挑战。非洲中等教育的入学率仍然较低，尤其是在过去的十多年里，撒哈拉以南非洲国家的中等教育入学率并没有明显提升，2020年中等教育入学率仅为43.91%，比世界平均水平低20多个百分点（见表3-18）。这意味着大量的非洲劳动力没有掌握很好的技能。这一点从成人识字率指标也能够看到，2020年撒哈拉以南非洲成人识字率仅为67.27%，比世界平均水平低将近20个百分点（见表3-19）。2022年非洲15~24岁青年的识字率仅为78.6%，比世界平均水平低11.6个百分点，而非洲各次区域的各类青年识字率也都低于世界平均水平（见表3-20）。

表3-18　2012~2020年世界及撒哈拉以南非洲不同教育阶段入学率 单位：%

教育阶段		2012年	2013年	2014年	2015年	2016年	2017年	2018年	2019年	2020年
初等教育入学率	撒哈拉以南非洲	99.59	99.84	99.35	97.90	98.09	98.53	99.15	99.05	98.75
	世界	103.68	103.93	102.69	102.35	103.80	103.65	101.22	101.43	101.85
中等教育入学率	撒哈拉以南非洲	42.00	44.63	43.37	43.86	43.20	43.40	43.57	43.73	43.91
	世界	63.79	64.90	65.65	65.71	65.83	66.20	66.27	—	—

资料来源：根据世界银行的数据整理所得。

表3-19　　2012~2020年世界及撒哈拉以南非洲成人识字率　　单位：%

地区	2012年	2013年	2014年	2015年	2016年	2017年	2018年	2019年	2020年
撒哈拉以南非洲	61.49	62.35	63.00	63.60	64.31	64.69	66.14	67.06	67.27
世界	84.76	84.95	85.40	85.56	86.01	86.25	86.28	86.66	86.81

资料来源：根据世界银行的数据整理所得。

表3-20　　　　2022年不同区域各类青年识字率　　　　单位：%

地区	15~24岁	15~24岁女性	15~24岁男性
南部非洲	87.7	87.9	87.7
中部非洲	74.6	70.9	78.7

续表

地区	15~24岁	15~24岁女性	15~24岁男性
东非	82.7	82.8	82.7
北非	88.7	86.8	90.5
西非	68.0	62.0	74.6
非洲	78.6	76.1	81.4
世界	90.2	89.2	91.4

资料来源：根据经济合作与发展组织《2023年非洲发展动态：投资于可持续发展》的数据整理所得，参见 https：//www.oecd.org/dev/africa/development-dynamics/。

九、小结

从外部环境来看，不利的经济环境以及极端气候事件等制约了非洲的经济增长。一方面，全球范围内持续通货膨胀、紧缩货币政策等失衡的宏观经济条件使非洲国家的公共债务处于数十年来的最高水平，加上援助预算长期下降以及债务利息负担加重，导致非洲地区经济复苏缺乏后劲。另一方面，全球气候变化的冲击，尤其是大范围的干旱及洪水等极端气候事件，极大地增加了气候多变性和极端情况带来的压力，对非洲的农业生产、粮食安全、基础设施等造成灾难性损害，威胁非洲消除饥饿的能力，加剧了非洲大陆的极端贫困。

从非洲内部环境来看，缓慢的经济增长和稳定的人口增长、日益加剧的粮食危机、持续的地区冲突以及薄弱的发展条件等多重不利于发展的内部因素，导致难以有效推进非洲减贫进程。首先，非洲缓慢的经济增长难以有效驱动减贫发展。在较低的人口城镇化率、较高的人口增长压力下，缓慢的经济增长难以发挥其减贫效应，沉重的债务负担以及低水平的对外投资也导致非洲经济增长动力不足。其次，非洲农业生产环境脆弱、粮食生产能力低以及粮食自给率低，极大地增加了非洲各国粮食的市场脆弱性和风险性，导致粮食可及性大幅度下降。再者，地区冲突和不安全局势以及由此带来的大量难民扰乱了经济生产活动和市场，损害了农村生计和基础设施，加剧了非洲各国的贫困。最后，非洲地区发展的基础条件仍十分薄弱，不充分就业以及较低的人口素质等在很大程度上阻碍了减贫进程。

整体来看，非洲各国的近期前景极不确定，因为该地区的前景与全球经济发展以及部分国家所面临的紧迫的社会政治和安全局势息息相关。非洲地区资金短缺也将影响该地区的长期前景。资金短缺可能迫使各国减少卫生、教育和基础设施等关键发展部门的资源，削弱非洲各国的增长潜力①。如何有效推动非洲减贫进程，需要非洲各国、区域性组织等主体共同努力。

---

① 国际货币基金组织，《2023非洲区域经济展望》，参见https：//www.imf.org/en/publications/reo?sortby=Date&series=Sub−Saharan%20Africa（访问日期：2023年6月1日）。

第四章
非洲减贫主要议题及进展

　　非洲国家面临严重的贫困问题，长期依赖外来投资和援助以求改善。同时，这些国家也在努力增强自主发展能力。在政治方面，非洲国家加强政治民主建设和经济体制改革，自主提出各种非洲复兴计划，非盟成立后也提出了"非洲互查机制"来推动成员国的发展；在经济方面，非洲国家领导人制定的"非洲发展新伙伴计划"（NEPAD）也争取到了西方国家的支持，非盟制定了《2050年非洲海洋整体战略》以发展蓝色经济，非洲各国制定适宜的金融战略推动当地经济发展并为贫困家庭提供资金支持；在区域合作方面，西非国家经济共同体、东非共同体以及南部非洲发展共同体在基础设施、金融、教育、健康、安全等广泛领域展开合作，共同有效推动减贫事业发展。

一、非盟的减贫战略及进展

　　作为政治、经济和军事一体化的全非洲性的政治实体，非盟旨在帮助非洲发展经济，推进政治、社会和经济一体化进程，推动各领域的泛非合作，提高人民生活水平等；其成员包括55个非洲国家。非盟致力于实现泛非远景，即建设一个"由非洲民众推动，在国际舞台上充满活力、统一、繁荣与和平的非洲"。为了实现这一目标，非盟与国际机构加强了伙伴关系，共同推动非洲大陆自由贸易区建设和非洲基础设施发展计划的实施；中国同非盟长期保持友好合作，并向非洲提供援助，在气候变化、2030年可持续发展议程等重点国际问题上与非盟保持沟通；其他国家也支持非盟提出的各项政策，非盟的减贫进程也得到了国际机构的支持。消除贫困一直是非洲国家发展的重要议题。为了实现这一目标，非盟在2015年通过了一项名为《2063年议程》的远景规划并将此议程作为非盟的集体行动指南，以团结非洲人民为基础，旨在未来50年内建成地区一体化与和平繁荣的新非洲。

（一）非洲发展新伙伴关系计划

非洲发展新伙伴关系计划（NEPAD）涵盖了一系列旨在减少贫困、促进可持续发展的战略，其中包括提升获得教育和医疗保健的机会、促进私营部门投资和经济增长、倡导善治和民主，以及解决环境和气候变化问题。[①] 非洲面临的独特挑战主要在于其经济长期未能实现增长。特别需要注意的是，农业在绝大多数贫困社区中占据主要地位，因此，致力于消除极端贫困的努力必须以提升农业生产和生产力为核心目标。此外，非洲的商品在营销方面存在弱势和低效的问题，导致农民陷入贫困，他们面临着收成受损、商品价格偏低等问题，同时还受到中间商的剥削，影响其利润和收入。

（二）《非洲大陆自由贸易协定》

非洲大陆各国的汇率制度存在差异。目前，约有一半的经济体采用钉住汇率制，而另一半则选择了更具灵活性的汇率安排。2021年1月启动的《非洲大陆自由贸易协定》是非洲经济一体化建设的重要里程碑。该协议取消了成员国之间90%的关税，实现了服务、资金和人员等要素的无障碍流动，这将提升贸易的便利程度和自由化水平，激发非洲内部贸易的活力，促进区域供应链的发展，进一步提升市场的聚合力和竞争力。然而，在2023年非盟第36届首脑会议上，非盟委员会主席强调了国际形势的不确定性、地缘政治冲突的加剧以及全球经济治理体系面临的挑战，这些因素对非洲产生了深远影响。

（三）应对粮食安全战略

从非盟《2063年议程》对农业发展的规划来看，未来非洲的农业发展将侧重于引入外部的农业技术和经验以推动农业现代化，农业发展将关注社会和生态效益，包括改善粮食安全和环境保护。从《非洲农业综合发展计划》来看，要依靠内部力量解决粮食安全问题，非洲国家计划每年将财政预算的10%投入农业领域。然而，只有布隆迪、布基纳法索、刚果（布）、埃塞俄比亚、加纳、几内亚、马达加斯加、马拉维、马里、尼日尔、塞内加尔、赞比亚以及津巴布韦13个国家曾经实现过10%的投入目标，只有七个国家能够保持比较稳定的10%的农业投入；平均来看，非洲各国在农业领域的投入仅占公共支出的4%左右。

（四）基础设施建设战略

根据非盟《2063年议程》第一个十年规划（2014~2023年）的执行情况，

---

① 参见 https：//au.int/en/nepad。

非洲在加速非洲大陆自贸区建设以及促进经济社会可持续发展方面取得了显著进展。目前，已有54个非盟成员国签署了《非洲大陆自由贸易协定》。截至2022年11月，有44个成员国已提交批准文件，这使该协定成为自世界贸易组织成立以来，参与国家最多的自贸协定。在实践中，贸易一体化取得了积极进展。

2021年，非洲各国通过非盟峰会通过了《非洲基础设施发展计划（2021—2030年）》第二期优先行动计划中的71个优先项目。这些项目涵盖了交通、通信、能源、水利、农业等多个领域，涉及非盟40多个国家。这些计划的实施有助于提升非洲大陆的基础设施水平，推动经济发展和可持续增长。

（五）非洲大陆教育战略

非盟《2063年议程》确定了非洲发展的七大主题愿景，愿景反映了非盟对于非洲大陆教育的重视。非盟在实现2063愿景中追求建设公平、民主、尊重人权、正义和法治的非洲，并且广泛开展以科学、技术和创新为基础的技术革命，关爱儿童成长，让公民接受良好的教育。联合国教科文组织在撒哈拉以南非洲的女童教育援助工作与非盟存在协同作用，联合国教科文组织在女童教育方面强调的两性平等愿景与非盟完全一致。

非盟制定的《非洲大陆教育战略（2016—2025年）》确定了十二个战略目标及其行动领域，其中第五个目标是"促进性别平等和公平"，行动领域包括"确保成功升学、动员社区成为合作伙伴"等内容。此外，该战略强调要激发教师的积极性，利用信息技术保障受教育权利，发起全面有效的扫盲活动等。联合国教科文组织在撒哈拉以南非洲开展的女童教育援助行动符合该地区的教育战略。在国家层面，2017年非盟与其成员国就教育资格制度进行磋商；在区域层面，2015年完成了区域教育资格体系建设。非盟在非洲推行开放和远程学习，使非洲高等教育入学率从6%提升到50%以上。

（六）鼓励就业创业战略

1.鼓励女性与青年政策

非盟《2063年议程》鼓励非洲女性和青年积极参与农业生产，并在生产资料和资金方面提供政策支持。这包括制定和实施一系列政策和倡议，以确保女性能够获得土地等生产资料，同时推动至少30%的农业资金资助提供给女性。该议程也致力于促进女性和青年获取用于投资的资金，以改善他们的经济权益。

2. 非盟—联合国粮农组织与非洲青年一起开发农业机会

在2022年，联合国粮农组织与非盟联合发布了《非洲农业粮食系统青年准则》和《对青年敏感的价值链分析与发展》。这两份文件是由联合国粮农组织、工业发展组织以及非盟委员会合作实施的联合项目的成果。通过价值链技能发展培训、能力建设以及融资和市场准入讲习班，该项目为超过700名青年企业家提供了支持。这一举措提高了人们对青年就业和创业重要性的认识，为青年参与农业粮食系统创造了更有利的环境。

然而，尽管做出了这些积极的努力，非洲仍然面临一些挑战。收入低和科研经费不足是导致非洲人才外流的其中两个主要原因。绝大多数非洲国家的首要任务是解决国民的基本生存问题，因此用于科技发展和吸引人才的资金非常有限。在非洲，除南非之外，科技领域的投入仅占GDP的0.2%。因此，尽管取得了一些进展，非洲仍然在支持教育和就业方面面临着限制。

（七）金融支持战略

非盟制定了《2050年非洲海洋整体战略》，旨在支持和鼓励发展充满活力、环保和可持续的蓝色经济。2022年，在《联合国气候变化框架公约》第二十七次缔约方大会期间，世界银行宣布"蓝色经济增强非洲韧性计划"，进一步强调了蓝色经济对非洲可持续发展的重要性。

长期以来，非洲在减贫方面面临严峻的挑战。非盟作为非洲大陆唯一的区域组织，将保障非洲的减贫工作视为重要目标，并将落实联合国减贫战略作为实现这一目标的关键途径。尽管如此，从实际结果来看，非盟的政策设计与执行之间存在一定的差距。金融和教育环境对于非盟实施经济发展与减贫议程产生了不良影响。

二、非洲区域性组织的减贫战略

在非洲，区域性组织推动着非洲减贫工作的开展。其中，西非国家经济共同体、东非共同体以及南部非洲发展共同体为实现消除贫困目标制定了一系列减贫战略，包括2021年的《西非国家经济共同体2050年愿景》、南部非洲发展共同体制定的《2050年愿景》和《2020—2030年区域战略发展参考计划》、东非共同体制定的《国家发展规划（2020—2024年）》等，参见表4-1。

表4-1　　　　　　　　非洲部分区域性组织的减贫战略

组织	政策文件	减贫目标	具体措施
西非国家经济共同体	《西非国家经济共同体2050年愿景》	提高该区域民众的生活水平，减少贫困	充分利用人口红利来改善民众的生活条件，提高受教育水平，为青年和女性创造良好的就业机会，加强公共卫生体系的韧性
南部非洲发展共同体	《2050年愿景》和《2020—2030年区域战略发展参考计划》（RISDP2020-2030）	实现可持续经济增长、经济社会发展和消除贫困等目标	《2050年愿景》是一项长期目标，设置了该地区到2050年的愿景。RISDP2020-2030推动《2050年愿景》的实现。此外，RISDP还将确保协调支持跨境基础设施和服务的政策、战略和措施；同时，确定多样化的区域基础设施和服务，以促进货物、服务和技能以及包括可再生能源在内的区域能源市场的发展；信息和通信技术、水利以及交通运输
东非共同体	《国家发展规划（2020—2024年）》	有效推动减贫事业发展；未来，中非减贫合作机制还将在减债缓债和指导非洲国家部署减贫工作方面继续发挥作用	减贫战略目标涉及教育、健康、安全等广泛领域。制定减贫及增长战略；政府相关部门及时发布有关识别贫困和政策目标的信息，积极寻求国家和地方各级政府的参与，并咨询民间团体和私营部门
	《东非共同体2050年议程》	以结构性发展战略实现减贫并重建国家	各国的减贫措施：《卢旺达2020年发展规划》旨在通过经济结构转型开发人力资源，促进区域和全球经济发展；《坦桑尼亚2025年规划》旨在鼓励工作、创新和改革，创建学习型社会，改善基础设施并促进投资；《肯尼亚2030年发展规划》旨在实现东非共同体区域发展目标，履行区域和全球发展承诺；《乌干达2040年发展规划》旨在夯实经济基础，争取更多的合作机会。预计到2050年，东非共同体各成员国人均收入将增长10倍，使该地区达到中高收入水平

资料来源：根据各区域性组织公布的信息整理所得。

三、非洲各国的减贫战略和具体行动

非洲国家十分重视减贫，一些国家在减贫方面也取得了显著的成就，如博茨瓦纳。2000年以来，该国政府实施了各种旨在减少贫困和改善公民福祉的措施，在减贫方面取得了重大进展：贫困率持续下降，从1993年的47%下降至2002年的30.6%，2009年进一步降低到19.3%，2015年下降至16.3%[①]，仅为1993年的1/3。该国的经济增长和福利改善在很大程度上得益于国家层面明确的减贫战略导向。

案例4-1 博茨瓦纳国家减贫方案及实施进程

博茨瓦纳推出了两个关键减贫方案。

一是2002年启动实施的《消除贫困方案》（Poverty Eradication Programme，PEP），这一方案主要强调通过经济赋权、社会支持和农业发展来促进减贫，推动经济社会发展。（1）经济赋权：通过各种举措促进经济赋权，包括向有抱负的企业家提供小额贷款和赠款，进行技能培训以及进入市场和业务发展方面的支持；（2）社会支持：认识到社会保护的重要性，向老年人、残疾人和孤儿等弱势群体提供援助，包括现金转移以及医疗保健服务和教育援助；（3）农业发展：强调农业发展是减贫的一种手段，通过提供相关培训，使农民能够负担得起相关投入品，并改善与小规模农民的市场联系，以加强粮食安全和提高农村地区的收入水平。

根据《消除贫困方案》，实施的项目主要包括：青年创业计划；IPELEGENG计划——劳动密集型公共工程计划，旨在为有需要的个人提供临时就业；耕地农业发展综合支持计划（ISPAAD），通过提供补贴、技术咨询和市场准入来支持小规模生产农户。

二是2011年启动实施国家减贫战略（National Strategy for Poverty Reduction，NSPR），这一战略是博茨瓦纳国家减贫综合方案。关键战略包括：（1）经济多样化：通过促进旅游业、农业、制造业和服务业等部门的经济多样化，减少该国对钻石业的依赖；（2）人力资本开发：强调投资教育、医疗保健和技能发展，以使个人拥有摆脱贫困的必要技能。

通过实施各种方案和倡议，博茨瓦纳的《消除贫困方案》和《国家减贫战略》在解决贫困、促进经济赋权方面取得了可喜的进展。2023年11月

[①] 资料来源：博茨瓦纳统计局，博茨瓦纳核心福利调查。

发布的总统国情咨文指出，"到目前为止，已经制定了29个社会福利和经济方案，旨在通过获得体面生活的选择权来消除贫困、减少不平等和减轻公民的脆弱性。例如，基于社区的自然资源管理（CBNRM）和当地经济发展相关计划；五年来，政府已对选区社区计划投资了超过2.55亿普拉，以资助所有57个选区的4929个项目，这些项目累计雇用了19682人。未来，政府将在所有经济部门加强2022年《经济包容法》的实施和监测，以保护我们的公民，建立必要的框架来促进遵守，促进包容性参与，为目标公民提供资金和技能发展。"

资料来源：根据博茨瓦纳政府相关公开资料整理所得。

（一）非洲部分国家的减贫与农业发展计划

在上述战略的影响下，非洲国家也在积极调整本国的农业政策。这些政策在一定程度上有效应对了粮食安全问题，使农村贫困呈现下降的积极趋势。然而，需要指出的是，虽然各国农业政策在某种程度上取得了一些成效，但受益的仅为少数农民，而非广大农村人口。

1.坦桑尼亚：农业支持政策

2015年，坦桑尼亚推出了微型、小型和中型企业计划，旨在改善小农和渔业从业者的生计。该计划的实施带来了就业的增长和粮食安全的提升，同时也有助于减少农村贫困。在坦桑尼亚，相关政策涵盖了农业和畜牧业政策、农业部门发展计划，以及微型和中小型企业计划。

2.塞拉利昂：农业减贫战略

该战略是塞拉利昂2008~2012年的一项涉及多部门的国家战略。其核心目标在于提供稳定的电力供应，提升农渔业生产能力及其附加值，发展国家交通运输网络，同时通过提供更完善的社会服务来确保可持续的人类发展，主要着眼于解决粮食不安全与营养不良问题。

3.赞比亚：农户投入支持计划（FISP）和农场支持计划（FSP）

农户投入支持计划（FISP）旨在解决赞比亚在连续遭遇干旱和洪水后农作物产量下降的问题，尤其是玉米产量，这些灾害削弱了许多小农户的资产基础。农场支持计划（FSP）不仅有利于小规模农户的发展，还通过增加家庭收入，推动了农村发展和减贫工作。农场支持计划的受益人为弱势群体，而农户投入支持计划主要支持小规模农户。

> ### 案例4-2 非洲部分国家的农业措施与实施进展
>
> 2019年非洲各国农业全要素生产率目标的完成率仅为2%。虽然农业部门为60%以上的劳动人口提供了就业，并被视为大多数非洲国家的经济支柱，但却表现不佳。这在一定程度上是因为非洲各国农业机械化程度低、价值链薄弱以及对不可预测的降水的严重依赖。尽管进展成效欠佳，但一些国家还是不断努力提高农业生产率。例如，坦桑尼亚推动政府与私营部门合作，促进灌溉系统建设，以减少依赖不可预测的降水所存在的风险。此外，该国还采取措施促进价值链发展，提升土地利用，改善农村基础设施模式，包括配备采收后续设备和加强农村道路建设等具体措施。
>
> 资料来源：《2063年议程》第一个十年执行计划实施报告。

（二）非洲部分国家的基础设施建设计划

在撒哈拉以南非洲，政府对基础设施建设的支持较少。该地区大部分国家由于长期贫困和处于弱势，在吸引基础设施投资方面临挑战。资金有限使得这些非洲国家在发展基础设施项目时主要依赖联合国、世界银行、国际货币基金组织以及非洲开发银行等国际机构的支持。

1. 可持续农业创新数字村庄倡议（DVI）

目前，非洲有九个国家正在参与数字村庄倡议（DVI）的试点，这些国家分别是加纳、肯尼亚、利比里亚、马拉维、尼日尔、尼日利亚、塞内加尔（撒哈拉以南非洲国家）、索马里和津巴布韦。在塞内加尔（撒哈拉以南非洲国家），超过30万名农民已在当地的数字平台SAIDA上注册。该计划面临的主要障碍包括缺乏创业和技术教育或技能，投资不足，基础设施薄弱，监管和税收机构不完善。

2. 埃塞俄比亚：2020—2026年联合国可持续发展合作框架

该合作框架指出，在2020年至2026年，为了支持埃塞俄比亚实现联合国2030年可持续发展议程，联合国相关机构计划在埃塞俄比亚开展的工作和执行的预算总额约为71亿美元。这一合作框架的签署旨在通过联合国机构的协同行动，帮助埃塞俄比亚在各个领域实现可持续发展目标，以促进该国经济、社会和环境可持续增长[①]。

---

① 非盟研究中心，参见https://caus.tute.edu.cn/info/1085/1607.htm。

3.毛里塔尼亚：接受金融组织的资金援助

毛里塔尼亚政府的资源有限，通常需要向世界银行、国际货币基金组织、非洲开发银行等国际金融机构，以及阿拉伯经济和社会发展基金、伊斯兰开发银行等阿拉伯国家的金融机构寻求资金支持。近五年来，毛里塔尼亚政府总共获得了约50亿美元的援助，其中贷款约30亿美元，其余为援助和援助性贷款。这些资金大部分投向基础设施建设领域，主要投入电力（约9亿美元，占17%）、水利和供排水（约9亿美元，占17%）、公路（约5.6亿美元，占12%）、港口（约3.4亿美元，占7%），而投向农业、医疗、教育、粮食安全等领域的资金各占5%左右[①]。

4.马里：增长和减贫战略框架

增长和减贫战略框架（SFGPR）是马里的减贫战略。该战略涵盖了一系列旨在减少贫困的政策和计划，包括提高农业生产力，促进农村发展，改善医疗保健和教育等基本服务的可获得性，推动私营部门投资和经济增长，以及加强治理和促进民主。[②]

案例4-3 非洲部分国家基础设施措施与进展

非洲在增加发电量和配电量方面取得了一定的进展，已完成2019年目标的79%。在实现信息通信技术（ICT）普及率翻一番这一目标方面，非洲仅取得了部分进展。在整个非洲大陆，信息通信技术对GDP的平均贡献率仅略有增加，完成了2019年目标的39%。例如，在科特迪瓦，2013~2019年信息通信技术对GDP的贡献率由8%升至9%，而其2019年目标为12.8%。2019年该国使用移动电话的人口比例为72%，这要归功于该国光纤长度由2016年的2040公里增加至2018年的5180公里。又如，在加纳，由于信息通信技术领域基础设施的迅速发展，以及信息通信技术管理部门和监管框架的加强，该国2017年农村和城市地区信息通信技术普及率得以提升，达到98%。

资料来源：《2063年议程》第一个十年执行计划实施报告。

---

① 根据世界银行关于毛里塔尼亚的统计数据整理。

② 参见https：//www.worldbank.ora/en/country/mali/brief/stratedic-framework-for-arowth-and-poverty-reduction。

（三）非洲部分国家的教育发展相关政策

尽管非洲国家（如坦桑尼亚和赞比亚等）重视教育发展，但整体而言，非洲在教育方面仍面临诸多挑战，主要包括性别不平等、教育资源分配不平等以及整体教育水平落后。

1.坦桑尼亚

在坦桑尼亚，教育部门通过关注不同教育阶段来确保各个群体能够平等地接受教育，包括学前教育、中等教育、特殊教育以及高等教育。这些措施旨在确保所有人都能够受益于教育，不论他们是哪类群体。坦桑尼亚在教育领域的努力旨在确保人们能够获得平等、优质的教育，以增强个人能力和促进社会的整体发展。

2.赞比亚

性别平等和女性赋权项目（Gender Equity and Women's Empowerment Project）旨在支持赞比亚政府增加妇女获得生计支持的机会。项目的重点在于提供贷款，以支持妇女从事创收活动，从而改善她们的生计。此外，该项目还关注极端贫困家庭中的弱势少女，为她们提供中等教育机会，从而打破贫困的循环。

> **案例4-4 非洲部分国家的教育措施与实施进展**
>
> 整体而言，非洲的基础教育发展态势良好，虽然非洲整体入学率低于2019年90.7%的目标，但也从2013年的76.8%增至2019年的80.8%。在塞舌尔，2019年小学阶段入学率达到100%；在南非和多哥，该比例分别从2013年的88.1%和83%增至2019年的94.2%和93%；在埃塞俄比亚，入学率从2013年的85.7%升至2019年的97%；在布基纳法索，净入学率从2013年的63.2%升至2019年的74.3%。
>
> 许多国家在基础教育阶段入学率快速提升的同时，也实现了基础教育阶段的教育均等，其部分原因在于这些国家提供了免费的基础教育。此外，针对特定国家的各种干预措施也起到了一定作用。例如，布基纳法索推行教室建设国家专项规划，并划拨学校食堂建设专项公共预算，科特迪瓦则颁布了《义务教育政策法》，规定年满6周岁的儿童必须依法入学，接受义务教育，义务教育年限为6~16周岁。
>
> 资料来源：《2063年议程》第一个十年执行计划实施报告。

（四）非洲部分国家的就业政策

非洲部分国家针对特定群体制定了一系列就业战略，大力支持农村地区的青年就业，但是由于资金有限，大部分项目需要国际金融组织的支持。

1. 坦桑尼亚：青年农业综合企业倡议

坦桑尼亚制定了2022~2030年"建设更美好的明天——青年农业综合企业倡议"（BBT-YIA）战略，该战略旨在加强青年在农业领域的参与度，以实现可持续改善生计的目标。此外，该战略旨在到2030年将青年就业人口增加100万人，并将农业部门的增长率提升至10%。然而，由于坦桑尼亚的文化规范以及对妇女和残疾人的偏见，青年群体的依赖率和贫困率居高不下。因此，他们参与治理和政治进程的程度较低，在获得就业机会、教育和经济机会方面受到限制。

2. 马里：青年就业和技能发展项目

马里实施的青年就业和技能发展项目旨在促进青年，特别是农村地区的青年的技能发展，并为其提供农业和其他部门的就业机会。该项目得到了非洲开发银行的支持。

案例4-5　非洲部分国家的就业措施与实施进展

非洲优先考虑青年参与《2063年议程》的实施，十分重视为青年赋权，各国努力降低青年失业率以在一些程度上保障青年的权利，但是成效甚微，完成率低至-128%。

在埃塞俄比亚，青年失业率从2013年的22.8%增至2019年的25.2%；而在加纳，青年失业率从2013年的24.7%增至2019年的26.4%；尼日尔的青年失业率呈指数级增长，从2013年的3.1%上升至2019年的12.2%；博茨瓦纳的青年失业率在2019年达到25.6%；纳米比亚和中非共和国的青年失业率更是分别从2013年的41.7%和38.4%上升至2019年的48.5%和47%。也有少数国家的青年失业率有所下降，如埃及、卢旺达、塞内加尔和突尼斯的青年失业率分别从2013年的12.8%、21.3%、28.9%和38.4%降至2019年的9.9%、18.7%、14.2%和34.4%。

资料来源：《2063年议程》第一个十年执行计划实施报告。

（五）非洲部分国家采取的金融战略

1.尼日利亚：中央数字货币政策

撒哈拉以南非洲金融发展主要依靠外力，一些国家正在探索采用央行数字货币（CBDC）的可能性，如尼日利亚启动了eNaira。CBDC能够带来若干好处，如提高金融包容性，降低汇款成本，减少对那些可能阻碍货币传导和便利非法资金流动的私人加密货币的依赖。

2.坦桑尼亚：发展基金政策

政府推出妇女发展基金（WDF）和青年发展基金（YDE），通过这些基金为妇女和青年提供软性贷款以支持其发展[1]。这些基金的分配在社区部门的管理下，由理事会决定，其中妇女分配占5%，青年分配占5%。这种安排的初衷是为了帮助那些由于缺乏抵押品而难以从金融机构获得贷款的经济弱势妇女和青年。这些贷款是免息的，不需要支付利息[2]。

然而，坦桑尼亚针对青年、妇女和残疾人的金融贷款优惠政策虽然在一定程度上为年轻创业者提供了帮助，却也面临一些挑战。首先，由于青年群体对这种政策的接受程度不高，一些受益人在偿还贷款前消失，影响了政策的有效性。其次，目标群体在创业技能方面有所欠缺，这导致他们在实际创业过程中遇到困难。此外，整体商业环境不佳也影响了政策的实施。例如，2018~2019年，坦桑尼亚有16252家企业破产。此外，地方政府的收入动员不足，资金来源有限，这可能导致地方议会认为这些资金削弱了其他计划，进而影响了贷款基金的作用，妨碍预期受益人的发展[3]。

3.卢旺达：减贫计划

卢旺达推行了"愿景2020 Umurenge减贫计划"，旨在向贫困家庭提供资金支持。该计划在实践中面临一些挑战，包括付款延迟、监测与评估技能薄弱，以及对计划实施人员了解不足等问题。

社会援助基金也面临一系列问题，如政府政策不稳定、医疗设施老旧、罢工、缺乏必要的基础设施，以及地区冲突等，这些都对妇女和青年赋权项目产生影响。在这种背景下，生计赋权反贫困计划的实施也面临着一些困难，包括行政层面的问题、资金流入不稳定以及外界对政治干预的感知。同时，由于决策主要由中央层面制定，地方参与较少，这也为减贫计划的实施带来了阻力[4]。

---

[1][2][3][4] Rogers Rugeiyam. Impromptu Decisions: Tanzania's Local Government Authorities' challenge in Establishing and Managing the Women, Youth, and People with Disabilities Fund. Local Administration Journal, 2022, 15 (4): 345-361.

案例4-6　非洲部分国家的金融措施与实施进展

非洲在依靠自己进行融资方面总体表现较差，仅完成2019年目标的18%。在提升总税收占GDP比重方面进展缓慢，较2019年目标仅完成2%。但是，部分非洲国家也取得了一些进展。例如，卢旺达推行自力更生政策，大部分预算资金来自国内，故该国税收及贷款融资的国内预算份额从2005年的55%增至2018~2019年的84%。加纳政府推行一系列措施以增加国内收入，包括扩大税基，引入税务识别号，实行推定税制，实施消费税印章，运行无纸化港口系统，以及审查免税制度。通过此类方式，加纳公共预算中的国内收入份额从2015年的49.6%增至2018年的64.3%。塞内加尔的税收收入在预算收入中占比达到90%以上，税收收入占GDP的比重也从2014年的63.9%提升至2018年的69%，估计很快会超过72%。

资料来源：《2063年议程》第一个十年执行计划实施报告。

（六）撒哈拉以南非洲的主要减贫战略文件

为减少农村贫困，非洲各国采取广泛的行动，如现金转移、粮食援助、负担得起的医疗费用、儿童保护服务和应对威胁生命的紧急情况，以加强弱势群体的应对机制。为了使农业和粮食系统更具包容性和效率，各国都寻求提高农业生产力。非洲各国的减贫规划如表4-2所示。

表4-2　　　　　　　非洲部分国家的减贫规划

国家	政策文件	减贫目标	具体措施
布隆迪	国家十年发展规划（2018—2027年）	依照联合国2030年可持续发展目标、非盟《2063年议程》以及布隆迪的资源禀赋制定，目标是在2027年之前走出经济困境并减少贫困	该规划的长期目标是提升粮食自给自足率，提高农工商和采掘业的出口占比、实现出口结构多元化，开发能源和艺术产业，以基础设施的修建和维护工程刺激增长，提高教育、医疗和社保等基础社会服务的普及率，加强环境保护和土地合理规划，提高金融业治理水平和去中心化程度，发展地区和国际伙伴关系，以实现经济的协调发展

续表

国家	政策文件	减贫目标	具体措施
埃塞俄比亚	生产安全网计划（2019年）	解决农村地区长期粮食不安全问题	在长达六个月的淡季期间，每月向贫困家庭提供现金或粮食，以换取他们为建立社区而劳动。少数家庭受益于"直接支持"，这种支持为期12个月，提供给那些没有健壮成人的家庭
马达加斯加	马达加斯加倡议计划（2019—2023年）	刺激增长和减少贫困	发展畜牧业和农工业，以确保粮食安全，占领出口市场；发展健康与卫生服务，将社区健康作为优先事项；改善水、环境卫生和个人卫生，将Analanjirofo选为2020年马达加斯加Madio计划的试点地区，以促进饮用水、卫生设施和个人卫生的普及
索马里	第九个国家发展计划	提出三个首要的国家优先事项：政治稳定、提高安全和经济增长	减少索马里各地的不安全状况，加强索马里各机构的有效治理能力，从而提高包容性和减少暴力冲突；加强机构能力，使索马里公民在极端情况下更好地获得医疗卫生、教育和其他基本服务，并实施赋权妇女的战略；加强索马里各机构对有效政治和环境治理的承诺和能力，加快经济增长和建设以创造就业，特别强调为青年创造机会
安哥拉	安哥拉长期发展战略(2025年)	到2025年，贫困指数下降75%，消除极端贫困，大幅减少相对贫困和饥饿	增加和扩大对全民家庭性质的社会福利；制定适当的奖励措施，如获得土地和生产资料，安置流动人口，特别是流离失所者、复员者或难民；支持扩大生产性就业和公平报酬，以消除贫困和实现收入公平分配
喀麦隆	国家发展战略（2020—2030年）	大幅减少贫困，2030年将贫困率降至25%以下	通过大幅度减贫和缓解就业不足，改善人们的生活条件，提高人们获得基本社会服务的机会；通过加强农业、工业活动和农场现代化来提高生产力，从而显著减少农村贫困

续表

国家	政策文件	减贫目标	具体措施
刚果（金）	国家战略规划（2021—2024年）	减少贫困、粮食不安全和营养不良	通过农业转型、开放和创新的经济多样化以及推动促进青年和妇女创业，促进可持续、包容的经济增长，满足粮食需求
纳米比亚	第五个国家发展计划（2017/2018—2021/2022）	减少贫困与不平等，实现包容、可持续和公平的经济增长，培养有能力和健康的人力资源。到2022年，极端贫困人口比例降低到5.00%，基尼系数降低到0.5，人类发展指数增长到0.695	提高农业生产力和可持续性，帮助消除饥饿、粮食不安全和营养不良；将边缘社区纳入主流经济；将所有利益相关者的投资用于刺激经济增长、创造就业和减少贫困的活动；强化技能培训，建立有能力和健康的人力资源；加强社会保障，强化社会保障体系，提高部门行动的协调性
贝宁	政府行动方案（2021—2026年）	到2026年，将货币贫困率降低到36.5%	政府部门应推进素质教育和职业技术教育培训，促进高素质教育；全面推行社会资本保险计划，加强医疗卫生体系建设，实现有效的医疗卫生覆盖，提高民众基本社会服务和社会福利的可及性
利比里亚	繁荣与发展亲贫议程	通过扩大对农业、基础设施、人力资源开发和社会保障方面的投资，推动可持续和包容的经济增长，额外为100万利比里亚人提供更大的收入保障，并在六个地区中的五个地区将绝对贫困人口减少23%	为了在未来五年内实现该议程并最终实现《2030年愿景》的目标，战略和干预措施围绕四大支柱展开，这将为未来五年的发展提供路径
毛里塔尼亚	加速增长和共同繁荣战略	经济增长率超过12%，生产性资本进一步积累，减少非正规经济份额，经济发展更具竞争力、包容性与韧性	制定了两部分措施，第一部分为社会、经济、体制及环境评估，第二部分为战略方向及2016~2020年行动规划。目前，第一个五年规划已完成，主要涉及维护宏观经济稳定，提高自然资源转化能力，改善商业环境等。2021~2025年规划仍在制定过程中，第一、二部分涉及一些就业、商业发展、教育等领域的具体措施

资料来源：根据世界银行、联合国以及各国政府公布的资料整理得到。

四、小结

贫困问题在非洲国家十分突出。以2021年为例，全球政府收入总计约309133.66亿美元，而非洲国家的政府总收入仅占大约1.7%。为了摆脱贫困，非洲国家制定并实施了包括从拉各斯行动计划到《2063年议程》在内的一系列减贫战略。这些战略覆盖经济、社会、政治、文化、科技、对外关系等多个方面，展现了非洲总体发展战略的全面性和完善性。然而，与东亚、南亚等其他地区相比，非洲的减贫工作一直面临着投入多、成效微弱的困境。非洲国家减贫进程遭遇困境的一个重要原因是国家自主程度低、国家财政能力不足。2021年，非洲政府总收入为5275.7亿美元，但是政府总支出高达6708.81亿美元（见表4-3），而非洲人口约有14亿人，财政收入、支出与人口比例失衡，在减贫过程中严重依赖国际援助和投资。

表4-3　　　　　　　2021年非洲和全球公共财政情况

地区	人口 （亿人）	政府财政收入 （亿美元）	政府财政支出 （亿美元）	人均财政收入 （美元）	人均财政支出 （美元）
非洲	14.25 （17.97%）	5275.70 （1.71%）	6708.81 （1.80%）	370.22 （9.49%）	470.79 （10.03%）
世界	79.28	309133.66	372118.88	3899.26	4693.73

注：括号内为非洲占世界的比重。

资料来源：The Statistical Annex to the annual Africa's Development Dynamics（AFDD）report，https：//oe.cd/AFDD-2023。

从非洲国家内部来看，财政能力和执行力低是实施减贫战略和政策的主要障碍。由于经济发展水平低，再加上制度建设不完善和严重腐败，大部分非洲国家的财政汲取能力较弱，税收资源大量流失，无法筹集提供公共服务和实施减贫项目所需的巨大资金。同时，非洲国家财政能力不足，对资金的管理和利用不善，真正投入基础设施建设和减贫项目的资金很少。非洲减贫文件大多是非盟或者区域联盟指定的战略性文件，与非洲当地政府贫困治理现状脱节，没有涉及民众真正需要的教育、民生、基建项目，也因此收益甚微。非盟等制定的减贫政策能否被有效地贯彻落实，关系到减贫目标能否实现、贫困人口的利益能否得到保障。但是，大多数非洲国家的官僚机构能力不足、效率低下，政府工作人员的工作能力和素质较低，缺乏责任心，无法有效执行减贫战略，因此很多减贫政策的成效有限。

从外部角度来看，非洲国家对国际社会的援助和资金依赖程度较高，大部分非洲国家都背上了沉重的外债负担，而且西方援助的附加条件削弱了非洲国家制定自身减贫战略的自主权，阻碍了政府治理能力的提升。非洲国家的财政支出高度依赖国际社会提供的发展援助，为了获得援助资金，非洲国家在制定政策时更多地迎合援助国的要求，而不关心国内民众的真正需求，这催生了政府对公民不负责任。更重要的是，西方国家给予非洲的援助不但没有真正帮助其解决贫困问题，援助国过多地干预和指导受援国的政策制定和其他政府决策过程反而使非洲国家政府产生了依赖心理，使其自主探索适宜本国减贫政策的意愿下降，损害了政府的治理能力。总之，对外部资金的过度依赖导致非洲国家在减贫中丧失自主权，难以取得真正的成效。

总而言之，在今后的减贫实践中，非洲国家应在保持自主性的基础上，合理地利用外部援助。其关键在于不断提升国家能力，主动制定并执行适合本国实际的有效的减贫战略和政策。这将使非洲国家走上一条既符合自身特点，又具有可持续性的减贫发展道路。

第五章
国际社会对非洲的援助

非洲一直是国际社会关注的重点地区，国际社会不同类型的援助主体对非援助的理念和方式不同，并产生了不同的减贫效果。本章从比较的视角梳理了传统援助主体、新兴经济体对非援助的规模、领域和特点，进而将非洲置于国际社会中来深度理解非洲减贫与发展的状况。

一、传统援助主体对非发展援助

（一）传统援助主体对非发展援助的规模

国际官方发展援助是非洲解决发展问题的重要资金来源之一。但是，自2020年以来，非洲获得国际官方发展援助的规模呈下降趋势。

第一，从撒哈拉以南非洲获得的官方发展援助占全球官方发展援助总额的比例来看，从20世纪90年代开始，撒哈拉以南非洲获得的官方发展援助一直占全球官方发展援助总额的30%左右。2018年以来，撒哈拉以南非洲每年获得的官方发展援助都在500亿美元以上；2020年，撒哈拉以南非洲获得的官方援助创历史新高，达到669亿美元；到2021年，撒哈拉以南非洲获得的官方发展援助下降至623亿美元（见图5-1）。

第二，从人均获得的官方发展援助规模来看，1978~2021年，撒哈拉以南非洲人均获得的官方发展援助规模一直高于世界平均水平，并远高于南亚、拉丁美洲和加勒比地区、东亚和太平洋地区。自2012年开始，撒哈拉以南非洲人均获得的官方发展援助规模稳定在50美元左右，而其他地区则始终在20美元以下。从增长率来看，撒哈拉以南非洲人均获得的官方发展援助规模从21世纪初开始快速增长，由2000年的19.45美元增加至2020年的58.1美元，而其他地区最大增幅不足10美元。但是，从其自身的增长幅度来看，2021年撒哈拉以南非洲人均获得的官方发展援助则下降至52.73美元，较2020年下降了5.37美元（见图5-2）。

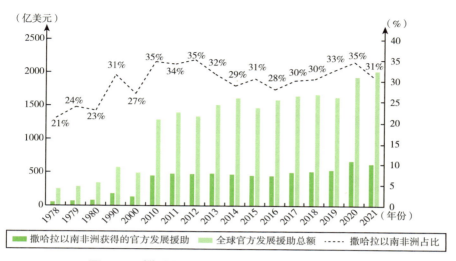

图5-1　撒哈拉以南非洲获得的官方发展援助

资料来源：世界银行。

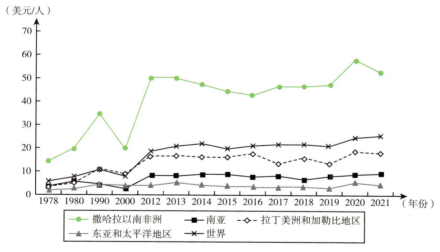

图5-2　世界及不同区域人均获得的官方发展援助

资料来源：https：//data.oecd.org。

第三，从国际多边机构对非洲的援助规模来看，2012年以来，撒哈拉以南非洲获得的援助额占国际多边机构援助总额的比重超过40%，2019年超过50%，并在2020年达到十年内最大规模——328.55亿美元。但是，从2020年开始，撒哈拉以南非洲从国际多边机构获得的援助占国际多边机构援助总额的比重开始下降，由 2019 年的 51.88% 下降至 2021 年的 45.79%，援助规模也由 2020 年的 328.55 亿美元下降至 2021 年的 260.36 亿美元（见表 5-1）。

表 5-1   2012~2021 年国际多边机构对撒哈拉以南非洲的援助规模及占比

单位：亿美元

	2012 年	2013 年	2014 年	2015 年	2016 年	2017 年	2018 年	2019 年	2020 年	2021 年
援助总额	403.23	426.64	436.49	418.29	415.18	439.54	433.54	447.44	661.11	568.57
撒哈拉以南非洲	176，32 (43.73%)	188，95 (44.29%)	184，48 (42.27%)	179，96 (43.02%)	173，1 (41.69%)	200，48 (45.61%)	205，18 (47.33%)	232，15 (51.88%)	328，55 (49.70%)	260，36 (45.79%)

资料来源：https：//data.oecd.org。

第四，从发展援助委员会（DAC）对非洲的官方发展援助规模来看，2019~2021 年，DAC 国家对非洲官方发展援助的规模基本平稳，维持在 250 亿美元左右，呈现倒"U"形发展趋势，援助额先增后降，分别为 231.4 亿美元、249.5 亿美元、245.8 亿美元。此外，官方发展援助更多流向撒哈拉以南非洲国家，2021 年有 197.2 亿美元用于对撒哈拉以南非洲国家的援助，占当年对非援助的 80%（见表 5-2）。

表 5-2   2019~2021 年 DAC 对非援助区域分布   单位：亿美元

地区	2019 年	2020 年	2021 年
非洲	231.40	249.50	245.80
撒哈拉以北非洲	30.60	31.50	35.40
撒哈拉以南非洲	185.10	205.00	197.20

资料来源：https：//stats-1.oecd.org/index.aspx?DatasetCode=CPA。

第五，西方国家对非双边援助规模有所下降。例如，日本对撒哈拉以南非洲的双边官方发展援助总体上呈现先增后降的趋势[1]，从 1970 年的 800 万美元快速增长至 2010 年 18.35 亿美元，而后缓慢下降至 2020 年 13.38 亿美元（见图 5-3）。又如，非洲是英国特定地区双边官方发展援助的最大受援地区，占 2021 年英国发展援助总额的 50.5%，但是随着官方发展援助总支出的下降，亦呈现减少趋势[2]。

---

[1]   参见 https：//www.jica.go.jp/english/publications/reports/annual/2022/fh2q4d000001doiv-att/2022_all.pdf。

[2]   2021 年英国援助支出决算报告 Statistics on International Development: Final UK Aid Spend 2021 指出，英国 2021 年官方发展援助与国民总收入的最终比率为 0.50%，官方发展援助支出为 114.23 亿英镑，比 2020 年减少 30.54 亿英镑（减少了 21.1%）。

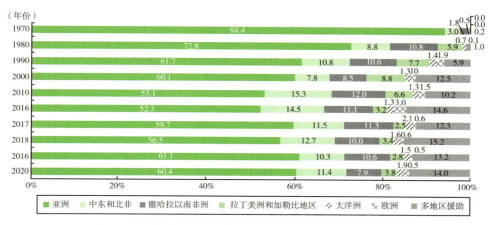

图5-3　按地区划分的日本双边官方发展援助趋势

资料来源：JICA，*2022 Japan International Cooperation Agency Annual Report*。

（二）传统援助主体对非发展援助的领域

第一，西方发展援助较为重视对社会发展领域的支持，缺少对大型公共基础设施建设和工业发展等领域的投入。西方发展援助尤为注重提高非洲国家和地区教育、健康、人口和公共卫生、供水以及治理能力（包括政府和非政府组织）等，从OECD-DAC的统计数据来看，每年超过1/3的援助资金流向这些社会发展领域[①]。2021年，投向教育、卫生、饮水安全等社会发展领域占援助总额的40.35%，表明西方发展援助的重点仍然是改善贫困人口的生存环境与减贫条件。但是，对交通、通信、电力以及涉农类经济基础设施的援助占比仅为13%，甚至低于占比16.43%的紧急人道主义援助，说明西方发展援助依旧很少支持欠发达国家的公共基础设施建设和工业发展，这是西方发展援助和中国援助的显著区别[②]。从国际开发协会的援助领域来看，2022年援助资源用于社会服务（教育、卫生、社会保护）、基础设施（能源、信息通信技术、交通、水务、核废物管理）、公共行政、农业、工业及贸易、金融等领域的占比分别为30%、33%、16%、11%、6%、3%[③]，而农业作为非洲最为重要的社会经济领域，获得的援助投入仅占11%。

第二，西方发展援助涉及很多领域，从援助本身来看，通常以提供软件

① 唐丽霞、李小云.西方发展援助的管理和实践评述［J］.复旦国际关系评论，2016，（2）：153-167.

② OECD（2023），ODA by sector（indicator）. doi：10.1787/a5a1f674-en（Accessed on 08 July 2023）.

③ 参见 https：//ida.worldbank.org/en/ida-financing。

能力建设为主，比较重视能力建设活动，较少采取直接提供生产资料援助的方式。这些援助方式通过各种培训促进当地组织机构、地方性非政府机构以及农民组织的发展，但由于援助资源的有限和援助管理等问题，援助资源被攫取，减贫经验难以向外扩展和传播，范围较为局限，更广泛的困难群体难以获利，忽视了非洲特殊的发展阶段与需求。

案例5-1　典型西方国家对非洲的援助项目

法国： 自 2018 年以来，法国提出"选择非洲"（Choose Africa）倡议，旨在为非洲的初创企业和中小微企业提供各种类型的资金和技术支持。法国与整个非洲大陆的250个当地合作伙伴合作，为4万多家中小微企业和数十万微型企业拨款35亿欧元，为8700家初创企业和中小微企业提供技术援助，未来五年将创造200万个直接和间接就业机会。此外，2022年初，法国成立法国专家局，将此作为法国负责技术合作的部际机构，在380个项目中聘用了约1000名专家，其业务量的65%均来自非洲。

德国： 德国国际合作机构（GIZ）与非盟合作，帮助其成员国界定非洲大陆上殖民时代的边界，划定6000多公里长的边界线，以帮助减少自然资源冲突和犯罪。为了从非洲大陆自由贸易区（AfCFTA）提供的非洲大陆经济一体化的机会中获益，德国国际合作机构协助推动各国批准非盟的《人员自由流动议定书》，以实现免签证旅行，为从事跨境工作和贸易提供便利。

日本： 2022年8月，日本国际协力事业机构（JICA）举行第八届非洲发展问题东京国际会议（TICAD 8），在"争取建立一个有弹性的、包容和繁荣的非洲"的口号下，日本国际协力事业机构提出在非洲建立弹性社会和经济的合作方向。例如，日本国际协力事业机构向肯尼亚、埃塞俄比亚、尼日利亚和卢旺达提供旨在建立产业生态系统的双边合作，建立青年企业家与各利益相关者（如投资者、教育机构和职能部门）联系的平台。

（三）传统援助主体对非发展援助的效果

第一，关于发展援助与受援国经济发展和减贫之间关系的结论尚未统一，但是纵观 70 多年来的国际发展援助尤其是对非援助，其在一定程度上促进了当地的发展，也使非洲成为世界上对援助依赖程度最高的地区。西方官方发展援助在本质上形塑了南北不平等的权力关系，在此权力关系下，不管叙事如何改变、政策如何修正，如果要求发展中国家按照西方发达国家追求现代化的核心动力不改变，就难以摆脱援助依赖性加强而有效性降低的结果。

从支撑数据来看，一方面，撒哈拉以南非洲获得的官方发展援助占国民总收入的比重稳定在3%左右，远远高于世界平均水平与其他地区，且差值不断扩大。到2020年，撒哈拉以南非洲获得的官方发展援助占国民总收入的比重（4.02%）比东亚和太平洋地区（0.05）高出3.97个百分点（见图5-4），说明该地区对官方发展援助有巨大的依赖性。

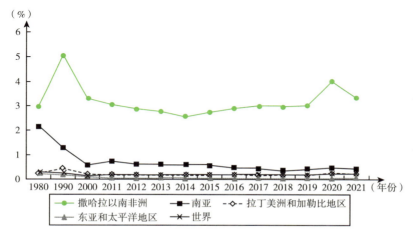

图5-4　世界及不同区域获得的官方发展援助占国民总收入的比重

资料来源：https：//data.oecd.org。

另一方面，全球共有75个国家有资格获得国际开发协会的援助资源，其中非洲国家有39个。从"国际开发协会毕业国家"概念来看，历史上共有11个非洲国家曾获得过毕业国家称号，其中仅有六个非洲国家（安哥拉FY14，埃及FY81、FY99，赤道几内亚FY99，斯威士兰FY75，摩洛哥FY75，突尼斯FY79）真正毕业；而喀麦隆、刚果（布）、科特迪瓦、尼日利亚和津巴布韦五个国家则在毕业后再度成为可以获得国际开发协会资源的国家，其减贫成效并不稳定①。在2022财年，国际开发协会前十大受援国中除了孟加拉国（获得21.61亿美元贷款），其他九个国家均来自非洲，分别是尼日利亚、刚果（金）、埃塞俄比亚、肯尼亚、尼日尔、乌干达、坦桑尼亚、莫桑比克和喀麦隆，分别获得的贷款是24亿美元、21.25亿美元、19.04亿美元、18亿美元、17.28亿美元、

---

① 参见https：//ida.worldbank.org/en/about/borrowing-countries/ida-graduates。

17.15 亿美元、16.5 亿美元、12.87 亿美元、11.2 亿美元①。

第二，援助条件是国际发展援助的核心，很多援助主体基于不同目标实施有条件的援助，国家的财政政策、贸易自由化、公共企业私有化和农业私有化等成为援助主体提供政策性贷款援助条件考量的重点。由于各种附加条件，发展中国家获得发展援助的成本越来越高。从国际多边机构来看，以世界银行为例，近年来对受援国的援助条件有所变化，贸易政策的重要性正在下降，公共部门的管理能力、公共财政管理、公共开支和公共部门改革日益成为重要的援助条件。同时，一些援助方案的实施还需要受援国制定特定的行动战略，并且该行动战略要接受援助机构的审查和评估，通过后方能获得援助资金的支持。以重债穷国减债计划和多边减债动议为例，这两项最主要的减债计划要求受援国制定减贫战略文件（PRSP），由世界银行体系对该战略进行两个阶段的审查，如果达到决策点，方可启动重债穷国计划，达到完成点，可启动多边减债动议。

从双边援助主体来看，一方面，受援国的政治条件直接影响援助机构对其提供援助项目。例如，受援国若发生"种族清洗"、军事政变或终止民主化进程、人权问题等，援助机构就会采取停止全部援助项目、停止续签新的援助项目、停止部分援助项目、全面减少援助配给四个不同级别的援助制裁。例如，美国依据 1961 年颁布的《对外援助法》向非洲提供援助，其援助项目的大多数执行机构是美国实体②，并在对非援助中把受援国的政治改革作为援助附加条件，如在支持改善当地的公共卫生条件的基础上附加"推进地区和平稳定与政治体制改革"等要求③。另一方面，双边援助带有明显的选择性与指向性，并非以贫困为援助的根本依据。例如，2021 年英国双边国别官方发展援助的前十位受援国中有六个是非洲国家，分别是尼日利亚（1.4 亿英镑）、埃塞俄比亚（1.2 亿英镑）、南非（1.02 亿英镑）、索马里（1.01 亿英镑）、南苏丹（0.96 亿英镑）、苏丹（0.94 亿英镑）。2022 年美国发展援助支出预算为 380 亿美元，其中近 25% 的预算仅用于十个国家，这十个国家中有六个为非洲国家，分别是埃塞俄比亚（11.3 亿美元）、南苏丹（8.21 亿美元）、刚果（8.14 亿美元）、尼日利亚（8.03 亿美元）、苏丹（4.88 亿美元）、索马里（4.75 亿美元）。2022 年法国

① 参见 https：//ida.worldbank.org/en/ida-financing。
② 联合战略计划，参见 https：//www.usaid.gov/results-and-data/planning/joint-strategic-plan/fy-2022-2026。
③ 周尚思，徐之明.中国与美国对非洲官方发展援助模式的比较分析［J］.山东社会科学，2021，316（12）：160-166.

国际发展援助规模前十的国家中有五个是非洲国家，分别为摩洛哥（5.97亿欧元）、科特迪瓦（3.61亿欧元）、南非（3.01亿欧元）、突尼斯（2.86亿欧元）和埃及（2.84亿欧元）。2022年，日本国际协力事业机构项目支持最多的非洲国家是坦桑尼亚，为392.45亿日元，其对加纳、肯尼亚、马拉维、吉布提的援助也都达到40亿日元以上（见表5-3）。

表5-3　2022年日本国际协力事业机构项目，按国家划分的总金额

单位：亿日元

国家	金额
坦桑尼亚	392.45
加纳	63.06
肯尼亚	56.20
马拉维	49.45
吉布提	40.95
塞内加尔	34.77
莫桑比克	23.90
卢旺达	22.03
乌干达	20.56
马达加斯加	18.48
南苏丹	17.66
埃塞俄比亚	17.07
赞比亚	16.86
刚果（金）	16.84
苏丹	12.82
科特迪瓦	12.71
尼日利亚	9.33
喀麦隆	8.86
布吉纳法索	8.30
南非	6.36
安哥拉	2.86
其他28个国家	149.64

注：该表仅列出了日本国际协力事业机构设有海外办事处的国家。表中数据经过四舍五入处理。

资料来源：世界银行。

二、新兴经济体对非发展援助

（一）新兴经济体对非援助概况

1.援助资金规模和类型

从援助资金规模来看，新兴经济体对非援助的总额呈上升态势，成为国际对非援助的重要补充力量。纵向来看，新兴经济体对非援助额由2011年的3.4亿美元升至2017年的5.2亿美元[1]，并在2018年增加至16.56亿美元，同比上涨77.27%[2]。但也有个别国家的援助比例呈下降趋势，如土耳其2015~2020年对非援助中，南部非洲的占比从9.66%下降到0.71%，北非的占比在2017年之后下降至0.001%[3]。横向来看，各国都重视对非援助，以2019~2020年援助撒哈拉以南非洲的均值为例：土耳其援助7577万美元、泰国援助152万美元、阿联酋援助107447万美元、沙特阿拉伯援助41946万美元[4]。

从援助资金类型来看，新兴经济体的援助更多采用赠款、贷款等形式。在直接赠款方面，阿联酋对非赠款达5.758亿美元[5]，印度提供5亿美元赠款用于能力建设和人力资源开发[6]。在优惠贷款方面，这些贷款主要用于非洲民生领域的重要项目和优先发展项目，以及用于购买援助国的机械设备或产品[7]。例如，印度进出口银行提供的50%以上的贷款都是针对非洲的发展项目，用于农业生产、食品加工、基础设施、信息技术、能源和制药等关键领域[8]；巴西外贸局向加纳和津巴布韦分别提供9500万美元和9800万美元贷款以进口巴西的农产品[9]。

2.援助地区流向

在援助地区选择上，新兴经济体侧重地理区位邻近、社会经济发展相似、资源条件丰富、文化传统相近的地区。阿联酋对非援助主要集中在西非、北非、东非，占比分别为63.3%、58.4%、47.3%[10]。印度集中在与之有传统友好关系的东南部非洲国家以及资源丰富的非洲国家[11]。巴西对非援助范围从最开始集

---

[1] 参见http：//world.people.com.cn/n1/2019/1018/c1002-31407967.html。
[2] 数据来自国际社会对非洲的援助—中国社会科学院西亚非洲研究所。
[3] Assessing Türkiye-Africa Engagements.
[4] OECD-DAC，参见http：//www.oecd.org/dac/financing-sustainable-development/development-finance-data/aid：at-a-glance.htm。
[5] United Arab Emirates Foreign Aid 2021.
[6] 温翠苹.21世纪中国与印度援助非洲对比研究［D］.北京：外交学院，2014.
[7] 唐丽霞、李小云.印度的对外援助评述［J］.南亚研究季刊，2013，154（3）：7-12，32，1.
[8] India's Development Cooperation in Africa: The Case of 'Solar Mamas' Who Bring Light.
[9] 参见http：//iwaas.cass.cn/xslt/fzlt/201508/t20150831_2609374.shtml。
[10] United Arab Emieates Foreign Aid 2021.
[11] Devex Emerging Donors Report.

中于葡语地区，到后来拓展到整个非洲大陆[①]。沙特阿拉伯对非援助主要针对伊斯兰国家[②]。土耳其对非援助主要集中在撒哈拉以南非洲[③]。

3.援助机制和形式

在援助机制上，新兴经济体积极构建三方合作机制，不断丰富国际发展合作的方式和路径。例如，印度联手日本，与非洲国家建立"亚非增长走廊"；土耳其联合日本举办"土耳其—日本—非洲伙伴关系"会议；巴西参与"南美—非洲峰会"和"印度—巴西—南非论坛"，与日本发展援助机构开展热带草原发展项目，与美国国际发展机构开展加强莫桑比克研究能力项目，与联合国粮农组织和世界粮食计划署在非洲五国开展向家庭农场提供粮食收购项目等[④]。在援助形式上，新兴经济体竞相召开对非峰会，推动双边合作向全方位、多层次、高质量方向发展。为进一步加强与非洲国家的政治、经济和文化关系，峰会外交成为各国对非外交的标配活动（见表5–4）。

表5–4　　　　　　　　　部分国家与非洲的峰会外交

国家	时间	会议名称	核心内容
印度	2008年	第一届印非论坛峰会	将科技列为印非合作的重点领域，提供54亿美元的信贷支持非洲国家在信息技术、通信和能源以及生物医药领域的发展，加强对非技术人才培训
	2011年	第二届印非论坛峰会	印度—非洲伙伴关系建立在能力建设、技术转让、贸易与基础设施发展三个支柱之上
	2015年	第三届印非论坛峰会	深化在清洁能源、公共交通、适应气候变化的农业等方面的合作，未来五年为非洲提供100亿美元优惠贷款和6亿美元无偿援助
土耳其	2008年	第一届土耳其—非洲峰会	加强伙伴关系以促进共同发展与繁荣；通过了《伊斯坦布尔宣言》和《非伙伴关系的合作框架》
	2014年	第二届土耳其—非洲峰会	加强可持续发展和一体化的新型伙伴关系模式；通过了《2015—2019年宣言和联合执行计划》，并提出对非政策的七项原则
	2021年	第三届土耳其—非洲峰会	加强各领域的伙伴关系与合作，包括建立和平与安全的环境，增加改善非洲基础设施的投资

---

①　参见http://iwaas.cssn.cn/xslt/fzlt/201508/t20150831_2609356.shtml。
②　陈沫.沙特阿拉伯对外援助的特点、动因与效应［J］.西亚非洲，2021，278（3）：113–136.
③　张春.土耳其对非洲地区的经贸合作［J］.阿拉伯世界研究，2012，139（2）：86–99.
④　唐露萍.发展中国家对外援助及其发展方向［D］.厦门：厦门大学，2014.

续表

国家	时间	会议名称	核心内容
俄罗斯	2019年	第一届俄罗斯—非洲峰会	向非洲提供政治和外交支持、国防和安全帮助、经济援助、疾病控制建议、人道主义救援援助、教育和职业培训等
	2023年	第二届俄罗斯—非洲峰会	通过了有关防止太空军备竞赛、国际信息安全领域合作、加强反恐合作的三份文件，以及《俄非伙伴关系论坛2023—2026年行动计划》

资料来源：根据印度、土耳其、俄罗斯以及非洲国家或相关组织公布的资料整理所得。

（二）新兴经济体对非援助特点

1.援助理念新颖

随着新兴市场和发展中国家经济实力的提升，新兴经济体在国际发展援助中的作用越来越大。与传统官方发展援助不同的是，新兴经济体坚持平等互利、互不干涉内政等南南合作理念，追求互惠互利的经济增长和长期贸易发展，通过经贸合作、知识交流、经验分享和人才培养等方式帮助受援国提高发展能力和治理能力，例如，中国注重人力资源培训、减贫经验分享；印度重视教育培训、信息技术等；巴西以农业、食品安全等领域技术援助为主[①]。新援助理念的出现不仅推动了国际发展援助领域的创新，使国际发展援助的效果更可持续，还进一步促使各方开始对西方主导的发展援助体系进行深刻反思。

2.援助领域广泛

新兴经济体对非援助涉及医疗、教育、安全等方方面面。

（1）医疗援助。一是提供医疗服务。例如，印度作为"世界药房"，将大量药品销往非洲；印度关爱眼睛基金会为非洲眼病患者提供免费手术。土耳其为非洲民众提供健康检查，并为无法在本国接受治疗的非洲患者提供救治[②]。在新冠疫情期间，印度、土耳其、巴西、阿联酋等国家向非洲国家提供医疗设备、疫苗等抗疫物资，印度还举办新冠疫情网络研讨会，以支持非洲抗击疫情[③]。二是培训医务人员。例如，印度利用远程电子医疗技术进行专业培训[④]，土

---

① 参见http：//world.people.com.cn/n1/2019/1018/c1002-31407967.html。
② 魏敏.正义与发展党执政后土耳其的对非政策述评［J］.中东研究，2020，11（1）：112-132，278.
③ 参见https：//user.guancha.cn/main/content?id=322649。
④ 张永宏，赵孟清.印度对非洲科技合作：重点领域、运行机制及战略取向分析［J］.南亚研究季刊，2015，163（4）：47-55，5.

耳其卫生部向非洲国家提供职业培训①，巴西派遣专家帮助非洲制定预防和治疗艾滋病的计划②。

（2）教育援助。一是建立培训机构。例如，印度为非洲国家提供了300多个培训项目，培训内容覆盖众多领域，有效促进了就业情况改善③。巴西在马里、布基纳法索、乍得、贝宁"棉花四国"分别建立农村经济研究所、环境和农业研究所、农业研究所和农业科学研究中心，提高棉花供应链的生产力和竞争力④。土耳其在非洲26个国家创办了175所学校⑤，超过11000名非洲年轻人在土耳其大学接受培训⑥。二是资助非洲学生。例如，2011~2015年印度为25000名非洲学生提供奖学金，2012~2021年土耳其向54个非洲国家的12600名学生提供奖学金资助⑦。

（3）安全援助。一是培训军事人员。例如，土耳其帮助索马里恢复安全和打击恐怖主义⑧。印度向非洲提供反恐培训，协助非洲东部和南部沿印度洋国家进行反海盗和专属经济区调查等活动，帮助非洲增强海上安全能力。二是参与维和活动。例如，土耳其参加了由联合国主导的七项维和行动中的四项，为非洲大陆的维和行动作出贡献。印度承诺继续支持在非洲的联合国维和行动，并在印度的联合国维和中心培训非洲军官。

3.援助重点突出

新兴经济体对非援助覆盖面很广，但重点集中在基础设施援助、技术援助、人道主义援助三个方面。

（1）基础设施援助。例如，印度为非洲国家建设医院、体育馆、学校等生活基础设施⑨。巴西在非承包道路、桥梁等建设工程⑩。沙特阿拉伯、阿联酋在非

---

① 魏敏.正义与发展党执政后土耳其的对非政策述评［J］.中东研究，2020，11（1）：112-132，278.

② 参见http：//www.holine.com/July/171902.htm。

③ 参见75 years of development cooperation，https://www.researchgate.net/publication/362790779_75_years_of_development_cooperation。

④ 参见https：//www.fx361.cc/page/2022/0916/11559757.shtml。

⑤ The Rise of Turkey in Africa.

⑥ 土耳其与非洲的伙伴关系：以发展为导向的方法，参见https://www.sohu.com/a/366732488_120073528#google_vignette。

⑦ Visualizing Turkey's Activism in Africa.

⑧ 陈洋.土耳其介入非洲之角事务的表现、原因和影响［D］.金华：浙江师范大学，2021.

⑨ 温翠苹.21世纪中国与印度援助非洲对比研究［D］.北京：外交学院，2014.

⑩ 参见http：//iwaas.cssn.cn/xslt/fzlt/201508/t20150831_2609356.shtml。

洲之角增加对房地产、酒店、交通等基础设施投资[①]。土耳其在非洲有着"基建狂魔"称号，2021年土耳其建筑商在撒哈拉以南非洲承担的项目占所有海外建筑项目的17%，高于2008年前的0.3%[②]。为了方便土非之间的人员流动和物流，土耳其航空公司开通了飞往非洲大陆61个目的地的航班。

（2）技术援助。例如，巴西对非援助的主要手段是技术合作，涉及热带农业、热带医学、职业技术教育、社会政策推广四大领域。土耳其通过资助农业基础设施和农业研究等方式向非转移技术。印度在信息技术领域内推广"泛非电信网络"计划，在非洲建造工业园、光纤电缆、网络数据处理中心等设施，为非洲53个国家提供远程教学、遥控医疗、电子政务、信息娱乐、资源测绘和气象业务等服务[③]；在农业技术领域内分享"绿色革命"经验，将耕种技术转让给非洲国家用于农业生产[④]，在"棉花四国"实施棉花技术援助方案，帮助其提高种植棉花的能力。

（3）人道主义援助。例如，印度主要提供自然灾害的救灾援助[⑤]。土耳其红新月会通过建造住房、学校、祈祷之家等公共设施，为数千个弱势社区提供服务[⑥]。阿联酋成立沙迦慈善协会以支持和援助学生、孤儿以及贫困家庭，修建学校、诊所以及清真寺，为灾民提供紧急救援，挖掘水井，提供食品与药品[⑦]。

三、小结

从援助内容上看，国际对非援助最初是简单的经济、军事以及包括教育、卫生在内的人道主义援助，在一定程度上帮助并促进了非洲国家的经济发展。20世纪90年代以来，国际对非援助逐渐强调良治和能力建设，对科技创新领域的援助亦有所增加，主要集中在技术、卫生、减贫和可持续发展等领域。例如，在国际援助与合作中，通过加强就业培训促进当地居民技能的提升，通过文体设施建设促进教育发展，通过对弱势群体的关注改善其生活条件，通过对营养卫生的关注改进生活习惯等。从援助效果来看，相关援助措施在一定程度上对减轻贫困、促进可持续发展具有重要意义。如果没有国际援助，许多非洲

---

① 王磊.中东国家在"非洲之角"动作频频［J］.世界知识，2018，1726（11）：52-53.

② Dipama, S., & Parlar, E. (2023). Assessing Turkey–Africa Engagements (APRI Policy Brief 2/2023). Berlin: APRI.

③ 冯立冰，郭东彦.印非峰会与印非合作机制的构建及影响［J］.国际论坛，2018（5）：15-22.

④ 温翠苹.21世纪中国与印度援助非洲对比研究［D］.北京：外交学院，2014.

⑤ 唐丽霞，李小云.印度的对外援助评述［J］.南亚研究季刊，2013，154（3）：7-12，32，1.

⑥ 陈洋.土耳其介入非洲之角事务的表现、原因和影响［D］.金华：浙江师范大学，2021.

⑦ 喻光龄.阿联酋对外援助研究2010—2016［D］.上海：上海外国语大学，2018.

国家将无法实现经济持续增长。"发展靠援助"形象地反映出非洲国家与外援国家的关系。然而，在过去50多年里，接受国际发展援助最多的非洲的经济增长和减贫并未有明显的进展，许多非洲国家仍长期处于"援助陷阱"之中①。

从宏观层面看，由西方主导的现代国际发展援助体系面临转型的压力。一方面，苦于援助的实际效果不佳；另一方面，受制于整体经济形势，西方发达国家的"援助疲劳"也日益加剧。从微观层面看，援助效果所面临的质疑仍然存在，部分传统援助主体在援助过程中依然附加条件，如要求受援国必须同意援助者制定的一系列经济和政治政策，要求受援国家必须在特定国家购买选择服务和产品，以及要求购买援助国产品并由指定公司或机构来执行项目等。这在一定程度上增加了项目实施的成本，使援助在某种意义上成为促进援助国的产品出口渠道和途径。此外，国际对非减贫援助还受到诸多条件的限制，如受援国的殖民历史、援助国和受援国之间的政治战略关系、受援国自身的经济水平和贫困程度、受援国政治政策和援助国的一致性、不同国家分类（重债穷国、脆弱国家）等，在一定程度上减损了对非援助减贫的效果。

随着新兴经济体积极地向非洲提供援助，印度、巴西等新兴经济体开始成为提供国际发展援助的生力军。与传统的"援助国—受援国"主从关系不同，新兴援助国将自己视为发展伙伴，而非援助国。新发展援助是基于经验共享和知识共同创造的平行过程。新兴经济体在国际对非援助领域的迅猛崛起不容忽视，对长期以西方传统援助理念为中心的"援助—受援"范式构成挑战，推动国际发展援助理念变革，使国际社会越来越重视构建平等发展合作伙伴关系的新型国际发展合作思想，进而使国际发展合作的结构发生根本性变化②。

---

① 李小云.为何国际发展援助常常无效，参见http://jer.whu.edu.cn/jjgc/5/2016-01-07/2119.html。
② 胡勇.国际发展援助转型与印度对非发展合作［J］.外交评论（外交学院学报），2016，33（6）: 131-156.

第六章
中非合作论坛框架下中非减贫合作的新发展与未来

　　非洲是全球贫困问题最严重的地区，是全球减贫的主要区域，减贫发展面临严峻挑战。中国消除极端贫困，提前十年完成联合国 2023 年可持续发展议程的减贫目标，显著缩小了世界贫困人口的版图。在中非合作论坛的框架下，中国减贫理念和方案获得了非洲国家的深刻认同，中非不断加强双方在减贫领域的合作，取得了一系列重大成果。中非减贫合作的经验总结与推广将促使中非减贫合作进一步深化，对于中国减贫经验的国际化、非洲减贫乃至全球减贫事业的发展有着重要意义和深远影响。

一、中非减贫合作的基础——中国减贫的巨大成就

　　中国在减贫方面的巨大成就是中非减贫合作的基础。2020 年底，中国如期打赢了脱贫攻坚战，现行标准下 9899 万农村贫困人口全部脱贫，832 个贫困县全部摘帽，12.8 万个贫困村全部出列，区域性整体贫困得到解决，提前十年实现了联合国 2023 年可持续发展议程的减贫目标。联合国秘书长古特雷斯称赞"中国是为全球减贫作出最大贡献的国家"。中国在减贫方面取得的巨大成就不仅仅让数亿贫困人口摆脱贫困，更为全球减贫提供了新方案。

（一）中国减贫经验之一：精准扶贫、精准脱贫

　　经历了小规模救济式扶贫、体制改革推动扶贫、大规模开发式扶贫、整村推进式扶贫阶段，中国在消除贫困方面取得了显著的成绩，但也面临诸多新挑战。一方面，贫困标准的提高导致贫困人口数量增加，而经济增长放缓也使其对减贫的贡献减弱。另一方面，扶贫工作依然存在"大水漫灌""扶贫资金使用存在漏出""扶贫效率存在较大提升空间"等现象。针对这些问题和不足，

习近平总书记于2013年提出了精准扶贫理念，并作出了一系列新决策新部署，中国扶贫开发的路径开始从"大水漫灌"向"精准滴灌"转型；2015年，习近平总书记发出打赢脱贫攻坚战的总攻令，2017 年，党的十九大把精准脱贫作为三大攻坚战之一进行全面部署，决战决胜脱贫攻坚。中国政府坚持"精准扶贫、精准脱贫"战略，组织实施了人类历史上规模空前、力度最大、惠及人口最多的脱贫攻坚战[①]，并取得了全面胜利。

　　习近平总书记提出的精准扶贫思想引领精准扶贫精准脱贫方略顶层设计，从宏观层面谋求区域发展资源的配置优化，以切实做到"扶真贫、真扶贫"，加快实现推进贫困治理体系和治理能力现代化的主要目标。从主要内容看，精准扶贫的核心在于做到"六个精准"，实施"五个一批"，解决"四个问题"。其中，"六个精准"是精准扶贫的基本要求，主要包括扶持对象精准、项目安排精准、资金使用精准、措施到户精准、因村派人精准、脱贫成效精准等；"五个一批"是精准扶贫的实现途径，主要是指发展生产脱贫一批、易地搬迁脱贫一批、生态补偿脱贫一批、发展教育脱贫一批、社会保障兜底一批；"四个问题"则是精准扶贫的关键环节，具体指的是解决好扶持谁、谁来扶、怎么扶、如何退等问题。建档立卡和驻村工作队是贯彻落实宏观顶层设计，推进基层精准扶贫实践的两大支柱，分类施策则是精准扶贫的核心。一方面，为了提高扶贫的指向性、针对性和有效性，全国上下开展"建档立卡"工作，逐村逐户开展贫困识别，对识别出的贫困村、贫困户建档立卡，通过"回头看"和甄别调整，不断提高识别准确率，很好地解决了"扶持谁"问题。同时，全国累计选派300多万县级以上机关、国有企事业单位干部参加驻村帮扶（2020年，在岗的第一书记20.6万人、驻村干部70万人），加上197.4万乡镇扶贫干部和数百万村干部，增强了一线扶贫力量，打通了精准扶贫"最后一公里"，切实解决了"谁来扶"的问题。另一方面，分类施策是开展精准扶贫的核心，也是我国特困地区发展滞后、相对贫困凸显等贫困新特征的现实要求。中国坚持分类施策，因人因地施策，因贫困原因施策，因贫困类型施策，通过实施"五个一批"工程，因地因人制宜，扶到点上扶到根上，很好地解决了"怎么扶"问题。在如何推动落实减贫的基础上，精准脱贫阶段还明确了贫困县、贫困村、贫困人口退出标准和程序，指导各地科学合理制定脱贫滚动规划和年度计划，对拟退出的贫困县组织第三方进行严格评估，有关政策保持稳定，很好地解决

---

①　唐丽霞.发展示范与资源提供：中国对"全球南方"的重要意义［J］.人民论坛·学术前沿，2023（23）：70-79.

了"如何退"问题。中国以开发式扶贫、精准扶贫精准脱贫为核心，探索出来的是一套经过实践检验的贫困治理体系，能够为其他发展中国家的减贫实践提供有效经验、理论参考，更为全球有效地进行减贫治理贡献出"中国方案"。

（二）中国减贫经验之二：益贫性宏观经济增长和专项扶贫共同驱动

大量对中国减贫因素的研究一致认为中国减贫最重要的驱动力是长期高速经济增长。从1978年到2008年的30年间，中国经济年均增长9.8%，同期贫困发生率从63%下降到不足10%。中国经济增长的益贫性主要来源于快速经济增长创造了大量非农就业机会，大量农业人口转移到城市从事非农工作。在长期高速经济增长的背景下，社会经济结构出现了两大转型：大量的农村人口转移到非农产业就业，农业从业人口数量和比例快速下降，城镇化率不断提升；农民收入结构转型，工资性收入占比上升，家庭经营性收入下降。这两大转型是中国减贫最主要的动力之源。

在保持经济快速增长的同时，中国政府还长期实行针对贫困地区和贫困人群的扶持政策体系，使经济增长成果惠及更多民众。1980年，国家财政设立支援经济不发达地区发展资金。自财政扶贫专项资金设立以来，中央财政为地方补助的扶贫资金规模由最初的5亿元逐年增加到了2020年的1396亿元。1986年，中国政府成立国务院扶贫开发领导小组并下设办公室，从此扶贫成为中国政府的一项重要职能，也标志着中国正式进入政府主导的大规模开发式扶贫阶段。成立专门的扶贫机构、安排专门的财政扶贫资金投入以及采取专门针对贫困人口的行动等措施构成了中国特色的开发式扶贫行动体系。

（三）中国减贫经验之三：中国减贫政策的长期性、连续性和阶段性

中国取得的减贫成就得益于其减贫政策的长期性、连续性和阶段性。自1980年起，每隔几年，中国政府就会根据当时的社会经济发展水平和贫困问题的特点出台整体性的减贫政策，确定当前阶段减贫的重点、目标、路径和资源保障等。

1984年，为解决山区、少数民族聚居地区、革命老区和边远地区的贫困问题，中共中央、国务院发布《关于帮助贫困地区尽快改变面貌的通知》，提出单纯救济不如经济开发的扶贫理念，并明确了扬长避短、集中投入的发展思路，这是中国从"输血式"扶贫向"造血式"扶贫的转变。1987年，《关于加强贫困地区经济开发工作的通知》提出"七五"期间解决贫困地区大多数群众温饱问题的目标。1994年，中国历史上首个有明确目标、明确对象、明确措施、明确期限的扶贫纲领性文件——《国家八七扶贫攻坚计划（1994—2000

年）》发布，明确提出要集中人力、物力、财力，动员社会各界力量，力争用七年左右的时间，到2000年底基本解决当时全国农村8000万贫困人口的温饱问题。1996年，中共中央、国务院发布《关于尽快解决农村贫困人口温饱问题的决定》，提出要继续加大扶贫工作支持力度，保证到2000年顺利完成八七扶贫攻坚计划。2001年颁布的《中国农村扶贫开发纲要（2001—2010年）》中，"巩固温饱成果"成为重要目标之一，扶贫工作从以攻为主转向攻守结合，扶贫瞄准单位从贫困县向贫困村和贫困户延伸。2011年，为实现全面建成小康社会奋斗目标，《中国农村扶贫开发纲要（2011—2020年）》印发，提出了"两不愁三保障"的目标。2015年，中共中央、国务院发布《关于打赢脱贫攻坚战的决定》，更加明确了到2020年消除现行标准下绝对贫困，实现"两不愁三保障"的目标。2020年打赢脱贫攻坚战以后，中国政府并未停止对欠发达地区和低收入人口的支持，在全面推进乡村振兴战略的大背景下，设置了五年的衔接过渡期，巩固脱贫攻坚成果。

（四）中国减贫经验之四：减贫工具的瞄准性和普惠性

中国减贫行动一直非常注重发挥资源的有效性，在减贫工具的使用上既有普惠式政策安排，也有瞄准式政策安排。2000年以来，随着经济发展水平提高和财政能力增强，越来越多普惠式政策开始实施，包括农业补贴、城乡居民基本养老保险、城乡居民基本医疗保险、义务教育等政策。因病致贫和因学致贫曾是农民家庭贫困的重要原因，这些政策的实施减少了农民的医疗和教育负担。普惠的居民养老保险政策、以土地为主要发放依据的农业补贴政策以及已经基本实现"应保尽保"的最低生活保障制度等都增加了农民的转移性收入，这些收入成为很多没有劳动能力的农村贫困人口的主要收入来源，发挥了重要的兜底保障作用。

瞄准性也是中国减贫政策有效的重要因素。中国瞄准性政策安排主要有两种机制：一种是区域瞄准，用来分配中央财政扶贫资源；另一种是群体瞄准，用来识别贫困人口并对其提供有针对性的扶贫措施。区域瞄准主要识别贫困县，这是各种扶贫资源投向的重点。中国的县域瞄准最早开始于1986年，确定了331个国家级贫困县，此后又经历了三次重大调整，国家级贫困县数量有相应的增减变化。中国还实行了比较严格的群体瞄准。建档立卡是中国在精准扶贫阶段采取的瞄准方式，为准确识别农村贫困人口，中国政府以2013年农民人均纯收入2736元为贫困线，同时将容易识别的衣、食、住房、教育、医疗作为指标对贫困人口进行综合考量，截至2014年底，共识别出贫困户 2948 万户，贫困人口 8962 万人[①]；从 2015 年起，每年对贫困人口进行查缺补漏，累计共识别建档立卡贫困人口 9899 万人。这些建档立卡贫困人口除获得普惠式扶持外，还会在住房安全、劳动就业、教育医疗、产业发展等方面获得额外支持。

（五）中国减贫经验之五：减贫行动的开发性和保护性

开发式扶贫是中国减贫的重要特点。这主要表现在三个方面：第一，通过改善贫困地区基础设施条件，提高贫困地区产业发展能力，促进其区域整体性经济发展；第二，通过提升贫困农户参与就业和产业发展的能力，包括技能培训、提供产业发展支持等，提高贫困农户自我发展的能力；第三，通过引进小额信贷模式、培育和发展社区互助资金等，培育贫困农户的金融意识，并为农户发展产业提供金融支持。近年来，中国政府助推电商扶贫、旅游扶贫、光伏扶贫以及资产扶贫等模式，都是希望通过市场的力量将贫困农户手中有限的资源转化成为资产，使贫困农户成为市场的主体。在贫困人口中，有相当大比重的人没有劳动能力，还需要通过兜底保障对其进行帮扶，中国还采取了以现金转移支付和构建社会安全网为主的保护性措施，包括各项补贴政策、最低生活保障制度等。

（六）中国减贫经验之六：减贫主体的政府主导和社会参与

中国减贫由政府主导，同时也鼓励社会参与。中国政府有着强大的社会动员能力，聚集了大量的社会资源，构建起有中国特色的社会参与扶贫机制。开始于 1996 年的东西协作帮扶建立了东部发达地区对口支持西部欠发达地区发展的正式机制；正式开始于 2012 年的定点帮扶让中央和国家机关单位、军队和武警部队、国有大中型企业、民主党派中央机关以及高等院校都参与到了扶贫工作中；开始于 2015 年的"万企帮万村"行动搭建了民营企业和贫困村之间的帮扶关系。为了营造全社会共同参与扶贫工作的良好社会环境，2014 年国务院办公厅出台了《关于进一步动员社会各方面力量参与扶贫开发的意见》，扶贫志愿活动、扶贫公益行动等逐渐成为扶贫的重要力量。

二、中国对非援助

非洲一直是中国对外援助的重点地区。根据《新时代的中非合作》白皮

---

① 国务院关于脱贫攻坚工作情况的报告［EB/OL］.（2017-08-29）［2023-07-19］.http：//www.npc.gov.cn/zgrdw/npc/xinwen/2017-08/29/content_2027584.htm.

书，2013~2018年中国对外援助额为2702亿元人民币，其中对非洲国家的援助占比44.65%，包括无偿援助、无息贷款和优惠贷款（见图6-1）。与其他地区相比，非洲获得的中国援助规模最大，金额最多。中国对非援助涉及经济社会生活的方方面面，受到非洲国家政府和人民的广泛欢迎和支持。中国已宣布免除与中国有外交关系的非洲最不发达国家、重债穷国、内陆发展中国家、小岛屿发展中国家截至2018年底到期未偿还政府间无息贷款。新冠疫情发生后，中国宣布免除15个非洲国家2020年底到期的无息贷款债务。从内容和方式来看，中国对非援助主要有三大特点。

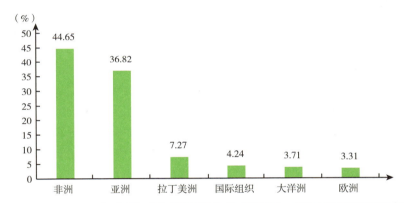

图6-1　2013~2018年中国对外援助资金分布情况，按区域及国际组织划分

资料来源：《新时代的中国国际发展合作》白皮书。

　　第一，中国对非援助是非洲基础设施建设的重要资金来源，中国十分重视非洲基础设施发展对减贫的作用。其一，中国对非援助充分考虑非洲地区多为发展中国家，基础设施条件较差，且在基础设施建设方面缺乏先进的生产技术和生产设备的现实情况，因此将对非援助重点放在基础设施领域，占比约为68.64%[①]。中国目前参与了35个非洲国家的基础设施项目，涉及发电（尤其是水电）、运输（尤其是铁路）、信息和通信技术（主要是设备供应）等多个领域。2000~2020年，中国援助非洲建成公路铁路超过13000公里，建设了80多个大型电力设施，援建了130多个医疗设施、45个体育馆、170多所学校，为非洲培训各领域人才共计16万余名，打造了非盟会议中心等一系列中非合作

　　① 胡建梅，单磊.中国对非援助、基础设施和受援国经济增长：基于中介效应模型的实证分析[J].国际经济合作，2022（5）：53~68，95.

"金字招牌"[①]。其二，中国对非援助关注基础设施对于减贫的作用，通过向非洲国家提供资金、技术、设备和人才来帮助其提升基础设施水平，对非洲国家的经济增长产生正向作用，提高减贫效应。

第二，中国十分重视对非民生援助，在农业、卫生、教育等领域发挥积极作用，并通过提供援助，分享社会发展经验，帮助非洲国家提高社会综合发展水平，为非洲经济发展创造内生动力。在粮食安全领域，中国既重视在援助中增强非洲国家农业生产能力，又不断培养农业科研和技术人才。截至2019年底，中国向37个亚非国家派遣了81个农业技术专家组，共计808人次，并在非洲国家援建22个农业技术示范中心，为有关国家试验并推广高产新品种，指导农民提高生产能力，增强发展信心。在卫生健康领域，非洲疫情发生后，中国开展了新中国成立以来涉及范围最广、实施难度最大的人道主义援助行动。中国向非洲53国和非盟提供了120批检测试剂、防护服、呼吸机等紧急抗疫物资援助。在教育领域，1999~2018年，非洲来华留学生数量整体维持高速增长态势，到2018年，非洲学生总数已达81562人[②]。其中，东非、西非、南部非洲的来华留学生数量显著领先于北非和中非[③]。此外，中国加大对非职业教育援助，同联合国设立统计能力开发信托基金，为59个发展中国家的近900名政府统计人员提供培训。

第三，中国对非援助不仅依靠双边渠道，也更加注重多边合作，加强与联合国粮农组织、信托基金、非盟等组织机构的合作。其一，中国加大捐资力度，向世界银行国际开发协会、亚洲发展基金、全球环境基金等机构增加捐资额度。截至2018年底，向非洲开发银行集团捐资9.39亿美元、8亿元人民币，支持非洲地区减贫、粮食安全、贸易、医疗、灾害管理、教育和环保等领域的发展。其二，中国注重与世界银行、非洲开发银行等双多边金融机构加强交流合作，共同为有关国家提供资金支持，如出资20亿美元与非洲开发银行设立"非洲共同增长基金"，涉及供水卫生、交通运输、农业发展、青年就业等领域。[④]

① 《新时代的中非合作》白皮书，参见http：//www.scio.gov.cn/zfbps/ndhf/2021n_2242/202207/t20220704_130719.html。

② 参见http://www.moe.gov.cn/jyb_xwfb/gzdt_gzdt/s5987/201904/t20190412_377692.html.

③ 李冰，黄文杰.非洲来华留学生发展变化趋势与对策研究：基于1999~2018年数据的统计分析[J].云南师范大学学报（对外汉语教学与研究版），2021，19（6）：82-89.

④ 《新时代的中国国际发展合作》白皮书，参见http://www.scio.gov.cn/zfbps/ndhf/2021n_2242/202207/t20220704_130669.html。

随着"一带一路"倡议和全球发展倡议的深入发展，中国落实中方承诺，不断加大对非援助力度，扩大同非洲的投融资合作，加强同非洲国家在农业、制造业等领域的互利合作，帮助非洲国家把资源优势转化为发展优势，实现自主发展和可持续发展。

三、中非减贫合作的政策框架及发展脉络

推动和指导中非减贫合作的政策框架主要有两个层面。第一个层面是全球发展合作目标，其中最为重要的是联合国可持续发展框架。第二个层面是中非之间达成的合作战略和框架，主要包括中非合作论坛及其后续行动计划、《中国对非洲政策文件》和《中国和非洲联盟加强中非减贫合作纲要》等。

（一）联合国可持续发展框架和中国应对方案

2010年9月，在联合国千年目标峰会上，很多国家倡议启动2015年后发展议程的讨论，经过几年的讨论和磋商，2015年联合国大会提出了可持续发展框架。联合国可持续发展框架一共有17项可持续发展目标和169个具体目标。值得注意的是，在千年发展目标中贫困和饥饿是作为一个整体目标呈现的，但可持续发展框架将贫困和饥饿分开，作为两个可持续发展目标，即目标1"在全世界消除一切形式的贫困"和目标2"消除饥饿，实现粮食安全"，这凸显出可持续发展框架对贫困问题的重视。

联合国可持续发展框架已经成为指导各国国内自身发展和国际发展合作的普遍性的政策框架和目标导向。中国先后发布了《落实2030年可持续发展议程中方立场文件》《中国落实2030年可持续发展议程国别方案》以及《中国落实2030年可持续发展议程进展报告》，明确提出中国将不断深化南南合作，帮助其他发展中国家做好2030年可持续发展议程的落实工作，尤其是在《中国落实2030年可持续发展议程国别方案》中，对于目标1、目标2、目标3、目标4、目标9、目标10、目标11、目标14和目标17中具有国际减贫意义的具体目标，中国政府都提出了相应的承诺和方案。该方案成为中国推动全球国际发展合作和可持续发展目标实现的重要指导性方案，对中非减贫合作也同样具有指导性意义（见表6-1）。

表6-1　　　　　　　　　　中国落实可持续发展议程的部分方案

目标	具体目标	中国方案
目标 1：在全世界消除一切形式的贫困	1.a 确保从各种来源，包括通过加强发展合作充分调集资源，为发展中国家，特别是最不发达国家提供充足、可预见的手段以执行相关计划和政策，消除一切形式的贫困	落实习近平主席 2015 年 9 月出席联合国可持续发展峰会期间宣布的南南合作援助基金、"6 个 100"项目等务实举措，帮助其他发展中国家发展经济，改善民生，消除贫困。在援外框架下推动更大范围、更高水平、更深层次的国际减贫合作
	1.b 根据惠及贫困人口和顾及性别平等问题的发展战略，在国家、区域和国际层面制定合理的政策框架，支持加快对消贫行动的投资	利用"减贫与发展高层论坛""中国—东盟社会发展与减贫论坛""中非合作论坛—减贫与发展分论坛"等平台，分享中国减贫的理念、经验和做法，探讨将更多投资引入减贫领域
目标2：消除饥饿，实现粮食安全，改善营养状况和促进可持续农业	2.a 通过加强国际合作等方式，增加对农村基础设施、农业研究和推广服务、技术开发、植物和牲畜基因库的投资，以增强发展中国家，特别是最不发达国家的农业生产能力	计划到 2022 年与联合国粮农组织合作执行 10 个左右南南合作国别项目，在"一带一路"建设农业合作框架下，与沿线国家和区域在农作物育种、畜牧、渔业、农产品加工与贸易等领域开展合作
目标3：确保健康的生活方式，促进各年龄段人群的福祉	3.c 大幅加强发展中国家，尤其是最不发达国家和小岛屿发展中国家的卫生筹资，增加其卫生工作者的招聘、培养、培训和留用	加大对其他发展中国家，尤其是最不发达国家和小岛屿发展中国家卫生医疗设施、人员和技术培训的援助，帮助其他发展中国家加强卫生领域筹资
目标 4：确保包容和公平的优质教育，让全民终身享有学习机会	4.b 到 2020 年，在全球范围内大幅增加发达国家和部分发展中国家为发展中国家，特别是最不发达国家、小岛屿发展中国家和非洲国家提供的高等教育奖学金数量，包括职业培训和信息通信技术、技术、工程、科学项的奖学金	落实习近平主席 2015 年 9 月出席联合国可持续发展峰会期间宣布的"到 2020 年，向发展中国家提供 12 万个来华培训和 15 万个奖学金名额，为发展中国家培养 50 万名职业技术人员"的举措。面向其他发展中国家，特别是最不发达国家、小岛国和非洲国家，提供更多人力资源、发展规划、经济政策等方面咨询培训，加强科技教育合作和援助
	4.c 到 2030 年，大幅增加合格教师人数，具体做法包括在发展中国家，特别是最不发达国家和小岛屿发展中国家开展师资培训方面的国际合作	为其他发展中国家提供短期教育培训，在培训班计划和招生方面积极考虑最不发达国家和小岛国对师资培训的需求
目标 9：建造具备抵御灾害能力的基础设施，促进具有包容性的可持续工业化，推动创新	9.2 促进包容可持续工业化，到 2030 年，根据各国国情，大幅提高工业在就业和国内生产总值中的比例，使最不发达国家的这一比例翻番	推进"一带一路"建设，通过国际产能和装备制造合作推动其他发展中国家，特别是最不发达国家的工业化发展。通过共建中小企业国际合作园（区）的方式，共同推动中小企业发展
	9.a 向非洲国家、最不发达国家、内陆发展中国家和小岛屿发展中国家提供更多的财政、技术和技能支持，以促进其开发有抵御灾害能力的可持续基础设施	在南南合作框架下，加大对其他发展中国家的技术支持和援助力度，帮助其加强可持续基础设施建设，提高抵御灾害等相关能力建设

续表

目标	具体目标	中国方案
目标10：减少国家内部和国家之间的不平等	10.b 鼓励根据最需要帮助的国家，特别是最不发达国家、非洲国家、小岛屿发展中国家和内陆发展中国家的国家计划和方案，向其提供官方发展援助和资金，包括外国直接投资	敦促发达国家履行官方发展援助承诺，向发展中国家提供更多的资金、技术和能力建设等方面的支持。丰富对外援助模式，为其他发展中国家提供更多人力资源、发展规划、经济政策等方面咨询培训
目标11：建设包容、安全、有抵御灾害能力和可持续的城市和人类住区	11.c 通过财政和技术援助等方式，支持最不发达国家就地取材，建造可持续的、有抵御灾害能力的建筑	支持最不发达国家建造可持续的基础设施，在节能建筑领域推动与相关国家技术合作，帮助最不发达国家培养本地技术工人
目标13：采取紧急行动应对气候变化及其影响	13.b 促进在最不发达国家和小岛屿发展中国家建立增强能力的机制，帮助其进行与气候变化有关的有效规划和管理，包括重点关注妇女、青年、地方社区和边缘化社区	通过中国设立的气候变化南南合作基金，帮助最不发达国家和小岛屿发展中国家加强应对气候变化能力建设，包括应对工作的整体规划和管理等方面。关注上述国家妇女、青年、地方社区和边缘化社区在应对气候变化领域的特殊困难，并提供力所能及的帮助
目标14：保护和可持续利用海洋和海洋资源以促进可持续发展	14.7 到2030年，增加小岛屿发展中国家和最不发达国家通过可持续利用海洋资源获得的经济收益，包括可持续地管理渔业、水产养殖业和旅游业	通过南南合作向最不发达国家和小岛国提供水产养殖技术支持，包括推广养殖节能减排、循环水养殖技术、网箱养殖减排技术等。推动可持续渔业管理和旅游方面的南南合作
目标17：加强执行手段，重振可持续发展全球伙伴关系	17.2 发达国家全面履行官方发展援助承诺，包括许多发达国家向发展中国家提供占发达国家国民总收入0.7%的官方发展援助，以及向最不发达国家提供占比0.15%~0.2%援助的承诺；鼓励官方发展援助方设定目标，将占国民总收入至少0.2%的官方发展援助提供给最不发达国家	推动各国执行《亚的斯亚贝巴行动议程》，要求发达国家全面履行官方发展援助承诺并设定时间表和路线图，从资金、技术、能力建设等各方面为发展中国家提供帮助
	17.3 从多渠道筹集额外金融资源用于发展中国家	积极参与南南合作，落实好南南合作援助基金，推动中国—联合国和平与发展基金积极发挥作用。推进亚洲基础设施投资银行、金砖国家新开发银行建设，发挥丝路基金作用，吸引国际资金共建开放多元共赢的金融合作平台
	17.16 加强全球可持续发展伙伴关系，以多利益攸关方伙伴关系作为补充，调动和分享知识、专长、技术和财政资源，以支持所有国家，尤其是发展中国家实现可持续发展目标	积极参与全球发展合作，推动建立更加平等均衡的全球发展伙伴关系。坚持南北合作的主渠道地位，呼吁南南合作和三方合作发挥更大作用，欢迎国际组织、私营部门、公民社会等参与落实可持续发展目标

资料来源：根据《中国落实2030年可持续发展议程国别方案》等相关规划整理所得。

（二）中非合作论坛框架下中非减贫合作的发展脉络

中非减贫合作主要在中非合作论坛的框架下展开。中非合作论坛是中非之间在南南合作范畴内的集体对话机制，成立于2000年，现已成为中非合作的重要机制化框架和重要交流平台。自2000年首届中非合作论坛以来，历届中非合作论坛部长级会议都将减贫作为重要讨论内容，并发布一系列后续行动计划。在中非合作论坛的框架下，中非双方开展了多种类型的减贫合作，取得了可喜的成果。中非合作论坛框架下的中非减贫合作经历了三个发展阶段。

第一，共识达成阶段。从第一届中非合作论坛到第三届中非合作论坛，中非双方开始在减贫方面达成共识，但尚未形成专门性合作机制。第一届中非合作论坛发布的《中非经济和社会发展合作纲领》首次明确将债务减免、农业合作、医疗卫生、人力资源开发等与减贫息息相关的领域作为合作重点。第三届中非合作论坛发布的《中非合作论坛北京峰会宣言》强调要加强中非在减贫领域的合作，把中非减贫合作推向深入，其后续行动计划《中非合作论坛—北京行动计划（2007—2009年）》提出双方"认为加强农业合作，对双方消除贫困、促进发展以及保障粮食安全将发挥积极作用"[1]。双方对减贫的认识和重视程度逐步加深，与减贫相关的多个领域被列为合作重点，但减贫合作始终未作为独立议题被重点讨论，交流合作机制也并未建立。

第二，经验交流阶段。第四届至第六届中非合作论坛开始聚焦减贫经验交流分享，中非减贫合作也开始走上机制化。第四届中非合作论坛发布的《中非合作论坛—沙姆沙伊赫行动计划（2010—2012年）》中，减贫合作首次作为一个单独的版块出现在，双方认识到"消除贫困是双方面临的艰巨任务"，并"将扩大在减贫领域的合作与交流"[2]。2010年，首届中非减贫与发展会议召开，双方就千年发展目标、中国减贫经验、非洲新扶贫战略、南南合作等广泛议题展开了深入研讨。自此，减贫合作正式成为中非合作的重要议题之一，中非减贫与发展会议这一政府间对话交流机制也初步建立。2015年，第六届中非合作论坛发布的《中非合作论坛—约翰内斯堡行动计划（2016—2018年）》将减贫经验交流列为重要计划之一，并将中非减贫与发展会议正式纳入中非合作论坛的总体框架内，成为中非合作论坛的配套机制，中非减贫交流合作机制正式建

---

[1] 中非合作论坛—北京行动计划（2007—2009年），参见http：//www.focac.org.cn/zywx/zywj/200909/t20090917_8044399.htm。

[2] 中非合作论坛—沙姆沙伊赫行动计划（2010—2012年），参见http：//et.china-embassy.gov.cn/chn/zgxx/policy/200911/t20091112_7213871.htm。

立[①]，对于确保双方的合作规划落到实处发挥了重要作用。

第三，深化合作阶段。自第六届中非合作论坛以来，中非减贫合作进入深化合作阶段，开始实施减贫示范工程和项目，合作机制更加完善，伙伴关系进一步深化。第六届中非合作论坛发布的《中非合作论坛—北京行动计划（2019—2021年）》提出要"广泛动员中非企业、社会组织、研究机构等各方力量共同参与中非减贫合作，逐步建立政府间、社会间的多层次减贫对话机制"[②]，促进减贫经验交流，并实施减贫示范工程和试点项目，将减贫合作落到实处。第八届中非合作论坛部长级会议提出实施"九项工程"，将减贫惠农工程作为重点工程之一，聚焦农业合作，通过实施农业合作项目、开展技术交流、建设中非农业发展与减贫示范村、支持在非中国企业承担社会责任等方式促进减贫，合作形式更加多样化。

此外，随着全球减贫与发展的不断推进，全球减贫目标、中非减贫合作相关议题已从减贫迈入减贫与乡村发展。2023年减贫治理与全球发展（怒江）国际论坛会议与2021年中非减贫与发展会议的主题均关注乡村发展。《中非合作论坛—达喀尔行动计划（2022—2024年）》中，减贫合作部分的标题也从减贫经验交流变为减贫与乡村发展合作交流，可见乡村发展、乡村振兴已成为全球减贫的新目标蓝图。2015年发布的《中国对非洲政策文件》明确将"分享和推广减贫经验"作为中非合作的主要内容之一。这与上述中非合作论坛提出的减贫合作重心一致。

四、中非减贫与发展合作方式

（一）合作与交流机制更加成熟

随着中非减贫与发展合作的不断深入，以中非合作论坛为总体框架的政府间、社会间多层次减贫与乡村发展对话机制逐步建立，成为减贫合作与经验交流的重要平台。

1.政府间对话机制呈现体系化发展

中非合作论坛及其配套机制——中非减贫与发展会议已成为中非减贫与发展合作中稳定的政府间集体对话机制与重要平台，为中非官方合作提供了重要

---

① 中非合作论坛—约翰内斯堡行动计划（2016—2018年），参见http：//www.scio.gov.cn/XWfbh/xwbfbh/wqfbh/44687/47454/xgzc47460/Document/1716759/1716759.htm。

② 中非合作论坛—北京行动计划（2019—2021年），参见http：//www.cidca.gov.cn/2018-09/07/c_129949203.htm。

支撑。该会议通过邀请政府官员、国际组织代表、专家学者、企业代表、公民社会代表等群体参会，为中非减贫合作出谋划策，深化了中非在减贫与发展领域的交流合作。2022 年，在第十二届中非减贫与发展会议上，中非减贫与发展伙伴联盟正式成立，中非伙伴关系进一步深化。此外，作为中非减贫经验交流重要机制，中非共享发展经验高级研讨会等理论研讨会也为中非减贫经验交流和推广提供了重要平台。

2. 社会层面对话机制日趋丰富

由民间组织、企业家、智库等构成的多层次、多领域减贫对话机制逐步建立，民间对话日益频繁。中非民间论坛为推动中非民间务实合作作出了重要贡献；中非智库论坛为中非之"智"助力中非之"治"提供了支持，二者业已成为中非合作论坛机制化配套活动。2021 年，中国在非企业社会责任联盟正式成立；2022 年，中非职业教育联合会成立，并将举办中非职业教育论坛。

由此可见，多层次的中非减贫与乡村发展对话机制日趋成熟，为中非双方加强减贫与发展合作、推进减贫经验交流、积极应对全球减贫与发展挑战提供了良好的基础。

（二）合作内容和形式更加丰富

中非减贫合作内容从减贫经验交流逐步拓展到具体的、多领域的合作项目。从中非合作论坛发布的主要文件来看，第三届至第六届中非合作论坛主要提出要通过举办研讨会、培训班、论坛等方式开展中非减贫经验交流与对话，其主要目的是让非洲国家认识和了解中国减贫经验。第七届和第八届中非合作论坛则先后提出要实施"减贫惠民合作计划"和"减贫惠农工程"，可见中非开始逐步实施一些具体的减贫合作项目。"减贫惠民合作计划"以基础设施建设等民生工程为主，在非洲实施"幸福生活工程"和以妇女儿童为主要受益者的减贫项目。"减贫惠农工程"聚焦农业合作，通过实施农业合作项目、派遣农业专家、开展技术交流、建设农业发展与减贫示范村、向中国在非企业发起"百企千村"活动等方式促进减贫，合作形式更加多样化。首批四个中非现代农业技术交流示范和培训联合中心已挂牌成立[①]；肯尼亚纳库鲁郡马坦吉提萨村"中非农业发展与减贫示范村"挂牌成立，中国援尼日利亚农业技术示范中心项目投入运营。

[①] 弘扬中非友好 加强团结合作 打造中非共同发展的新时代——王毅国务委员在中非合作论坛第八届部长级会议成果落实协调人会议上的致辞，参见 https://www.mfa.gov.cn/web/wjbz_673089/zyjh_673099/202208/t20220819_10745611.shtml。

中非减贫合作领域不断扩大。一方面，基础设施建设、医疗卫生、人力资源等传统领域的合作仍是合作重点。新冠疫情期间，中方向非洲27国提供了1.89亿剂新冠疫苗[①]。中国政府也致力于通过职业教育合作、派遣专家、举办培训班、来华交流等多种方式提升非洲人力资源水平。近年来，中非职业教育合作成为中非人力资源合作的重要方式，自"未来非洲—中非职业教育合作计划"倡议提出以来，中非已形成15对合作伙伴关系，对200余名非洲学生开展联合培养，为300余名非洲校长和骨干教师提供培训和实训[②]，为非洲培养高技术技能水平的本土人才。另一方面，双方积极将减贫与最新发展议题相结合，增进减贫的带动效应。中非逐渐探索产能发展、清洁能源、气候变化、数字经济等方面的减贫意义，更有助于增强非洲可持续发展的能力，进而促进减贫。例如，双方举办"非洲绿色长城"建设研修班，组织非洲国家的官员参与学习荒漠化防治，缓解干旱、实现土地可持续治理[③]。

五、中非减贫合作的未来：方向与远景

2021年11月底，中非合作论坛第八届部长级会议通过了《中非合作2035年愿景》，提出了未来15年中非合作的主体框架，为中非合作的未来指明方向。根据该愿景确定的目标任务，中非合作将"以支持非洲培育内生增长能力为重点，以促进中非合作转型升级、提质增效为主线，巩固传统合作，开辟新兴领域，创新合作模式，推动中非共建'一带一路'高质量发展"[④]。

（一）持续深化中非减贫合作

目前，非洲发展面临着基础设施滞后、人才不足、资金短缺三大"瓶颈"。近年来，中非减贫合作相关政策框架不断明确双方合作的重点。未来，中国将通过助推非洲工业化、助力非洲农业现代化、全面参与非洲基础设施建设、加强中非金融合作等一系列措施深化与非洲的经贸合作，并通过对非洲的援助、支持非洲加强公共卫生防控体系和能力建设、扩大教育和人力资源开发合作、分享和推广减贫经验等举措加强中非减贫与发展合作。

---

① 中非合作论坛—北京行动计划（2019—2021年），参见http://www.cidca.gov.cn/2018-09/07/c_129949203.htm。

② 中非职业教育联合会宣告成立，参见https://news.eol.cn/yaowen/202205/t20220512_2225019.shtml。

③ 中国助力"非洲绿色长城"建设，参见http://www.focac.org.cn/chn/zfzs/202205/t20220512_10685226.htm。

④ 参见《中非合作2035年愿景》。

（二）积极支持非洲国家减贫与发展能力建设

在过去的几十年里，中国贫困问题的解决离不开政府主导，通过发挥政府在整合全社会资源、制定国家发展战略等方面的优势，出台一系列政策、选择经济与社会发展模式，从而推进国家减贫进程和效果提升。这种能力不仅体现在治理能力上，还体现在财政能力与资源动员能力上，中国政府能够安排较大规模的资金用于专项扶贫行动。但非洲国家政府一般性支出有赖于国际援助，进行专项扶贫投入更为困难。除具体行动计划层次外，更要注重减贫与发展的能力建设。未来，中非减贫合作可以更多地考虑促进非洲国家减贫与发展方面的能力建设，提升非洲本土减贫行动的效果。

（三）加强"小而美"的减贫项目合作

重点关注以村为单元的减贫示范，扩大对减贫示范村建设的支持，在非洲打造成功运用中国减贫经验的示范村。非洲的村庄形态和中国具有很强的相似性，在非洲大陆开展村级减贫示范和动员中国企业参与，有助于非洲国家在减贫行动中不仅聚焦贫困人口，还聚焦贫困人口生活的区域，将区域发展作为减贫的一个前提；同时，也有助于非洲国家理解减贫不仅仅是政府的责任，不只是要争取国际援助的支持，企业和私营部门也能在减贫中发挥重要作用，从而扩大非洲国家动员社会资本的能力，解决减贫中资源供给不足的问题。

（四）继续开展各种形式的减贫交流活动

中国和非洲之间的各种减贫交流活动为非洲国家了解和理解中国减贫经验作出了重要贡献，越来越多的非洲国家认识到中国减贫经验的有效性，并表现出强烈的学习意愿。针对不同群体组织不同形式的交流活动；同时扩展参与各种交流活动的主体，让更多的人了解中国的减贫经验。

全球减贫与发展经验分享系列
The Sharing Series on Global Poverty
Reduction and Development Experience

2024 Annual Report on Poverty Reduction and Development in Africa

Edited by International Poverty Reduction Center in China

2024 Annual Report on Poverty Reduction and Development in Africa

Research Group

Leaders of the Research Group:

Tang Lixia, Liu Junwen

Members of the Research Group:

Li Xiaoyun, Liu Yifeng, Fang Yongxin, Zhou Zisheng,

Luo Yanni, Xi Zhenhua, GongYaqi,

Xu Liping, He Shengnian, Liu Huanhuan, Yao Yuan,

Zhao Wenjie, Liu Haoran, Yuan Baibing,

Abdoul Razak Toure, Aghaton Elias Madonda, Zikusooka Harriet Sarah,

Osman Tarawalie, Baxter Bwalya Musonda

Preface

    The eradication of poverty has always been a wish to be fulfilled. The history of humankind is the history of relentless struggle against poverty. As the world's largest developing country with a population of 1.4 billion, China had long been plagued by poverty because of its weak foundations and uneven development. Ending poverty, improving people's well-being and realizing common prosperity are the essential requirements of socialism and important missions of the Communist Party of China (CPC). In order to fulfill this solemn political commitment, over the past century, the CPC has united and led the Chinese people to wage a long and arduous struggle against poverty with unwavering faith and will. After the launch of reform and opening up, China has carried out well-conceived and well-organized initiatives for development-driven poverty alleviation on a massive scale, and devoted its focus to releasing and developing productive forces and to ensuring and improving public wellbeing, securing great and unprecedented achievements in the process. Since the 18th CPC National Congress, the CPC Central Committee with Xi Jinping at its core, has prioritized poverty elimination in its governance. President Xi Jinping has assumed leadership, made plans and directed in person in order to implement the basic policy of a targeted strategy in poverty alleviation and mobilize the whole Party, the entire nation and all sectors of society, thus scoring the largest battle against poverty and benefiting the largest number of people in human history.

    The complete victory in the battle against poverty is inseparable from the organic combination of a capable government and an effective market. Over the eight years since the 18th CPC National Congress, the CPC Central Committee, with Xi Jinping at its core, has centrally and uniformly led the fight against poverty, leveraged the political advantages of the country's socialist system with Chinese characteristics which can bring together the resources necessary to accomplish great tasks, and placed poverty reduction in a prominent position in national governance, providing strong political and organizational guarantees for the fight against poverty. The active participation of market and social forces has been widely mobilized, with the implementation of actions such as the "Ten Thousand Enterprises Helping Ten Thousand Villages" campaign, to encourage private enterprises, social organizations and individual citizens to participate in the fight against poverty, and facilitate the agglomeration of factors such as capital, talent and technology in poverty-stricken areas. By the end of 2020, all of the 98.99 million rural residents, 832 counties, and 128,000 villages that fell below the current poverty line had been lifted out of poverty. Regional poverty had been eliminated on the whole, and the arduous task of eradicating absolute poverty had been completed. China has built the largest education, social security, and healthcare system in the world, and achieved rapid development in step with large-scale poverty reduction, and economic transformation in step with the elimination of extreme poverty.

China has always been an active advocate, strong promoter and important contributor to the international cause of poverty reduction. According to the World Bank's international poverty line, since reform and opening up in 1978, the number of people lifted out of poverty in China accounted for more than 70 percent of the global total and 80 percent of that in East Asia and the Pacific over the same period. China is home to nearly one fifth of the world's population. Its complete eradication of extreme poverty – the first target of the United Nations 2030 Agenda for Sustainable Development – 10 years ahead of schedule, is a milestone in the history of the Chinese nation and the history of humankind, making an important contribution to the global poverty alleviation.

On the basis of the national conditions and the understanding of the patterns underlying poverty alleviation, China has pioneered a Chinese path to poverty alleviation, given shape to Chinese theory on fighting poverty, and created a "China example" of poverty reduction. Adherence to the people-centered development philosophy, and unswervingly following the path of common prosperity are the fundamental driving force behind China's poverty reduction.

Highlighting poverty alleviation in the governance of China, all CPC members, from top leaders to the grassroots officials work together towards the same goal. China has strengthened top-level design and strategic planning, mobilized forces from all quarters to participate in poverty alleviation, improved the institutional system for poverty eradication and maintained the consistency and stability of policies. Eradicating poverty through development, China's experience with poverty alleviation has proven that development is essential to solving many of its problems, including poverty and is the most reliable path towards a more prosperous life. Pressing ahead with poverty alleviation based on reality, China has constantly adjusted and reformed its strategies and policies as circumstances and local conditions change. The strategy of targeted poverty alleviation has been the magic weapon for winning the battle against poverty, while the development-driven approach has emerged as the distinctive feature of China's path to poverty reduction. Letting the poor residents play the principal role, China has committed to mobilizing the enthusiasm, initiative, and creativity of impoverished people and inspiring them with the motivation to fight poverty, so that they can benefit from success in the undertaking of poverty alleviation and at the same time contribute to development in China.

Following the decisive victory in the fight against poverty, the Chinese Government has set out a five-year transition period for counties lifted out of poverty for consolidating and expanding these achievements, and comprehensively promoting rural revitalization. In accordance with the deployment of the 20th CPC National Congress, on the new journey of comprehensively promoting the rejuvenation of the Chinese nation on all fronts through a Chinese path to modernization, China is advancing rural revitalization across the board, building a beautiful and harmonious countryside that is desirable to live and work in, and moving towards the higher goal of realizing the all-round human development and common prosperity for all. China's exploration and practice of consolidating and expanding the achievements in poverty alleviation and rural revitalization will continue to provide new Chinese experience and wisdom for human poverty reduction and rural development, and contribute to the promotion of building a community with a shared future for mankind free of poverty.

In the face of new trends and features in the international situation, President Xi Jinping has put forward the Belt and Road Initiative, the Global Development Initiative and other common global actions, with poverty reduction as a key area of cooperation, and has endeavored to promote the building of a community with a shared future for mankind free of poverty and with common development. It has become a global consensus to strengthen the sharing of international experience in poverty reduction and rural development and to contribute to the global poverty reduction and development process.

To this end, since 2019, the International Poverty Reduction Center in China (IPRCC) and the Bill & Melinda Gates Foundation have jointly implemented international cooperation projects. With persistence in carefully planning the project topics from a policy-based and future-oriented perspective, we are committed to leading the frontier hot spots and research trends of poverty reduction and rural development at home and abroad. We have always insisted on bringing China's poverty reduction and rural development experience into line with international standards, explaining China's poverty reduction and rural revitalization path through the international discourse system, and promoting the international dissemination of China's poverty reduction and rural development experience. So far, more than 30 research projects have been implemented, and a number of research results in various forms and with wide influence have been formed, some of which have been released in relevant international exchange activities.

In order to implement the Global Development Initiatives and further promote global exchanges and cooperation on poverty reduction and rural development, IPRCC has carefully sorted out the research results and launched four series of books, including "The Sharing Series on Global Poverty Reduction and Development Experience", "The Sharing Series on China's Poverty Reduction and Development Experience", "The Sharing Series on International Rural Development Experience", and "The Sharing Series on China's Rural Revitalization Experience".

The Sharing Series on Global Poverty Reduction and Development Experience aims to track the progress of global poverty reduction, analyze the trends of global poverty reduction and development, summarize and share the experiences of countries in poverty reduction, and provide knowledge products for promoting the United Nations 2030 Agenda for Sustainable Development and participating in global poverty governance. This series mainly includes global poverty reduction knowledge products, such as *Annual Report on International Poverty Reduction* and *Theory and Frontier Issues in International Poverty Reduction*, as well as regional poverty reduction knowledge products covering Africa, ASEAN, South Asia, Latin America and the Caribbean.

The Sharing Series on China's Poverty Reduction and Development Experience aims to tell the story of China's poverty reduction, share China's poverty reduction experience with the international community, and provide practical experience for the majority of developing countries to achieve poverty reduction and development. This series focuses on China's experience and practices in targeted poverty alleviation, poverty eradication as well as consolidation and expansion of poverty eradication achievements, and forms knowledge products for sharing China's poverty reduction experience based on international perspectives.

The Sharing Series on International Rural Development Experience focuses on the history, policies and practices of international rural development, compares the experiences and practices of rural development between China and other countries, and provides knowledge products for exchange and mutual understanding for the cause of global rural development. This series mainly includes *Annual Report on International Rural Revitalization*, *Comparative Analysis Report on International Experience in Rural Governance*, *Urban-Rural Integrated Development and Rural Revitalization in Counties*, and other research results.

The Sharing Series on China's Rural Revitalization Experience focuses on telling the story of China's rural revitalization, summarizing the experiences, practices and typical cases of rural revitalization in time, and providing references for domestic and foreign policy makers and researchers. This series mainly focuses on rural development, rural planning, common prosperity and other topics, summarizes relevant policies, experiences and practices, and develops and compiles typical cases based on international perspectives.

Finally, I would like to extend my heartfelt appreciation to all the relevant project teams, publishers and editors who have worked diligently for the publication of the series, as well as the government agencies, universities and research institutes, social organizations and friends from all walks of life who have shown their concern and support for IPRCC. All these series have been generously funded by the Bill & Melinda Gates Foundation and have received careful guidance and assistance by the China Office of the Gates Foundation, for which we would like to express our heartfelt thanks.

Global poverty reduction and rural development are dynamic and ever-changing. The book is far from exhaustive, so we look forward to receiving comments from the readers of the books.

Liu Junwen

Director General of the International Poverty Reduction Center in China

January, 2024

Executive Summary

Poverty is a global challenge. Africa, as the continent with the highest poverty rate, is the focus of global poverty reduction and development. Despite the relatively rapid economic growth in Africa since the beginning of the 21st century, the overall uneven development cannot be concealed. On the one hand, the problem of multidimensional poverty in Africa is escalating, especially for vulnerable groups and rural areas. The challenges in health, education and living standards resulting from the COVID-19 pandemic will persist over a long period of time, and it is imperative to improve people's living standards. On the other hand, the food security and nutrition situation in Africa are also deteriorating. Multiple crises, including conflicts, natural disasters, diseases and economic predicaments, have led to escalating food insecurity. By 2022, the food shortage rate and food insecurity rate in Africa were as high as 19.7% and 60.9%, respectively, more than twice the global average. The even more worrying thing is that , African countries still lag far behind the global average in terms of basic health indicators such as life expectancy, fertility rate and infant mortality rate.

Poverty in Africa is driven by multiple factors such as macroeconomic conditions, food crisis, weather impacts, regional conflicts, and weak development conditions. First, sluggish economic growth can hardly drive poverty reduction. The heavy debt burden and low-level foreign investment lead to weak economic growth momentum in Africa. Given low urbanization rate and high pressure of population growth, slow economic growth can hardly play a role in reducing poverty, and the per capita gross national income (GNI) of most African countries is still at a very low level. Second, the output of major food crops in Africa is insufficient due to the fragile agricultural production environment, low grain production capacity and serious shortage of agricultural factor input in Africa. The fragile food supply system and high dependence on major food imports have greatly exacerbated the fragility of the food market and the instability of food accessibility. Third, due to insufficient emergency response capacity and imperfect measures, it is generally difficult for African countries to effectively cope with the impacts of global climate change, especially extreme weather events such as widespread droughts and floods, which have caused disastrous damages to agricultural production, food security and infrastructure in Africa. Fourth, regional conflicts and insecurity and the ensuing large number of refugees have disrupted economic production activities and markets, compromised rural livelihoods and infrastructure, and aggravated poverty in African countries. Fifth, the basic conditions for development in Africa remain very weak. The access to electricity and Internet as well as basic transportation facilities are seriously lagging behind, while underemployment and low population quality have also been hindering the process of poverty reduction in Africa to a great extent.

Poverty eradication has always been an important issue in African countries and even at the international level. African countries are constantly strengthening their capacity for independent development. **On the political front**, African countries have been strengthening the development of political democracy and the reform of economic system. They have also independently put forward various plans for African renewal. Following the establishment of the African Union (AU), the Africa Peer Review Mechanism (APRM) was proposed to promote the development among member States. **On the economic front**, African leaders have formulated the New Partnership for Africa's Development (NEPAD), and won the support of Western countries. The African Union has developed *2050 Africa's Integrated Maritime (AIM) Strategy* to develop the blue economy, while African countries have formulated appropriate financial strategies to promote local economic development and provide financial support to poor families. **In terms of regional cooperation**, the Economic Community of West African States (ECOWAS), the East African Community (EAC), and the Southern African Development Community (SADC) have been promoting the development of poverty reduction in an extensive range, covering infrastructure, finance, education, health and security, among other sectors. Despite some achievements made in the above poverty reduction practices, much remains to be done. **From the perspective inside Africa**, the national financial capacity of African countries is low, leading to poor implementation effect of poverty reduction strategies and policies. **From the perspective outside Africa**, African countries are highly dependent on international aid and funds, and most of them are burdened with heavy foreign debts. More importantly, the conditions attached to Western aid weaken the autonomy of African countries in formulating their own poverty reduction strategies, and hinder the improvement of the governance capacity of their governments.

Over a long period of time, the international community has been delivering large-scale assistance to Africa, with different results. **From the perspective of traditional donors' aid to Africa**, the sectors covered by assistance of developed countries differ from the needs of Africa, which are ignored. On the one hand, Western development aid focuses on social development, but rarely supports large-scale public infrastructure construction and industrial development in underdeveloped countries. On the other hand, Western aid usually focuses on soft capacity building, and rarely directly provides means of production. Therefore, instead of promoting local development, such assistance has rendered Africa the region with the highest dependence on aid in the world, while developing countries' cost of obtaining development aid is getting higher and higher due to various conditions attached. **From the perspective of assistance from emerging economies to Africa,** China, India, Brazil and other countries have transformed from traditional recipient countries to emerging donor countries, becoming important complementary forces of international aid to Africa. The scale of aid funds from emerging economies to Africa is rising, and the focus is on providing assistance to African regions with geographical proximity, similar socio-economic development, rich resources and similar cultural traditions. In addition, emerging economies rely on the tripartite cooperation mechanism and summit diplomacy to provide Africa with multi-level, multi-sector and multi-form assistance, mainly infrastructure assistance, technical assistance and humanitarian assistance.

The next part focuses on China's aid to Africa. **From the perspective of**

cooperation, China has scored immense achievements in poverty reduction, which are rooted in long-term practice, including the mode of macroeconomic growth and government-sponsored poverty alleviation projects complementing each other. China's poverty reduction policy is long-term, continuous and phased, and both inclusive and targeted policy instruments are adopted to ensure the effective use of resources. In addition, China has developed a unique mechanism of social participation in poverty alleviation. Such practices provide a solid foundation for China-Africa cooperation on poverty alleviation. **The policy framework of China-Africa cooperation on poverty reduction** mainly includes two contents: the first is the global development cooperation goal, the most important of which is the United Nations sustainable development framework, regarded by the Chinese government as a universal policy framework and orientation to guide its domestic development and international development cooperation; and the second is the cooperation strategy and framework reached between China and Africa, including the Forum on China-Africa Cooperation (FOCAC), and its follow-up action plan, and the Program for Strengthening China-Africa Cooperation on Poverty Reduction, among others. Currently, China-Africa cooperation on poverty reduction is mainly carried out under the framework of FOCAC, which has gone through three stages: reaching consensus, sharing experience and institutionalizing, and deepening cooperation. **From the perspective of the approaches to cooperation on poverty reduction**, the cooperation and exchange mechanism is more mature. The contents and forms of cooperation have been enriched, extending from the poverty reduction experience exchange to experience specific and multi-sector cooperation projects.

Therefore, **China-Africa cooperation on poverty reduction should focus on supporting Africa to cultivate endogenous growth forces under the guidance of** *China-Africa Cooperation Vision 2035*, with more attention focused on the following aspects. First, continue to deepen China-Africa cooperation on poverty reduction. Second, actively support African countries in capacity building for poverty reduction and development. Third, Strengthen cooperation on "small and beautiful" poverty reduction projects. Finally, continue to carry out various forms of poverty reduction exchange activities.

Chapter 1 Introduction

1.1 Research Background and Significance

1.1.1 Research background

Poverty is a global challenge facing the world today. Africa, as the continent with the highest poverty rate, is a key region of global poverty reduction and development. Poverty eradication is an important issue in African countries, and even at the international level. Over the past few years, the COVID-19 pandemic, extreme weather events and economic impacts have aggravated the social vulnerability of the entire African continent. Many African countries are plagued with such problems as low income, serious food shortage and serious debt crisis. The extreme poverty rate and the number of people living in extreme poverty in Africa have increased significantly, the reduction of multidimensional poverty has regressed, and the problem of multidimensional poverty is especially serious for vulnerable groups and rural areas. The report of *Global Multidimensional Poverty Index* (MPI) released by the United Nations Development Programme (UNDP) in 2023 demonstrates that, about 580 million poor people live in Sub-Saharan Africa, and the proportion of extremely poor in some African countries such as South Sudan and Equatorial Guinea is even higher than 70%. Accompanying poverty is the problem of food security and hunger.According to *The State of Food Security and Nutrition in the World* (SOFI) released in 2022, more than one third of the people affected by hunger (about 280 million) lived in Africa in 2021, and it is predicted that, by 2030 the number of undernourished people in Africa would increase from nearly 280 million to more than 310 million, the number of extremely poor in Africa would account for 86% of the world's total, and Africa would remain the region would the most concentrated population living in extreme poverty and the highest poverty rate in the world. Accelerating the process of poverty reduction in Africa is an important challenge to achieve the primary Sustainable Development Goal of the United Nations in 2030, "eliminating all forms of poverty in the world".

From the perspective of international aid, Africa remains the key region of poverty reduction in the world, and poverty is also the main area of international aid to Africa. While international aid to Africa has drawn extensive attention, it has been constantly questioned for the slow process of poverty reduction in Africa. On the one hand, international aid to Africa flows to Sub-Saharan Africa, which is of great significance to eliminate poverty and promote sustainable development by emphasizing good governance, boosting local capacity building, strengthening scientific and technological innovation, and promoting employment. For example, with the assistance and support of United Nations agencies, African countries have signed the strategic document of *United Nations Sustainable Development Cooperation Framework*, setting short-term goals for poverty reduction and development of African countries with the assistance of United Nations agencies. On the other hand, Africa, as the region receiving the largest amount of international development aid, has made no obvious progress in economic growth and poverty reduction, thus, some scholars have raised the view that, African countries have been in the "aid trap" for a long time. The African continent, especially Sub-Saharan Africa, is becoming the center of poverty in the world. **In addition, the trend of international aid to Africa is constantly changing.** As emerging economies are more and more active in providing assistance to Africa, China, India, Brazil and other emerging economies have become the main force in providing international development aid. Different from the traditional donor-recipient "master-slave" relationship, emerging donors regard themselves as development partners rather than donors, and new development aid is a parallel process based on experience sharing and knowledge co-creation. The rapid rise of emerging economies in the field of international aid to Africa is of great significance, which poses a challenge to the long-standing "donor-recipient" paradigm centered on the traditional western aid concept.

From the perspective of local poverty reduction strategies in Africa, under the guidance of *Agenda 2063* of the Africa Union (AU), African countries have developed and implemented national poverty reduction and development strategies to accelerate the process of poverty eradication. However, it is difficult for African countries to ensure the implementation of poverty reduction policies due to the low degree of their national autonomy and insufficient national financial capacity. African countries have developed corresponding national development strategies and poverty reduction plans to promote growth and reduce poverty, such as the Poverty Eradication Action Plan (PEAP) in Uganda, the Poverty Reduction and Growth Strategy (2022-2026) in the Republic of Congo. According to AU's *Agenda 2063* and other local strategic documents, African countries have successively launched a number of projects such as the construction of a free trade zone on the African continent and the Digital Village Initiative (DVI) for Sustainable Agricultural Innovation to accelerate infrastructure construction. The AU has specially formulated a comprehensive poverty reduction plan, namely New Partnership for Africa's Development (NEPAD), in an attempt to encourage private sector investment and economic growth, reduce poverty and promote sustainable development on the African continent by stimulating inclusive economic growth, and economic and institutional reform, promoting microfinance institutions and projects, and improving marketing systems. However, due to inadequate internal economic development and limited financial capacity, the African continent relies heavily on the assistance and investment of the international community in the process of poverty reduction, and poverty reduction strategies and policies see poor implementation effects. In addition, African countries have long been highly dependent on the aid and funds from the international community, and the heavy debt burden and the restrictive conditions attached to aid have continuously reduced the autonomy of African countries in formulating their own poverty reduction strategies, and hindered the improvement of their government capabilities, leading to the dilemma of "policy without action".

It is noteworthy that China-Africa cooperation on poverty reduction is an important field of China-Africa cooperation, having achieved remarkable results under the FOCAC. China, having made remarkable achievements in poverty reduction since the reform and opening up, is committed to poverty reduction and development around the world, especially in Africa plagued with the most serious poverty problem. The FOCAC is an important institutionalized framework and exchange platform for China-Africa cooperation, and poverty reduction is an important discussion content in previous ministerial meetings of the FOCAC. Under this framework, China-Africa cooperation on poverty reduction has experienced three stages of development: consensus-reaching, experience exchange and substantive cooperation. With the deepening of China-Africa cooperation on poverty reduction and development, a multi-level inter-governmental and inter-social dialogue mechanism between poverty reduction and rural development with the overall FOCAC framework has been gradually established. The field of cooperation on poverty reduction has expanded from the exchange of poverty reduction experience to infrastructure construction, human resources training, agricultural cooperation, debt relief and other fields, and the focus of cooperation on poverty reduction has also expanded from "poverty reduction" cooperation to "poverty reduction and rural development". The current practice of China-Africa cooperation on poverty reduction shows that China-Africa cooperation on poverty reduction has shifted from experience sharing to experience transfer, with more attention paid to the applicability and transferability of Chinese experience in African countries. In the future, China-Africa cooperation will, based on the goals determined in *China-Africa Cooperation Vision 2035*, continue to focus on supporting Africa's endogenous growth capacity, centering on promoting the transformation and upgrading of China-Africa cooperation, improving quality and efficiency, consolidating traditional cooperation, opening up new fields, innovating cooperation models, and promoting the high-quality development of China-Africa co-construction of the Belt and Road Initiative.

In the wake of the COVID-19 pandemic, poverty in Africa is deepening. Therefore, it is necessary to further review the basic situation of poverty in

Africa, elucidate the main reasons for Africa's backwardness, systematically study and analyze the main body, scale and characteristics of international aid to Africa from the perspective of international development, and summarize the key contents such as the evolution of macro strategies and policies in Africa, poverty reduction issues and their implementation effects, so as to further optimize and improve China's policies on cooperation with Africa on poverty reduction, better share the beneficial experience of China in consolidating and expanding the achievements of poverty alleviation and rural revitalization strategy, constantly promote the steady development of China-Africa cooperation on poverty reduction while the world is undergoing changes, and at the same time promote more effective responses to the global issue of poverty reduction and development.

1.1.2 Research significance

By reviewing and analyzing the current situation of poverty and the progress of poverty reduction in Africa, the overall information and key cases of international aid to Africa, and China's aid to poverty reduction in Africa, we can, first, update the needs and practices of poverty reduction in Africa in time and understand the evolution and future development direction of basic concepts, macro strategies and main policies of poverty reduction in African countries; second, present the basic cooperation situation of international aid to Africa, the areas of concern, and the lack and problems of aid; and third, clarify the basic framework and characteristics of China's international poverty reduction assistance to Africa, provide necessary support for deepening China-Africa partnership for poverty reduction and development, help China better grasp the opportunities and challenges of China-Africa cooperation, provide guidance for China to carry out pragmatic cooperation with Africa, then develop cooperation programs that meet the interests and needs of both sides, and promote the Belt and Road construction and the development of new South-South cooperation.

Generally speaking, reviewing and summarizing the latest progress in poverty reduction and development in Africa and the effectiveness of international development cooperation projects with Africa will help international development cooperation agencies to understand the poverty situation and poverty reduction needs in Africa, provide basis and guidance for the international community to formulate more effective and sustainable aid policies and projects to promote poverty reduction and development in Africa. Meanwhile, Africa is an important partner for China to implement the Belt and Road Initiative and promote South-South cooperation. The study of this book can help China to better carry out international cooperation on poverty reduction, summarize and disseminate Chinese experience and model in poverty reduction, offer Chinese solutions and Chinese wisdom to promote global poverty reduction governance, enhance China's influence in international poverty reduction, and better build a community with a shared future for mankind.

1.2　Research Objectives and Methods

1.2.1　Research objectives

This book mainly studies poverty reduction and development in Africa from three aspects. First, analyze and review the basic situation of poverty in Africa, especially in Sub-Saharan Africa, in the light of macro-policy documents, statistical data and academic research results. Second, by reviewing relevant literature and important cases, summarize the main progress of international aid to Africa, analyze the practices and characteristics of Western developed countries and emerging economies in their aid to Africa and their poverty reduction effects, and examine shortcomings. Third, drawing on the beneficial experience of China in poverty elimination and rural revitalization, think about the key points and advantages of cooperation on poverty reduction between China and Africa, and map out the prospects and strategies of cooperation on poverty reduction between China and Africa under the framework of the Global Development Initiative (GDI) and the Forum on China-Africa Cooperation (FOCAC).

1.2.2　Research methods

To achieve the above research objectives, this book mainly adopts the methods of literature analysis, case study and predictive analysis, and effectively employs relevant data to fully demonstrate the status of poverty reduction and development in Africa. **First, conduct macro-analysis through literature review.** Through the collection and arrangement of documents, this research reviews the data, theories and main concerns related to the poverty reduction process and issues in Africa, delineates the poverty reduction picture in Africa, and provides an important basis for the current situation of poverty in Africa and its driving factors. Meanwhile, in the light of the data of international organizations, local reports on poverty reduction in Africa and other series of data, and bulletins, analyze and sort out the system framework, overall context and specific projects of international assistance to Africa at this stage, and analyze the relevant international standards, strategic cooperation and agreements, evaluation system, poverty reduction results and shortcomings (see Table1-1). **Second, conduct meso and micro analysis of typical cases.** This research will make full use of the resources of international students from Africa, with special attention to the practice of poverty reduction in Sub-Saharan Africa. Against this background, we will sort out important issues, projects and progress of poverty reduction, observe the adaptability of endogenous poverty reduction strategies and external assistance, and make a comparative analysis to shape the accessible space for case studies. **Third, conduct predictive analysis through data summary.** Combined with the analysis of international aid to poverty reduction and the progress of poverty reduction in Africa, as well as the developments and overall background of poverty reduction, the predictive analysis method is adopted to summarize the main experience and contribution of China's poverty reduction assistance to Africa, and put forward the future development trend, so as to provide reference for better development of poverty reduction assistance in Africa.

Table 1-1   **Main Reference Materials of International Reports**

Type	Source	Title / URL
United Nations system	UN	The Sustainable Development Goals Report 2022
		2022 Global Multidimensional Poverty Index (MPI)
		OPHI and UNDP Regional MPI Brief Sub-Saharan Africa: An Age Group Analysis of the 2021 Global MPI
		The State of Food and Agriculture 2019: Moving Forward on Food Loss and Waste Reduction
		Climate Change and Poverty in Africa:Challenges and Initiatives
		2023 Global Report on Food Crises
		How the United Nations System Supports Ambitious Action on Climate Change
	OCHA	Southern Africa Humanitarian Snapshot
		South Sudan Humanitarian Needs Overview 2022
		West and Central Africa: Weekly Regional Humanitarian Snapshot
	WFP	An Analysis of the Impacts of Ongoing Drought across Eastern Horn of Africa
		2022: A Year of Unprecedented Hunger
	WMO	State of the Climate in Africa 2021
		State of Climate Services report: Water
	FAO	Annual Review 2021
		Statistical Yearbook:World Food and Agriculture 2022
	UNDP	Measuring the Multiple Dimensions of Poverty in Africa
		Human Development Report 2021-22 Uncertain Times, Unsettled Lives: Shaping our Future in a Transforming World
	UNICEF	The Climate Crisis Climate Change Impacts, Trends and Vulnerabilities of Children in Sub-Saharan Africa
	IOM	Mozambique Cyclone Eloise Response Plan
Financial Institution	WB	Africa's Pulse: An Analysis of Issues Shaping Africa's Economic Future
		Poverty and Climate Change Reducing the Vulnerability of the Poor through Adaptation
		Macro Poverty Outlook Country-by-country Analysis and Projections for the Developing World
		Climate Change Complicates Efforts to End Poverty
		Revised Estimates of the Impact of Climate Change on Extreme Poverty by 2030
	IMF	Africa Regional Economic Outlook 2023
		Climate Change and Chronic Food Insecurity in Sub-Saharan Africa

Continued

Type	Source	Title / URL
Professional Organization	IPCC	Climate Change 2022, Impacts, Adaptation and Vulnerability, Summary for Policymakers
	IFPRI	2023 Global Food Policy Report:Rethinking Food Crisis Responses
Other Organizations	IFRC	Emergency Appeal, Algeria, Forest Fires
	CIDCA	Forum on China-Africa Cooperation: Sharm el-Sheikh Action Plan
		Forum on China-Africa Cooperation: Johannesburg Plan of Action (2016-2018)
		Forum on China-Africa Cooperation: Beijing Action Plan (2019-2021)
		Forum on China-Africa Cooperation: Dakar Action Plan (2022-2024)
		China-Africa Cooperation Vision 2035
	African Development Bank	African Economic Outlook 2023:Mobilizing Private Sector Financing for Climate and Green Growth in Africa
Data Base	World Bank Open Data	https://data.worldbank.org.cn/
	UNCTAD	https://unctad.org/statistics
	OECD Statistics	https://stats.oecd.org/Index.aspx?DataSetCode=TABLE5A#
	FAOSTAT	https://www.fao.org/faostat/zh/#data/FS
Other	Devex	Devex Emerging Donors Report

Source: Based on the reference materials.

Chapter 2　Overview of Poverty in Africa after COVID-19

Since the beginning of the 21st century, Africa has been experiencing relatively rapid and continuous growth, with its politics and macro-economy becoming more stable. Africa has turned from a "hopeless continent" to a "promising continent", a "leaping lion",and a "center of world economic growth". Some optimists claim that the 21st century will be the African century, believing that Africa is expected to become "China of tomorrow" or "new India"[1,2]. Sub-Saharan Africa, in particular, with a population of over 1 billion, is a diversified continent, where the population under the age of 25 will account for half by 2050. The abundant supply of human and natural resources renders the region the potential to achieve inclusive growth and eliminate poverty.[3] With the largest free trade zone in the world and a vast market with a population of 1.2 billion, the African continent is creating a new development path that makes use of its resources and population potential. However, the overall economic development and prosperity of Africa cannot conceal the development difficulties faced by African countries. Africa remains the region with the slowest socio-economic transformation and the key region for global poverty reduction and development. In addition, African countries and different industrial sectors see different degrees of growth, which leads to different poverty reduction and development between

---

1　Africa: "Desperate Continent" or "Rising Star"？ See:https://www.focac.org/chn/zfgx/jmhz/t1486100. htm, accessed on June 1, 2023.

2　Ewout Frankema, Marlous van Waijenburg. Africa rising? A historical perspective［J］. African Affairs, 2018,117 (469):543-568.

3　Based on data from the World Bank website.

Africa and other regions, among different regions and different countries in Africa.

Although Africa is the region plagued with the most serious poverty problem in the world, and its economic and social development is subject to serious impacts from the COVID-19 pandemic and climate change, yet with the advent of the post-COVID-19 era, African countries have been actively introducing various policies and measures and seeking opportunities for international cooperation, dedicating to social and economic development. After the COVID-19 pandemic, the economic growth of the African continent began to recover, and the overall social and economic development improved. This chapter, based on relevant data from the United Nations system, the World Bank, the International Food Policy Research Institute and other international organizations, attempts to make a detailed analysis of the extreme poverty rate, multidimensional poverty level, hunger index, food security and nutrition, income inequality and human development level in African countries around the core indicators measuring poverty reduction and development, in order to clarify the different situation of poverty reduction and development at the regional and country levels despite overall backwardness of the whole continent, and make an overall judgment on poverty in Africa in the wake of the COVID-19 pandemic.

2.1   Africa's Economy Begins to Show Recovery Growth

Africa's economic growth has begun to recover, and the economic growth rate of some countries have recovered to or even exceeded the pre-COVID-19 level. Table 2-1 shows that, according to the data of the International Monetary Fund (IMF), before the pandemic, the economic growth rate of the African continent reached 2.99%, slightly higher than the world average of 2.84% and much higher than the 0.17% growth rate of Latin America and the Caribbean. In 2020, affected by the COVID-19 pandemic, the African continent generally suffered negative economic growth except for East Africa, and the overall economic growth rate was −1.74%, which was still better than the world average (−2.85%) and Latin America and the Caribbean (−6.78%). From 2021, the economic growth of the Africa began to recover, registering a medium-speed economic growth in each region, but the intensity of economic growth was weaker than the world average. However, by 2022, except for southern Africa, the economic growth rate of other regions was higher than the world average.

Table 2-1   Trends of Economic Growth in Different African Regions, 2015-2022 (%)

Region	2015	2016	2017	2018	2019	2020	2021	2022
Southern Africa	1.45	0.58	1.31	1.43	0.27	-5.79	4.46	2.47
Central Africa	2.64	-0.28	1.26	2.24	2.88	-0.34	3.23	4.10
East Africa	6.21	4.96	5.18	4.71	5.21	0.71	5.37	4.32
North Africa	3.73	3.10	4.67	4.19	2.96	-1.77	5.36	4.06
West Africa	3.15	0.78	2.87	3.22	3.72	-0.63	4.39	3.89
Africa	3.44	2.17	3.48	3.40	2.99	-1.74	4.85	3.78
Latin America and the Caribbean	0.36	-0.61	1.35	1.20	0.17	-6.78	7.01	3.96
Asia (excluding high-income countries)	6.32	6.82	6.28	6.08	4.96	-0.59	7.34	4.42
World	3.48	3.28	3.75	3.64	2.84	-2.85	6.28	3.46

Source: IMF World Economic Outlook Database, April 2023.

At the country level, affected by the COVID-19 pandemic, African countries generally experienced negative economic growth in 2020. Table 2-2 shows that, according to the relevant data from OECD, 34 African countries had negative economic growth rates in 2020, and some countries had serious economic stalls, such as Mauritius, Namibia, Libya, Zimbabwe, Angola, and Cabo Verde. By 2021, however, only two African countries had negative GDP growth rates, namely Chad and Equatorial Guinea. In 2022, only two African countries had negative GDP growth rates, namely Sudan and Libya, which mainly resulted from the impact of regional conflicts on economic growth.

Table 2-2   GDP Growth Rate of African Countries, 2019-2022 (%)

Country	2019	2020	2021	2022	Country	2019	2020	2021	2022
Niger	6.14	3.55	1.40	11.11	Cameroon	3.42	0.54	3.65	3.38
Cabo Verde	5.67	-14.78	7.00	10.50	Nigeria	2.21	-1.79	3.65	3.25
Seychelles	3.09	-7.72	7.91	8.84	Ghana	6.51	0.51	5.36	3.22

Continued

Country	2019	2020	2021	2022	Country	2019	2020	2021	2022
Mauritius	2.89	-14.60	3.50	8.30	Zimbabwe	-6.12	-7.82	8.46	3.03
Rwanda	9.47	-3.36	10.87	6.76	Algeria	1.00	-5.10	3.40	2.93
Côte d'Ivoire	8.31	1.70	7.00	6.70	Gabon	3.92	-1.86	1.48	2.85
Congo, Dem.Rep.	4.49	1.67	6.23	6.63	Angola	-0.70	-5.64	1.09	2.84
Egypt	5.53	3.51	3.31	6.61	Congo,Rep.	1.03	-6.20	1.50	2.78
South Sudan	0.86	-6.49	5.33	6.55	Sierra Leone	5.25	-1.97	4.10	2.77
Botswana	3.03	-8.73	11.84	6.43	Eritrea	3.84	-0.53	2.89	2.62
Ethiopia	9.04	6.06	6.27	6.36	Tunisia	1.59	-8.82	4.41	2.52
Benin	6.87	3.85	7.16	6.02	Djibouti	5.55	1.20	4.81	2.50
Togo	5.46	1.76	5.26	5.40	Chad	3.42	-2.14	-1.10	2.49
Kenya	5.11	-0.25	7.52	5.37	Burkina Faso	5.69	1.93	6.90	2.47
Mauritania	5.43	-0.94	2.45	4.96	Comoros	1.76	-0.20	2.11	2.43
Uganda	7.78	-1.30	6.00	4.93	Lesotho	-1.97	-3.90	2.10	2.09
Liberia	-2.52	-2.97	5.01	4.81	South Africa	0.30	-6.34	4.91	2.04
Senegal	4.61	1.33	6.07	4.71	Burundi	1.84	0.34	3.12	1.83
Tanzania	6.99	4.82	4.95	4.69	Somalia	2.70	-0.28	2.94	1.70
Gambia	6.22	0.59	4.27	4.44	Equatorial Guinea	-5.48	-4.24	-3.19	1.57
Guinea	5.62	4.92	4.29	4.29	Morocco	2.89	-7.19	7.93	1.13
Madagascar	4.41	-7.14	5.74	4.21	Sao Tome and Principe	2.21	3.02	1.88	0.89
Mozambique	2.31	-1.20	2.33	4.15	Malawi	5.45	0.91	4.57	0.80
Namibia	-0.84	-8.04	2.66	3.84	Eswatini	2.70	-1.56	7.88	0.47
Mali	4.76	-1.24	3.05	3.70	Central African Republic	2.97	0.96	0.98	0.38
Guinea-Bissau	4.50	1.50	6.40	3.50	Sudan	-2.50	-3.63	0.50	-2.50
Zambia	1.44	-2.79	4.60	3.44	Libya	-11.20	-29.46	28.33	-12.81

Source: Based on the data from OECD's *Africa's Development Dynamics 2023: Investing in Sustainable Development*, see https://www.oecd.org/dev/africa/development-dynamics/.

From the perspective of the economic size of various countries, due to the impact of the pandemic, the economic aggregate of 28 African countries in 2020 was lower than that of 2019; only 10 countries' economic aggregates in 2021 were lower than the 2019 level. By 2022, only five countries' economic aggregates were lower than the 2019 level, namely the Republic of Congo, Libya, Mauritius, Namibia and Eswatini. Except for Libya, the difference between the economic aggregates and that of 2019 was already very small. Based on the forecast of the International Monetary Fund on economic growth rate, the economic aggregates of African countries will all return to the level of 2019, and achieve substantive growth (see Table 2-3).

Table 2-3   GDP of African Countries, 2019-2022 (US$100 million)

Country	2019	2020	2021	2022	Difference (2020-2019)	Difference (2021-2019)	Difference (2022-2019)
Angola	693.09	536.19	674.04	1214.17	-156.90	-19.05	521.08
Burundi	25.77	26.50	27.80	38.94	0.73	2.03	13.17
Benin	143.92	156.52	171.45	174.13	12.60	27.53	30.21
Burkina Faso	161.78	179.34	197.38	195.68	17.56	35.60	33.90
Botswana	166.96	149.3	176.15	191.76	-17.66	9.19	24.80
Central African Republic	22.21	23.27	25.16	24.62	1.06	2.95	2.41
Côte d'Ivoire	585.39	613.49	700.43	700.46	28.10	115.04	115.07
Cameroon	396.71	407.73	453.38	437.16	11.02	56.67	40.45
Congo, Dem. Rep.	517.76	487.17	553.51	628.59	-30.59	35.75	110.83
Congo, Rep.	127.50	104.83	133.66	125.30	-22.67	6.16	-2.20
Comoros	11.95	12.25	12.96	12.33	0.30	1.01	0.38
Cabo Verde	19.82	17.04	19.36	22.24	-2.78	-0.46	2.42
Djibouti	30.89	31.81	34.83	36.46	0.92	3.94	5.57
Algeria	1,717.67	1,450.09	1,630.44	1,954.15	-267.58	-87.23	236.48
Egypt	3,030.81	3,652.53	4,041.43	4,752.31	621.72	1,010.62	1721.5
Ethiopia	959.13	1,076.58	1,112.71	1,203.69	117.45	153.58	244.56

Continued

Country	2019	2020	2021	2022	Difference (2020-2019)	Difference (2021-2019)	Difference (2022-2019)
Gabon	168.74	153.15	202.17	219.31	-15.59	33.43	50.57
Ghana	683.38	700.43	775.94	728.39	17.05	92.56	45.01
Guinea	134.43	141.78	160.92	204.69	7.35	26.49	70.26
Gambia	18.14	18.12	20.38	21.33	-0.02	2.24	3.19
Guinea-Bissau	14.40	14.32	16.39	17.05	-0.08	1.99	2.65
Equatorial Guinea	113.64	100.99	122.69	164.51	-12.65	9.05	50.87
Kenya	1003.80	1006.67	1103.47	1159.89	2.87	99.67	156.09
Liberia	33.20	30.4	35.09	39.74	-2.80	1.89	6.54
Libya	692.52	503.57	428.17	440.66	-188.95	-264.35	-251.86
Lesotho	24.54	22.31	24.96	24.80	-2.23	0.42	0.26
Morocco	1,289.20	1,213.48	1,428.66	1,380.52	-75.72	139.46	91.32
Madagascar	141.05	130.51	144.73	152.33	-10.54	3.68	11.28
Mali	172.80	174.65	191.40	190.48	1.85	18.60	17.68
Mozambique	153.90	140.29	157.77	179.40	-13.61	3.87	25.50
Mauritania	80.66	84.05	99.96	103.21	3.39	19.30	22.55
Mauritius	144.36	114.01	115.29	127.72	-30.35	-29.07	-16.64
Malawi	110.25	121.82	126.27	125.12	11.57	16.02	14.87
Namibia	125.42	105.82	123.11	123.45	-19.60	-2.31	-1.97
Niger	129.16	137.44	149.15	152.22	8.28	19.99	23.06
Nigeria	4,481.20	4,321.99	4,408.34	4,773.76	-159.21	-72.86	292.56
Rwanda	103.56	101.84	110.70	127.03	-1.72	7.14	23.47
Sudan	323.38	270.35	343.26	494.23	-53.03	19.88	170.85
Senegal	233.99	244.93	276.25	274.62	10.94	42.26	40.63
Sierra Leone	40.77	40.63	40.42	39.39	-0.14	-0.35	-1.38
Somalia	64.85	68.83	76.28	81.58	3.98	11.43	16.73
Sao Tome and Principe	4.27	4.73	5.27	5.52	0.46	1.00	1.25
Eswatini	44.95	39.82	47.43	44.62	-5.13	2.48	-0.33

Continued

Country	2019	2020	2021	2022	Difference (2020-2019)	Difference (2021-2019)	Difference (2022-2019)
Seychelles	16.84	12.61	14.54	19.26	-4.23	-2.30	2.42
Chad	113.15	107.15	117.8	119.09	-6.00	4.65	5.94
Togo	72.20	75.75	84.13	81.73	3.55	11.93	9.53
Tunisia	419.06	425.38	466.87	466.01	6.32	47.81	46.95
Tanzania	611.37	624.10	678.41	770.63	12.73	67.04	159.26
Uganda	353.53	376.00	405.30	488.41	22.47	51.77	134.88
South Africa	3,885.32	3,376.20	4,190.15	4,057.05	-509.12	304.83	171.73
Zambia	233.09	181.11	221.48	285.00	-51.98	-11.61	51.91
Zimbabwe	218.32	215.10	283.71	330.20	-3.22	65.39	111.88

Note: Data are not available for Eritrea and South Sudan.

Source: Based on the World Development Indicators (WDI) data updated on May 10, 2023, calculated in 2023 US dollars.

2.2 The Level and Quality of Urbanization Have Improved in Africa

Since the 21st century, the urbanization rate of African countries has maintained a relatively stable growth, rising from 34.95% in 2000 to 43.99% in 2021, with an increase of over 9 percentage points. At the regional level, the urbanization rate in Southern Africa and North Africa is relatively high and the urbanization speed is slow; the urbanization level is relatively low and the urbanization speed is fast in Central Africa, West Africa and East Africa, which are key regions in Africa to promote urbanization development. Especially in East Africa, many countries are in the stage of rapid urbanization.

At the country level, the urbanization rate of almost all African countries has grown to varying degrees. In 2021, the urbanization rate of 17 African countries was higher than the world average (56.47%). However, in terms of growth speed, the growth of urban population in Africa has slowed down. In 2021, the annual growth rate of urban population dropped to 3.53%, only 0.11% higher than that in 2000. Some countries, such as Zimbabwe and Mauritius, has even seen deurbanization. See Table 2-4 and Figure 2-1.

Table 2-4   **Urbanization Level and Growth Rate of African Countries in 2021 (%)**

No.	Country	Urbanization level	Urbanization growth rate	No.	Country	Urbanization level	Urbanization growth rate
Southern Africa (65.38%)				23	Ghana	57.99	5.91
1	Botswana	71.56	5.34	24	Mauritania	56.13	8.03
2	South Africa	67.85	3.84	25	Nigeria	52.75	8.35
3	Namibia	53.01	10.52	26	Liberia	52.57	4.61
4	Lesotho	29.48	7.92	27	Côte d'Ivoire	52.18	4.61
5	Eswatini	24.37	3.88	28	Benin	48.97	5.93
North Africa (56.16%)				29	Senegal	48.60	4.98
6	Libya	80.99	1.83	30	Mali	44.68	9.55
7	Djibouti	78.22	0.89	31	Guinea-Bissau	44.62	4.90
8	Algeria	74.26	3.92	32	Sierra Leone	43.37	5.20
9	Tunisia	69.89	2.26	33	Togo	43.36	6.72
10	Morocco	64.07	4.41	34	Guinea	37.26	5.09
11	Egypt	42.86	0.30	35	Burkina Faso	31.24	11.04
Central Africa (51.14%)				36	Niger	16.75	2.83
12	Gabon	90.42	2.10	East Africa (29.77%)			
13	Sao Tome and Principe	75.07	5.60	37	Seychelles	57.97	3.83
14	Equatorial Guinea	73.56	3.41	38	Somalia	46.73	6.65
15	Congo, Rep.	68.28	3.46	39	Zambia	45.19	6.49
16	Angola	67.46	5.16	40	Eritrea	41.99	8.13
17	Cameroon	58.15	5.38	41	Mauritius	40.78	-0.33
18	Congo, Dem.Rep.	46.24	6.76	42	Madagascar	39.21	9.35
19	Central African Republic	42.65	5.00	43	Mozambique	37.63	7.74
20	Chad	23.78	4.87	44	Tanzania	35.95	11.20
West Africa (48.30%)				45	the Sudan	35.59	4.31
21	Cabo Verde	67.10	3.58	46	Zimbabwe	32.30	0.02
22	Gambia	63.22	5.51	47	Comoros	29.61	3.47

Continued

No.	Country	Urbanization level	Urbanization growth rate	No.	Country	Urbanization level	Urbanization growth rate
48	Kenya	28.49	9.15	52	Malawi	17.70	7.20
49	Uganda	25.55	12.95	53	Rwanda	17.57	3.00
50	Ethiopia	22.17	11.62	54	Burundi	14.06	13.48
51	South Sudan	20.51	7.45	**Sub-Saharan Africa**		**43.99**	**5.61**

Source: Based on the World Development Indicators (WDI) data updated on May 10, 2023.

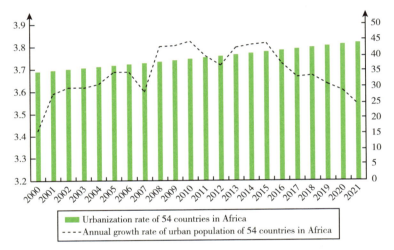

Figure 2-1   Urbanization in African Countries, 2000-2021 (%)

Source: Based on the World Development Indicators (WDI) data updated on May 10, 2023.

2.3   The Human Development Level Has Been Significantly Improved in African Countries

The Human Development Index (HDI), which refers to the geometric mean of the life expectancy index, the education index and the GNI index, is used to examine the human development level of different countries internationally. The HDI is between 0 and 1, and the closer it is to 1, the higher the level of human development is. Table 2-5 shows that in Sub-Saharan Africa, the HDI has been gradually increasing since 2000, reaching 0.552 in 2019, the highest level in history. According to the HDI data released by the United Nations Development

Programme (UNDP), the HDI of African countries has increased to varying degrees from 2000 to 2021, with Ethiopia rising from 0.287 to 0.498, registering the largest increase of more than 73%, while Angola, Rwanda, Niger, Burkina Faso and Sierra Leone all grew by more than 50%.

By 2021, eight countries in Africa are at a high level of human development (0.700-0.799), namely Mauritius, Seychelles, Algeria, Egypt, Tunisia, Libya, South Africa and Gabon. Seventeen countries are in the middle level of human development (0.550-0.699), with their HDI being between 0.550 (Côte d' Ivoire) and 0.693 (Botswana). In the same period of time, 28 countries saw a low level of human development (less than 0.550), including 13 countries with an HDI below 0.500 and 2 countries with an HDI below 0.400 (South Sudan with a HDI of 0.385 is the lowest)[1]. Compared with the world average (0.732), only three countries in Africa, namely Mauritius, Seychelles and Algeria, were above the average in 2021, while the human development level of the other 50 countries was all below the world average.

Table 2-5 Ranking of African Countries' Human Development Index (HDI)

Country	Ranking	1990	2000	2015	2019	2020	2021	2015-2021 ranking change	2000-2021 growth rate(%)
High level of human development (0.700-0.799)									
Mauritius	63	0.626	0.681	0.795	0.817	0.804	0.802	2	17.77
Seychelles	72	–	0.744	0.796	0.802	0.793	0.785	-8	5.51
Algeria	91	0.591	0.649	0.740	0.748	0.736	0.745	2	14.79
Egypt	97	0.572	0.633	0.706	0.735	0.734	0.731	13	15.48
Tunisia	97	0.576	0.658	0.733	0.745	0.737	0.731	1	11.09
Libya	104	0.666	0.712	0.699	0.722	0.703	0.718	10	0.84
South Africa	109	0.632	0.633	0.716	0.736	0.727	0.713	-4	12.64
Gabon	112	0.610	0.635	0.699	0.709	0.710	0.706	2	11.18
Medium level of human development (0.550-0.699)									
Botswana	117	0.586	0.585	0.702	0.717	0.713	0.693	-6	18.46

1　See: https://hdr.undp.org/data-center/documentation-and-downloads, accessed on June 1, 2023. No data available for Somalia.

Continued

Country	Ranking	1990	2000	2015	2019	2020	2021	2015-2021 ranking change	2000-2021 growth rate(%)
Morocco	123	0.447	0.521	0.654	0.682	0.679	0.683	3	31.09
Cabo Verde	128	–	0.569	0.663	0.676	0.662	0.662	-4	16.34
Ghana	133	0.460	0.507	0.607	0.631	0.632	0.632	5	24.65
Sao Tome and Principe	138	0.485	0.501	0.596	0.622	0.619	0.618	4	23.35
Namibia	139	0.579	0.546	0.628	0.639	0.633	0.615	-7	12.64
Eswatini	144	0.545	0.471	0.575	0.615	0.610	0.597	4	26.75
Equatorial Guinea	145	–	0.512	0.603	0.605	0.599	0.596	-6	16.41
Zimbabwe	146	0.509	0.452	0.582	0.601	0.600	0.593	-1	31.19
Angola	148	–	0.375	0.582	0.595	0.590	0.586	-3	56.27
Cameroon	151	0.452	0.442	0.560	0.583	0.578	0.576	2	30.32
Kenya	152	0.474	0.481	0.561	0.581	0.578	0.575	0	19.54
Congo, Rep.	153	0.522	0.491	0.590	0.570	0.574	0.571	-9	16.29
Zambia	154	0.412	0.418	0.562	0.575	0.570	0.565	-4	35.17
Comoros	156	–	0.464	0.544	0.560	0.562	0.558	0	20.26
Mauritania	158	0.397	0.465	0.544	0.563	0.556	0.556	-2	19.57
Côte d'Ivoire	159	0.427	0.457	0.513	0.550	0.551	0.550	8	20.35
Low level of human development (lower than 0.550)									
Tanzania	160	0.371	0.398	0.520	0.548	0.548	0.549	2	37.94
Togo	162	0.410	0.446	0.514	0.535	0.535	0.539	4	20.85
Nigeria	163	–	–	0.516	0.538	0.535	0.535	1	–
Rwanda	165	0.319	0.340	0.515	0.534	0.532	0.534	0	57.06
Benin	166	0.359	0.416	0.529	0.530	0.524	0.525	-6	26.20
Uganda	166	0.329	0.394	0.517	0.525	0.524	0.525	-3	33.25
Lesotho	168	0.479	0.452	0.503	0.524	0.521	0.514	3	13.72
Malawi	169	0.303	0.374	0.491	0.519	0.516	0.512	4	36.90
Senegal	170	–	0.388	0.505	0.513	0.513	0.511	-1	31.70
Djibouti	171	–	0.361	0.493	0.512	0.510	0.509	1	41.00

Continued

Country	Ranking	1990	2000	2015	2019	2020	2021	2015-2021 ranking change	2000-2021 growth rate(%)
Sudan	172	0.336	0.424	0.508	0.514	0.510	0.508	-4	19.81
Madagascar	173	–	0.443	0.504	0.510	0.501	0.501	-3	13.09
Gambia	174	0.343	0.404	0.478	0.503	0.501	0.500	1	23.76
Ethiopia	175	–	0.287	0.460	0.498	0.498	0.498	6	73.52
Eritrea	176	–	–	0.483	0.495	0.494	0.492	-2	–
Guinea-Bissau	177	–	–	0.472	0.490	0.483	0.483	2	–
Liberia	178	–	0.438	0.473	0.484	0.480	0.481	0	9.82
Congo, Dem. Rep.	179	0.386	0.376	0.463	0.482	0.479	0.479	1	27.39
Sierra Leone	181	0.312	0.318	0.453	0.480	0.475	0.477	1	50.00
Guinea	182	0.269	0.345	0.440	0.467	0.466	0.465	1	34.78
Burkina Faso	184	–	0.296	0.418	0.452	0.449	0.449	2	51.69
Mozambique	185	0.238	0.303	0.440	0.456	0.453	0.446	-2	47.19
Mali	186	0.237	0.317	0.416	0.433	0.427	0.428	1	35.02
Burundi	187	0.290	0.297	0.428	0.431	0.426	0.426	-2	43.43
Central Africa Republic	188	0.338	0.329	0.384	0.411	0.407	0.404	2	22.80
Niger	189	0.216	0.262	0.376	0.406	0.401	0.400	2	52.67
Chad	190	–	0.291	0.389	0.403	0.397	0.394	-1	35.40
South Sudan	191	–	–	0.412	0.393	0.386	0.385	-3	–
Sub-Saharan Africa	–	**0.407**	**0.430**	**0.534**	**0.552**	**0.549**	**0.547**	–	**27.21**

Note: No data available for Somalia.

Source: The United Nations, see:https://hdr.undp.org/data-center/documentation-and-downloads, accessed on June 1, 2023.

The rising level of human development in Africa means that the quality of life, life expectancy and education level in this region have been improved to some extent. By 2020, the life expectancy at birth in Sub-Saharan Africa had risen to 63.5 years, and the average years of education had gradually risen to about 6 years (see Table 2-6). However, compared with the world average, except for North Africa, where the basic health indicators have basically reached the average level, there remains a big gap in health indicators, such as life expectancy at birth, total fertility rate, infant mortality rate and mortality rate of children under five in the other four sub-regions on the African continent. Therefore, African countries need to accord great importance to the improvement of people's livelihood and well-being in their future development strategies.

Table 2-6 **Basic Health Indicators of African Countries, 2020**

Region	Life expectancy at birth (years)	Life expectancy at birth, female (years)	Life expectancy at birth, male (years)	Fertility rate, total (births per woman)	Mortality rate, infant (per 1,000 live births)	Mortality rate, under5 (per 1,000 live births)
Southern Africa	61.9	64.9	58.8	3.7	40.0	54.6
Central Africa	60.9	63.1	59.0	4.9	46.5	66.6
East Africa	64.9	67.4	62.4	3.9	37.0	52.1
North Africa	71.9	74.4	69.7	2.9	20.4	25.4
West Africa	61.5	63.1	59.8	4.6	49.3	73.2
Africa	63.5	65.8	61.3	4.1	40.7	57.9
World	71.7	74.5	69.1	2.6	19.9	26.5

Source: Based on the data from OECD's *Africa's Development Dynamics 2023: Investing in Sustainable Development*, see: https://www.oecd.org/dev/africa/development-dynamics/.

2.4 Poverty Remains the Primary Problem in Economic and Social Development of Africa

Africa is the region with the slowest socio-economic transformation and the largest concentration of least developed countries (LDCs) in the world, where poverty reduction and development are facing grim challenges.

By 2023, most of the 54 countries in Africa suffer from such problems as low income, serious food shortage and serious debt crisis. According to the latest classification of 46 least developed countries in the world by the United Nations[1], 51 low-income food-deficit countries by the United Nations Food and Agriculture Organization (FAO)[2] and 39 heavily indebted poor countries by the World Bank[3]. There are 33 least developed countries in Africa, 36 low-income food-deficit countries and 33 heavily indebted poor countries.

According to the three dimensions of least developed countries, low-income food-deficit countries and heavily indebted poor countries, 28 African countries are classified into all these three dimensions at the same time, namely Benin, Burkina Faso, Burundi, Central African Republic, Chad, Comoros, the Democratic Republic of the Congo, Eritrea, Ethiopia, Gambia, Guinea, Guinea-Bissau, Liberia, Madagascar, Malawi, Mali, Mauritania, Mozambique, Niger, Rwanda, Sao Tome and Principe, Senegal, Sierra Leone, Somalia, Sudan, Togo, Uganda, and Tanzania. This also shows that the above-mentioned 28 African countries suffer from a deeper poverty level, more constraints in development and more complicated poverty-causing factors. Four countries are classified into two dimensions of heavily indebted poor countries and low-income food-deficit countries, namely Cameroon, the Republic of Congo, Côte d' Ivoire and Ghana. Two countries are classified into two dimensions of low-income food-deficit countries and least developed countries, namely South Sudan and Lesotho (see Figure 2-2). The classification of these three dimensions reflects that African countries' poverty reduction and development are facing severe challenges as a whole.

1   See the list of least developed countries (LDCs) of the United Nations, https://unctad.org/topic/least-developed-countries/list, accessed on June 3, 2023.

2   See the FAO's list of low-income food-deficit countries, https://www.fao.org/countryprofiles/lifdc/zh/, accessed on June 4, 2023.

3   See the world Bank's list of heavily indebted poor countries, https://data.worldbank.org/indicator/SP.POP.GROW?locations=XE, accessed on June 3, 2023.

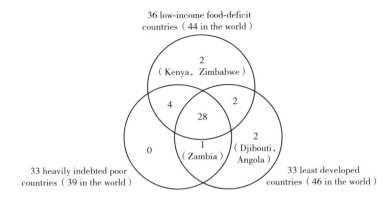

Figure 2-2　Overview of Poverty in African countries

Source: Based on the data from the United Nations, the World Bank and the United Nations Food and Agriculture Organization.

2.4.1　The problem of absolute poverty in Africa has become more prominent since the pandemic

Now and in the future, Sub-Saharan Africa is and will be the region with the largest concentration of poor people in the world. Since 1990, the issue of absolute poverty in the African region has become increasingly severe, with the number of people living in absolute poverty not decreasing but increasing. Figure 2-3 shows that, according to the World Bank's poverty line of US$2.15 per person per day, the number of people living in absolute poverty in Sub-Saharan Africa rose from 278 million in 1990 to 397 million in 2019, an increase of 43% over the same period. During the same period, the global number of people living in absolute poverty decreased significantly, from 2.011 billion in 1990 to 702 million in 2019, a reduction of over 65%. In terms of proportion, the share of the absolute poor population in Sub-Saharan Africa in the world has been continuously increasing from 13.82% in 1990 to 52.24% in 2017, meaning that more than half of the world's absolute poor population is concentrated in Sub-Saharan Africa. By 2019, this proportion had risen to 56.52%. In terms of the number of people living in absolute poverty, Sub-Saharan Africa has become increasingly the most concentrated region of poverty globally. Currently, 10% of the global population is still living in extreme poverty, with Sub-Saharan Africa being the most concentrated area with the highest poverty rate.[1] By the first half of 2020, affected by the COVID-19 pandemic, the number of people living in extreme poverty in Sub-Saharan Africa had risen to 449 million, with the extreme poverty rate hitting 40.17%[2]. According to the World Bank's forecast, by 2030, no obvious decline will be seen in the number of extremely poor people in Sub-Saharan Africa. Specifically, by 2025, the number of extremely poor people in Sub-Saharan Africa will amount to 431 million, accounting for 83.37% of the world's total, and by 2035, the number of extremely poor people in Sub-Saharan Africa will be 416 million, accounting for 86.85% of the world's total (see Table 2-7). That is to say, poverty will remain a severe challenge for Sub-Saharan Africa from now to the next two decades.

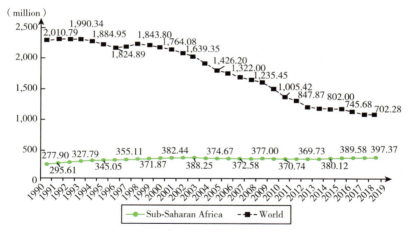

Figure 2-3   Number of People Living in Poverty in Sub-Saharan Africa under US$2.15 per person per day, 1990-2019 (2017 PPP, in millions)

Source: Poverty & Inequality Platform by the World Bank (https://pip.worldbank.org/home), compiled and accessed on June 1, 2023.

---

1   An Chunying. International Cooperation in Poverty Alleviation in Africa within the Framework of Global Poverty Governance [J]. Contemporary World, 2019 (10): 23-28.

2   Boao Forum For Asia, Report on Poverty Reduction in Asia, 2020[EB/OL].http://www.boaoforum.org.

Table 2-7 Global Changes of Population Living in Extreme Poverty (million)

Region	1990	1999	2005	2015	2018	2025	2030
Eastern Asia and the Pacific	987.1	695.9	361.6	47.2	34.0	7.0	3.0
Europe and Central Asia	13.3	36.7	22.9	7.1	5.0	3.0	2.0
Latin America and the Caribbean	62.6	69.7	54.9	25.9	26.0	22.0	19.0
Western Asia and North Africa	14.2	10.6	9.4	18.6	25.0	26.0	26.0
Southern Asia	535.9	534.4	510.4	216.4	121.0	20.0	5.0
Sub-Saharan Africa	277.5 (14.65%)	376.1 (21.76%)	387.7 (28.67%)	413.3 (56.16%)	437.0 (66.62%)	431.0 (83.37%)	416.0 (86.85%)
Other	4.3	5.0	5.3	7.3	8.0	8.0	8.0
World	1,894.8	1,728.6	1,352.2	735.9	656.0	517.0	479.0

Note:Data from 1990 to 2018 are actual figures, while those from 2025 to 2030 are estimated figures. ( ) =Proportion of Sub-Saharan Africa.

Source: https://www.worldbank.org/en/understanding-poverty.

According to the poverty line of US$2.15 per person per day released by the World Bank, among the 1.425 billion people in Africa, the number of people living in extreme poverty reached 375 million in 2022, and the extreme poverty rate hit 26.3%. At the sub-regional level, except for North Africa, the extreme poverty rates in the other four regions far surpass the world average, and more than three quarters of the poor people are concentrated in Southern Africa, East Africa and West Africa (see Table 2-8).

Table 2-8 Population and the Number of Poor under US$2.15, Africa and World, 2022

Region	Population (million)	Poverty rate (%)	Poor population (million)
Southern Africa	193.90	38.7	75.04
Central Africa	173.38	28.0	48.48
East Africa	415.98	28.8	119.65
North Africa	217.26	2.4	5.16
West Africa	424.34	22.1	93.84

Continued

Region	Population (million)	Poverty rate (%)	Poor population (million)
Africa	1,424.85	26.3	375.02
World	–	10.0	–

Source: Based on the data from OECD's *Africa's Development Dynamics 2023: Investing in Sustainable Development.*

At the country level, the total population of 45 African countries with data is 1.21 billion, of which the number of people living in poverty and extreme poverty are 340 million and 667 million, with the total poverty rate and extreme poverty rate reaching 28.1% and 55.1%, respectively. According to the US$2.15 poverty line, the poverty rate in 16 countries exceed 30%, including one country exceeding 70% (Malawi); four countries exceed 60% (South Sudan, Burundi, Mozambique, and Zambia) and two countries exceed 50% (Rwanda and Niger). The top five countries in terms of the number of extremely poor are Nigeria, Ethiopia, Tanzania, Mozambique, and Uganda. The total number of extremely poor in these five countries exceeds half of the total number of extremely poor in the African continent, accounting for 50.43% of the total. These countries suffer from the severest poverty problem in Africa (see Table 2-9 and Table 2-10).

Table 2-9   Number of People Living in Extreme Poverty under US$ 2.15 in Major Countries

No.	Country	US$ 2.15 poverty line	
		Poor population (million)	Proportion of total poor population in Africa (%)
1	Nigeria	67.53	19.86
2	Ethiopia	33.31	9.80
3	Tanzania	29.41	8.65
4	Mozambique	21.30	6.26
5	Uganda	19.94	5.86
6	Kenya	15.88	4.67
7	Malawi	14.30	4.21
8	Niger	13.26	3.90

Continued

No.	Country	US$ 2.15 poverty line	
		Poor population (million)	Proportion of total poor population in Africa (%)
9	Zambia	12.29	3.62
10	South Africa	12.28	3.61
11	Angola	11.07	3.26
12	Ghana	8.44	2.48
13	Burundi	8.39	2.47
14	South Sudan	7.34	2.16
15	Cameroon	7.17	2.11

Source: Based on the data from OECD's *Africa's Development Dynamics 2023: Investing in Sustainable Development.*

Table 2-10   **Population and Poverty Rate in 45 African Countries, 2022, US$2.15**

Country	Population (million)	Poverty rate (%)	Country	Population (million)	Poverty rate (%)
Angola	35.59	31.1	Sudan	46.87	15.3
Botswana	2.63	15.4	Tanzania	65.50	44.9
Eswatini	1.20	36.1	Uganda	47.25	42.2
Lesotho	2.31	32.4	Egypt	110.99	1.5
Malawi	20.41	70.1	Mauritania	4.74	6.5
Mozambique	32.97	64.6	Morocco	37.46	1.4
Namibia	2.57	15.6	Tunisia	12.36	0.1
South Africa	59.89	20.5	Benin	13.35	19.9
Zambia	20.02	61.4	Burkina Faso	22.67	30.5
Zimbabwe	16.32	39.8	Cabo Verde	0.59	4.6
Burundi	12.89	65.1	Côte d'Ivoire	28.16	11.4
Cameroon	27.91	25.7	Gambia	2.71	17.2
Chad	17.72	30.9	Ghana	33.48	25.2
Gabon	2.39	2.5	Guinea	13.86	13.8

Continued

Country	Population (million)	Poverty rate (%)	Country	Population (million)	Poverty rate (%)
Sao Tome and Principe	0.23	15.6	Guinea-Bissau	2.11	21.7
Comoros	0.84	18.6	Liberia	5.30	27.6
Djibouti	1.12	19.1	Mali	22.59	14.8
Ethiopia	123.38	27.0	Niger	26.21	50.6
Kenya	54.03	29.4	Nigeria	218.54	30.9
Mauritius	1.30	0.1	Senegal	17.32	9.3
Rwanda	13.78	52.0	Sierra Leone	8.61	26.1
Seychelles	0.11	0.5	Togo	8.85	28.1
South Sudan	10.91	67.3	45 African coutries	1,210.01	28.1

Note: Data are not available for 9 countries: the Central African Republic, the Republic of Congo, the Democratic Republic of the Congo, Equatorial Guinea, Eritrea, Madagascar, Somalia, Algeria, and Libya.

Source: Based on the data from OECD's *Africa's Development Dynamics 2023: Investing in Sustainable Development*.

2.4.2   Multidimensional poverty is deepening in Africa

The problem of multidimensional poverty in Africa is severe, and the negative impact of the COVID-19 pandemic still persists. The multidimensional poverty index (MPI) (ranging from 0 to 1) can reflect the poverty degree of different individuals or households by measuring the deprivations in terms of health, education and living standards. According to the regulations of relevant United Nations organizations, the closer the MPI is to 0, the lower the poverty level is; the closer the value is to 1, the deeper the poverty level is. *2022 Global Multidimensional Poverty Index* shows that, the global progress in reducing multidimensional poverty has regressed by 8 to 10 years, especially in countries with deep poverty and high MPI. In 2022, the MPI in Sub-Saharan Africa rose to 0.286, and the poverty rate reached 30.88%, both much higher than those in other parts of the world (see Table 2-11). Sub-Saharan Africa is also known as the region with the largest number of multidimensional poor people. In 2022, more than 579 million multidimensional poor people (48%) in the world lived in Sub-Saharan Africa[1], an increase of 5 percentage points over 2021. **The demographic composition and distribution of multidimensional poverty in Africa are also concentrated, especially in vulnerable groups and rural areas.** In 2021, the multidimensional poverty rate in Sub-Saharan Africa reached 59% for children and 47% for adults[2]. In addition, 70% (457 million people) in rural areas of Sub-Saharan Africa lived in multidimensional poverty, while the proportion in urban areas was 26% (99 million people).

Table 2-11　　　　**Multidimensional Poverty in Different Regions across the World, 2022**

Region	MPI	Extreme poverty rate (%)
East Asia and the Pacific	0.022	1.00
Europe and Central Asia	0.004	0.07
Latin America and the Caribbean	0.027	1.56
South Asia	0.091	6.92
Sub-Saharan Africa	0.286	30.88

Source: Based on the data of the Food and Agriculture Organization (FAO), see:https://www.fao.org/faostat/zh/#data/FS.

Low living standards play a decisive role in Africa's multidimensional poverty, followed by education and finally health. In 2022, Sub-Saharan Africa was the region with the highest contribution of living standards to multidimensional poverty, reaching 48.58%, 10 percentage points higher than South Asia (see Table 2-12). In the same period, the contribution of living standards in other parts of the world did not exceed 40%.

1　The data are derived from *2022 Global Multidimensional Poverty Index,* see: https://hdr.undp.org/content/2022-global-multidimensional-poverty-index-mpi#/indicies/MPI, downloaded on June 1, 2023.

2　*OPHI and UNDP Regional MPI Brief Sub-Saharan Africa: An age group analysis of the 2021 global MPI,* see: https://ophi.org.uk/wp-content/uploads/OPHI_and_UNDP_RMPIB_2022_SSA%E2%80%93Age%E2%80%93Group.pdf.

Table 2-12　　　　　**Contributions to Multidimensional Poverty in Different Regions, 2022**

Region	Contribution to multidimensional poverty (%)		
	Health	Education	Living standard
East Asia and the Pacific	27.92	35.24	36.84
Europe and Central Asia	53.25	24.57	22.18
Latin America and the Caribbean	39.77	24.91	35.32
South Asia	27.97	33.69	38.34
Sub-Saharan Africa	21.90	29.52	48.58

Source: Based on the data of the Food and Agriculture Organization (FAO), see https://www.fao.org/faostat/zh/#data/FS.

Based on multidimensional poverty contribution data of 48 countries, the living standard is the main influencing factor of multidimensional poverty in 37 countries, education is the main influencing factor in 10 countries, and health is the main influencing factor only in one country (Seychelles). Through analysis with a scatter plot, it is found that when the MPI is lower than 0.3, the contribution rate of health to the poverty index is higher; when the MPI is higher than 0.3, the living standard is the decisive factor of the MPI, and the influence of health on the poverty index is low at this time; when the MPI is between 0.3 and 0.35, education is the decisive factor of multidimensional poverty (see Figure 2-4). This shows that most African countries are subject to insufficient basic living security and deep multidimensional poverty.

Low living standards are also directly reflected in the consumption behaviors of the rural population. The authors, during a field research tour in rural Malawi, found the life logic of "living within one's means" in small packages or sporadic purchases common among local farmers.

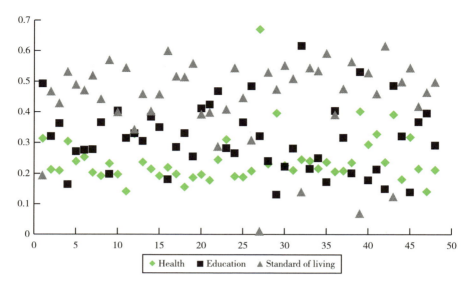

Figure 2-4   Scatter Plot of Contributions of Health, Education and Living Standard to Multidimensional Poverty

Note: Data are not available for Cabo Verde, Djibouti, Eritrea, Equatorial Guinea, Mauritius, and Somalia.

Source: Based on *2022 Global Multidimensional Poverty Index*.

Case 2-1   Malawi farmers' consumption behaviors

On the field research tour in rural Africa, we were often very puzzled to see that cooking oil was sold in bags of about 10 ml in humble village shops; small vendors selling along the way always packed peanuts or cashews into small bags of only a few dozen grams; in some countries, the face value of prepaid phone cards was US$1⋯ All things were sold in very small packages. It was almost impossible to see product promotion by increasing the quantity and reducing the price commonly that is generally used in China. Small packages and sporadic purchases must be more expensive. In the beginning, we could not understand why things were sold this way until we made a survey at a village in Tanzania. In Rudawe village, there was a very humble house with a humble long table. In the corner of the house, tea was being made on a stove made of three bricks. An African woman was sitting on the ground making a snack called Chapati. From time to time, villagers came here to buy Chapatis or drink tea. It was surprising that farmers did not prepare breakfast at home as their income was so low. Wasn't it cheaper and more cost-effective to cook by oneself? "How many Chapatis can you sell a day? How much does each cost?" We asked. The African woman said that it would take her 30,000 shillings to buy a bag of 25 kilograms of flour in the local market. These 25 kilograms of flour could make 375 Chapatis, each of which was sold at a price of 200 shillings. One bag of flour would be used for five days. And generally customers would eat it in the store with a cup of tea – such a set meal was 400 shillings. With rough calculation, it can be found that if farmers buy flour to make Chapatis, one Chapati only cost 80 shillings, but why did poor farmers come to buy Chapatis that cost 200 shillings each every day? Just then, a woman dropped by to buy Chapatis, so we asked her why she didn't buy flour to make Chapatis herself. "I don't have the budget to buy a whole bag of flour, which costs 30 thousand shillings. That's a lot of money. I help others weed, collect corn and do other farm work, only earning 3 thousand shillings a day. 3 thousand shillings are my family's budget for the whole day, so I can only buy a few Chapatis every day. That's why I come here every day." It turns out that, these ultra-small packaged goods are actually to meet the basic needs of local people with limited consumption power. Although their income is very low, they also want to use mobile phones, so they buy a US$1 phone card; and as they want to have a little snack, they spend a little amount of money to get it. They live within their means with careful calculation, and follow their own logic to make their life more enjoyable.

There are also significant differences in multidimensional poverty index (MPI) across countries. According to the latest statistics of the United Nations, in 2022, among the 48 countries that data are available in Africa, there are 15 countries with a MPI value higher than 0.3, and 12 countries with a poverty index value lower than 0.1 (see Figure 2-5).

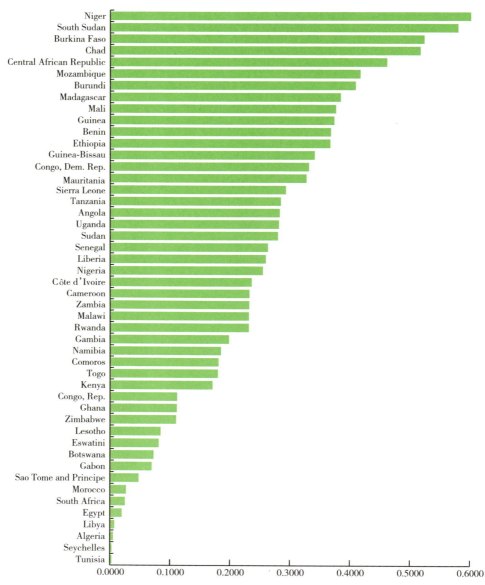

Figure 2-5   Multidimensional Poverty Index of 48 African Countries, 2022

Note: Data are not available for Cabo Verde, Djibouti, Eritrea, Equatorial Guinea, Mauritius and Somalia.

Source: Based on *2022 Global Multidimensional Poverty Index* (MPI).

2.4.3 Food security, nutrition and health face grim challenges in Africa

Multiple crises and conflicts, natural disasters, diseases and economic impacts in recent years have aggravated food insecurity across the African continent. In 2021, about 282 million people (20% of the total population) in Africa are confronted with food insecurity and malnutrition[1]. In 2022, the prevalence of food shortage, medium or serious food insecurity and food insecurity in Africa remained high, reaching 19.7%, 60.9% and 24%, respectively, far higher than other regions in the world and over twice the world's average (see Table 2-13).

Table 2-13	Food Security in Different Regions, 2022 (%)		
Region	Incidence of food shortage	Rate of medium or serious food insecurity	Rate of serious food insecurity
Europe	< 2.5	8.2	1.9
Latin America and the Caribbean	6.5	37.5	12.6
South Asia	15.6	40.3	19.4
Oceania	7.0	13.0	3.4
Africa	19.7	60.9	24.0
Sub-Saharan Africa	22.1	66.6	26.3
World	9.2	29.6	11.3

Source: Based on the data of the Food and Agriculture Organization, see: https://www.fao.org/faostat/zh/#data/FS.

The food security situation is especially severe in Sub-Saharan Africa, as the prevalence of food shortage and the population subject to food shortage have been significantly increasing since 2010. In 2019, the prevalence of food shortage reached 20.1%, with 214 million people facing food shortage. After the COVID-19 pandemic, the problem of food shortage was aggravated. In 2022, the prevalence of food shortage hit 22.1%, and the number of people with food

---

1   International Food Policy Research Institute. *Global Food Policy Report 2023*. See:https://ebrary.ifpri.org/digital/collection/p15738coll2/id/136641, accessed on June 1, 2023.

shortage amounted to nearly 250 million. Meanwhile, the prevalence of moderate and/or serious food insecurity and the prevalence of severe food insecurity in this region are at the highest level in the world, being respectively 66.6% and 26.3% (see Figure 2-6).

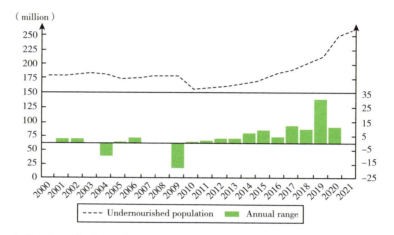

Figure 2-6   Population with Food Deficit in Sub-Saharan Africa, 2000-2021

Source: Based on the data of the Food and Agriculture Organization, see: https://www.fao. org/faostat/zh/#data/FS.

The rate of moderate or severe food insecurity and the population with food insecurity in Africa continue to rise. In 2022, the rate of moderate or serious food insecurity in Africa rose to 60.9%. At the sub-regional level, Central Africa has the most prominent food insecurity problem, followed by East Africa. The prevalence of food insecurity in these two regions is three times the world average, and the rate of moderate or serious food insecurity rate reaches 69.2% and 78.4%, respectively, making these two sub-regions the hardest hit area of food insecurity (see Table 2-14). The number of people with food insecurity has also continued to increase. In 2021, about 116.3 million people in Africa were in moderate or severe food insecurity,[1] an increase of 25.5 million compared with 2019, and the number of people with severe food insecurity increased by more than 13 million.

---

1   International Food Policy Research Institute. *Global Food Policy Report 2023*. See: https://ebrary.ifpri. org/digital/collection/p15738coll2/id/136641, accessed on June 1, 2023.

Table 2-14   Food Security in Different Regions of Africa, 2022 (%)

Region	Prevalence of undernourishment	Prevalence of moderate or severe food insecurity	Prevalence of severe food insecurity
East Africa	28.5	69.2	27.7
Central Africa	29.1	78.4	39.1
North Africa	7.5	32.4	12.0
South Africa	11.1	25.9	12.5
West Africa	14.6	66.4	22.0
Africa	19.7	60.9	24.0

Source: Based on the data of the Food and Agriculture Organization, see: https://www.fao.org/faostat/zh/#data/FS.

In terms of absolute number, food security in the Democratic Republic of the Congo is the most severe, with more than 27.3 million people in moderate or severe food insecurity, and the number of people subject to food insecurity in Ethiopia (23.6 million), Nigeria (19.45 million) and Sudan (11.7 million) is also over 10 million.

In terms of growth, between 2021 and 2022, the population of three African countries with severe food insecurity increased by over 500,000: Nigeria (+900,000), Somalia (+900,000) and Kenya (+800,000). In addition, in a certain period of time reported in the *Global Report on Food Crisis 2022*, 376,000 people from seven countries or regions were hungry, including 214,000 people in Somalia (accounting for 57%) and 87,000 people in South Sudan (accounting for 23%). Burkina Faso and Nigeria also identified the number of people in famine, with 18,000 people and 3,000 people, respectively （see Figure 2-7）. In these countries, hunger and food insecurity pose a direct threat to life safety.

The sustained growth of the rate of moderate or severe food insecurity and food insecure population in Africa makes it more challenging to achieve the goal of eliminating hunger by 2030.

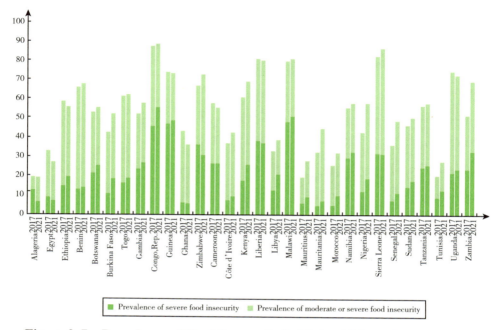

Figure 2-7   Prevalence of Food Insecurity in Major African Countries (%)

Source: Based on the data of the Food and Agriculture Organization, see:https://www.fao.org/faostat/zh/#data/FS, accessed on June 1, 2023.

The high dependence on food imports has also seriously threatened food security in Africa. The food self-sufficiency rate in African countries is generally low, and the dependence on food imports is high. Affected by the perennial drought in the Horn of Africa, the internal supply of grains in African countries has been declining, while the external dependence of African countries on grains has been greatly increasing, and the proportion of imported grain has been expanding. Table 2-15 shows that, in 2020, there were 26 countries in Africa with grain imports accounting for more than 20% of total imports. The proportion exceeded 30% in six countries, namely Seychelles, the Republic of Congo, Sao Tome and Principe, Liberia, Niger and Djibouti; the proportion exceeded 40% in four countries, namely Comoros, South Sudan, Guinea-Bissau and Burundi. In addition, the issue of food supply in Somalia is the most serious, where the abnormal climate and food insecurity have greatly affected the basic livelihood, and the food supply is heavily dependent on aid. Under the trend of rising global food prices and declining output, the high dependence on food imports has significantly threatened food security in Africa.

Table 2-15   **Food Imports of African Countries, 2020**

No.	Country	Proportion of food imports in total imports (%)	Net food imports (US$ millions)	No.	Country	Proportion of food imports in total imports (%)	Net food imports (US$ millions)
Food imports account for less than 10% (4)				Food imports account for 10%-20% (24)			
1	South Africa	6.25	-4,067	20	Central African Republic	18.00	74
2	Chad	6.43	60	21	Zimbabwe	18.15	734
3	Zambia	8.16	2	22	Eswatini	18.50	-225
4	Tanzania	9.35	-597	23	Madagascar	18.51	-273
Food imports account for 10%-20% (24)				24	Angola	18.73	1,721
5	Malawi	10.23	17	25	Sierra Leone	18.97	340
6	Burkina Faso	10.37	142	26	Mozambique	19.43	889
7	Congo, Dem. Rep.	10.61	595	27	Nigeria	19.84	5.785
8	Uganda	10.62	-580	28	Lesotho	19.86	289
9	Tunisia	11.19	601	Food imports account for 20%-30% (15)			
10	Namibia	11.24	-149	29	Equatorial Guinea	20.02	257
11	Ethiopia	11.51	-27	30	Libya	20.93	2.857
12	Botswana	11.73	687	31	Egypt	21.79	8.469
13	Mali	12.41	422	32	Ghana	21.93	-276
14	Morocco	12.97	-293	33	Mauritius	22.37	393
15	Eritrea	13.37	130	34	Côte d'Ivoire	22.94	-4,585
16	Gabon	16.11	535	35	The Sudan	23.02	1,012
17	Togo	16.47	133	36	Cameroon	23.11	183
18	Kenya	16.59	-152	37	Senegal	23.83	703
19	Rwanda	17.63	165	38	Algeria	23.84	7,973

Continued

No.	Country	Proportion of food imports in total imports (%)	Net food imports (US$ millions)	No.	Country	Proportion of food imports in total imports (%)	Net food imports (US$ millions)
39	Benin	24.39	709	48	Niger	36.28	686
40	Guinea	25.38	798	49	Djibouti	37.75	949
41	Gambia	26.98	152	**Food imports account more than 40%(4)**			
42	Mauritania	29.37	177	50	Comoros	41.77	104
43	Cabo Verde	29.86	170	51	South Sudan	42.42	412
Food imports account for 30%-40%(6)				52	Guinea-Bissau	50.56	20
44	Seychelles	30.28	-148	53	Burundi	77.16	52
45	Congo, Rep.	30.50	566	**Others**			
46	Sao Tome and Principe	32.60	34	54	Somalia	152.54	1533
47	Liberia	34.39	328				

Note: According to the data of FAO, Somalia's grain imports reached US$18 million in 2020, while total imports calculated by the World Bank in the same year were US$11.8 million, mainly due to Somalia's high dependence on international food aid.

Source: Based on *World Food and Agriculture Statistical Yearbook 2022* of the FAO, and the data of the World Bank.

Meeting the food and nutrition needs of the population to achieve zero hunger is the basic goal of poverty eradication in many African countries. However, the hunger situation in African countries is still serious, thus it is imperative to solve the hunger problem. According to the IFPRI's latest global hunger index ranking in 2022, African countries generally rank lower. Of the 49 African countries with data in 2022, only Tunisia, Algeria and Morocco have hunger indices below 10, while the other 46 countries all have hunger indices above 10 (in a state of severe hunger). Among them, 19 African countries have a hunger index of more than 20, 16 countries have a hunger index of more than 30 (of which 4 countries have a hunger index of more than 40), which means that the hunger situation is extremely severe (see Table 2-16).

Table 2-16   Global Ranking of Hunger Index of African Countries and its Changes

GHI Index Ranking of African Countries in 2022						2014-2022 GHI difference	2014-2022 GHI change rate (%)
Rank	Country	2000	2007	2014	2022		
26	Tunisia	10.3	7.6	6.7	6.1	-0.6	-9.0
32	Algeria	14.5	11.4	8.7	6.9	-1.8	-20.7
47	Morocco	15.8	12.4	9.6	9.2	-0.4	-4.2
54	Cabo Verde	15.3	11.9	12.1	11.8	-0.3	-2.5
57	Egypt	16.3	17.2	14.6	12.3	-2.3	-15.8
59	South Africa	18.1	17.2	12.7	12.9	0.2	1.6
62	Mauritius	15.3	14.1	13.0	13.4	0.4	3.1
67	Ghana	28.5	22.1	15.5	13.9	-1.6	-10.3
71	Senegal	34.2	22.8	17.6	15.6	-2.0	-11.4
73	Eswatini	24.7	22.9	18.4	16.3	-2.1	-11.4
74	Cote d'Ivoire	33.4	35.8	22.7	16.8	-5.9	-26.0
76	Gabon	20.9	20.3	16.5	17.2	0.7	4.2
78	Namibia	25.4	26.8	22.9	18.7	-4.2	-18.3
80	Cameroon	35.8	29.9	21.4	18.9	-2.5	-11.7
86	Botswana	27.7	25.8	20.5	20.0	-0.5	-2.4
87	Gambia	29.0	26.5	22.2	20.7	-1.5	-6.8
87	Malawi	43.3	32.5	24.1	20.7	-3.4	-14.1
87	Mauritania	31.8	28.3	26.3	20.7	-5.6	-21.3
90	Djibouti	44.3	35.8	27.4	21.5	-5.9	-21.5
91	Benin	33.8	26.9	23.2	21.7	-1.5	-6.5
92	Togo	39.3	30.2	26.1	22.8	-3.3	-12.6
93	Mali	41.7	35.7	26.1	23.2	-2.9	-11.1
94	Kenya	36.6	31.1	21.6	23.5	1.9	8.8
95	Tanzania	40.8	30.9	25.5	23.6	-1.9	-7.5
96	Burkina Faso	44.9	34.5	26.5	24.5	-2.0	-7.5
98	Angola	64.9	44.7	26.2	25.9	-0.3	-1.1
101	Comoros	39.5	31.7	29.1	26.9	-2.2	-7.6
102	Rwanda	49.9	35.9	29.5	27.2	-2.3	-7.8

Continued

GHI Index Ranking of African Countries in 2022					2014-2022 GHI difference	2014-2022 GHI change rate (%)
Rank	Country	2000	2007	2014	2022		
103	Nigeria	40.4	32.1	28.4	27.3	-1.1	-3.9
104	Ethiopia	53.6	42.6	27.4	27.6	0.2	0.7
105	Congo, Rep.	34.7	33.7	25.3	28.1	2.8	11.1
106	Sudan	–	–	29.3	28.8	-0.5	-1.7
108	Zambia	53.3	46	35.2	29.3	-5.9	-16.8
111	Guinea-Bissau	37.7	31.0	30.2	30.8	0.6	2.0
112	sierra leone	57.5	51.1	33.1	31.5	-1.6	-4.8
113	Lesotho	32.7	29.1	29.3	32.4	3.1	10.6
113	Liberia	48.2	39	34.8	32.4	-2.4	-6.9
115	the Niger	52.5	40.2	32.8	32.6	-0.2	-0.6
*	Guinea	–	–	–	20.0-34.9*	–	–
*	Mozambique	–	–	–	20.0-34.9*	–	–
*	Uganda	–	–	–	20.0-34.9*	–	–
*	Zimbabwe	–	–	–	20.0-34.9*	–	–
117	Chad	50.7	49	40.7	37.2	-3.5	-8.6
118	Congo, Dem.Rep.	48.0	43.2	38.7	37.8	-0.9	-2.3
119	Madagascar	42.5	37.2	37.3	38.7	1.4	3.8
120	Central African	48.8	46.8	44.6	44.0	-0.6	-1.3
*	Burundi	–	–	–	35.0-49.9*	–	–
*	Somalia	–	–	–	35.0-49.9*	–	–
*	South Sudan	–	–	–	35.0-49.9*	–	–

Note: Data are not available for five countries: Libya, Eritrea, Seychelles, Equatorial Guinea, and Sao Tome and Principe.

Source: Based on the global hunger index, see:https://www.globalhungerindex.org/, accessed on June 1, 2023.

2.5 The Imbalanced Regional Development Remains Very Prominent

Measured by per capita gross national income (GNI), 46 of the 54 countries in Africa are lower-middle income and low income countries, while the per capita GNI of one half of the African countries is lower than the average in Africa. Salient imbalanced development among different countries is found. Table 2-17 shows that, not only is there a great gap between high-income countries and low-income countries-for example, in 2021, the highest per capita gross national income (Seychelles: US$13,822) was 62 times the lowest (Burundi: US$222)-but also considerable gaps are found among countries at the same income level group (the lower the income, the greater the gap). The development level of African countries, especially Sub-Saharan Africa countries (GNI less than US$1,600), is the lowest in the world, and most low- and middle-income countries in Africa are caught in the "low-level equilibrium trap".

Table 2-17　Per Capita Gross National Income (GNI) of African Countries, 2021 (2021 current US$)

No.	Country	Per capita GNI	No.	Country	Per capita GNI	No.	Country	Per capita GNI
High income (13,205 and above)			11	Eswatini	3,658	24	Zimbabwe	1,730
1	Seychelles	13,821	12	Algeria	3,609	25	Cameroon	1,629
Upper-middle income (4,256-13,205)			13	Egypt	3,585	26	Senegal	1,602
2	Mauritius	9,241	14	Cabo Verde	3,229	27	Comoros	1,585
3	Gabon	7,283	15	Djibouti	3,095	28	Benin	1,354
4	South Africa	6,919	16	Côte d'Ivoire	2,472	29	Lesotho	1,246
5	Botswana	6,435	17	Sao Tome and Principe	2,386	**Low income (1,085 and below)**		
6	Libya	6,409	18	Ghana	2,303	30	Tanzania	1,063
7	Equatorial Guinea	5,596	19	Congo,Rep.	2,190	31	Guinea	1,050
8	Namibia	4,772	20	Mauritania	2,134	32	Zambia	1,038
Lower-middle income (1,086-4,255)			21	Kenya	2,050	33	Togo	975
9	Morocco	3,800	22	Nigeria	1,986	34	Ethiopia	920
10	Tunisia	3,681	23	Angola	1,799	35	Burkina Faso	846

Continued

No.	Country	Per capita GNI	No.	Country	Per capita GNI	No.	Country	Per capita GNI
36	Mali	833	43	Liberia	634	50	Sierra Leone	474
37	Rwanda	805	44	Malawi	623	51	Somalia	444
38	Guinea-Bissau	796	45	Niger	601	52	Burundi	222
39	Uganda	765	46	Congo, Dem. Rep.	542	53	Eritrea	–
40	Gambia	752	47	Central African Republic	492	54	South Sudan	–
41	Sudan	722	48	Madagascar	490	**Sub-Saharan Africa**		**1,577**
42	Chad	662	49	Mozambique	481			

Note: No data is available for Eritrea and South Sudan.

Source: Based on the World Development Indicators (WDI) data, updated on May 10, 2023.

Africa has a serious problem of income inequality. In terms of distribution, income inequality across Africa, among different sub-regions and countries is grim. The latest data shows that, the Gini coefficient in Africa has hit 0.416. Except for North Africa, the Gini coefficient of the other four sub-regions in Africa is higher than the world average, with the Gini coefficient of Southern Africa reaching 0.526. This also shows that despite the rapid economic growth in African countries before the pandemic, the extreme poverty and inequality in most countries have not been significantly improved during the development process, and the income inequality between regions and countries is still great (see Table 2-18).

Table 2-18   **Gini Coefficients by Region**

Region	Gini coefficient
Southern Africa	0.526
Central Africa	0.403
East Africa	0.397
North Africa	0.342
West Africa	0.381

Continued

Region	Gini coefficient
Africa	0.416
Latin America and the Caribbean	0.455
Asia	0.352
World	0.371

Source: Based on the data from OECD's *Africa's Development Dynamics 2023: Investing in Sustainable Development*, see: https://www.oecd.org/dev/africa/development-dynamics/.

According to the latest data of the World Bank, among 50 African countries with available data, only two countries, Guinea and Algeria, have a Gini coefficient below 0.3, while the other 48 countries are above 0.3, among which 26 countries are above 0.4 (and 9 countries are above 0.5) (see Table 2-19). From this, we can see that income inequality in many African countries is quite serious, and such problems as inequality in distribution are still prominent.

Table 2-19   **Gini Coefficients of African Countries**

Country	Year	Gini coefficient	Country	Year	Gini coefficient
South Africa	2014	0.630	Tanzania	2018	0.405
Namibia	2015	0.591	Morocco	2013	0.395
Zambia	2015	0.571	Gambia	2020	0.388
Central African	2008	0.562	Burundi	2013	0.386
Eswatini	2016	0.546	Malawi	2019	0.385
Mozambique	2014	0.540	Senegal	2018	0.381
Botswana	2015	0.533	Gabon	2017	0.380
Angola	2018	0.513	Benin	2018	0.378
Zimbabwe	2019	0.503	Chad	2018	0.375
Congo, Rep.	2011	0.489	Niger	2018	0.373
Burkina Faso	2018	0.473	Cote d'Ivoire	2018	0.372
Cameroon	2014	0.466	Mauritius	2017	0.368
Comoros	2014	0.453	Mali	2018	0.361
Lesotho	2017	0.449	Sierra leone	2018	0.357
South Sudan	2016	0.441	Liberia	2016	0.353

Continued

Country	Year	Gini coefficient	Country	Year	Gini coefficient
Rwanda	2016	0.437	Nigeria	2018	0.351
Ghana	2016	0.435	Ethiopia	2015	0.350
Uganda	2019	0.427	Guinea-Bissau	2018	0.348
Madagascar	2012	0.426	Sudan	2014	0.342
Cape Verde	2015	0.424	Tunisia	2015	0.328
Togo	2018	0.424	Mauritania	2014	0.326
Congo, Dem.Rep.	2012	0.421	Seychelles	2018	0.321
Djibouti	2017	0.416	Egypt	2019	0.319
Kenya	2015	0.408	Guinea	2018	0.296
Sao Tome and Principe	2017	0.407	Algeria	2011	0.276

Note: Data are not available for Eritrea, Equatorial Guinea, Libya, and Somalia.

Source: Based on the World Development Indicators (WDI) data, updated on May 10, 2023.

2.6 Summary

In summary, Africa is the region with the most serious poverty problem in the world, where the least developed countries, low-income food-deficit countries and heavily indebted poor countries are highly concentrated, especially in Sub-Saharan Africa. In recent years, the progress of poverty reduction has slowed down with little effect. In 2020, the number of people living in extreme poverty reached 449 million, and the extreme poverty rate reached 40.17%, making it the place with the highest concentration of people living in extreme poverty and the highest incidence of poverty in the world. According to the poverty line of US$2.15 per person per day issued by the World Bank in 2022, the number of poor people in Africa is 375 million, and the poverty rate has reached 26.3%. Multidimensional poverty in Africa is increasingly prominent, especially among vulnerable groups and in rural areas. The negative impact of the COVID-19 pandemic on health, education and living standards will persist for a long time, and the low living standards are the key issues that African countries urgently need to take measures to deal with. On the whole, the prevalence of food insecurity in Sub-Saharan Africa reached 22.1% in 2022, with nearly 250 million people suffering from food insecurity. The retrogression of food security and nutrition situation aggravated the food crisis in Africa. The moderate or severe food insecurity rate and the number of people suffering from food insecurity in various sub-regions continued to rise, and the extremely high dependence on food imports also posed a serious threat to food security in Africa. By 2022, the hunger index of African countries was high, and the hunger problem caused by food deficit remained the primary problem in Africa. In addition, the degree of inequality in distribution in Africa is generally high, and the income inequality in various sub-regions and countries is very serious. Relatively speaking, the level of human development in African countries has increased, but there is still a big gap in basic health indicators such as life expectancy, fertility rate and infant mortality rate.

Generally speaking, more than half of African countries have such problems as low income, serious food shortage and serious debt crisis, presenting severe challenges to poverty reduction and development. Africa, on the whole, is still at the stage of low development, the problem of insufficient and imbalanced regional development is increasingly prominent, the multi-dimensional progress of poverty reduction is blocked, and the poverty situation in various regions is grim, especially affected by multiple factors not conducive to development, such as the COVID-19 pandemic and global climate change. In order to understand the predicaments faced by African countries and the enormous differences in poverty reduction and development among African countries, it is necessary to further analyze the main causes of poverty in African countries in an effort to effectively cope with and promote the progress of poverty reduction and development in Africa.

Chapter 3　Main Causes for the Slow Progress of Poverty Reduction in Africa

Since the outbreak of the COVID-19 pandemic, persistent global inflation and tight monetary policy have led to an increase in the borrowing costs of African countries. Coupled with the long-term decline in aid budgets and the increased interest burden on public debt, Africa has to fight against the aggravation of macroeconomic imbalances. Rising food and energy prices have affected the most vulnerable groups in Africa. Public debt and inflation have been at the highest level in decades since 2022, and about half of the countries have experienced double-digit inflation[1]. According to the World Bank , the overall post-pandemic economic recovery in Sub-Saharan Africa has slowed down, with the economic growth rate dropping from 4.1% in 2021 to 3.6% in 2022.[2]

Poverty in African countries is largely caused by macroeconomic conditions, food crisis, climate disasters (especially droughts and floods), regional conflicts and weak development conditions, all of which affect the progress of poverty reduction in African countries. In the future, these internal and external factors will become more complicated, especially with regard to poverty reduction and development, which will be more and more affected not only by conflicts, but also by a series of impacts – especially the global impact of COVID-19 and regional conflicts on social economy, producing chain reactions in various regions and countries in Africa.

1　IMF, *Regional Economic Outlook for Africa*, see: https://www.imf.org/en/publications/reo?sortby=Date&series=Sub-Saharan%20Africa, accessed on June 1, 2023.

2　See: https://www.worldbank.org/en/region/afr, accessed on June 1, 2023.

3.1 Slow Economic Growth Can Hardly Drive Poverty Reduction

Africa's overall economic growth is relatively stable, but has slowed down, which cannot effectively promote poverty reduction. For a long time, the economic development of Sub-Saharan Africa has maintained a relatively stable growth, with the total GDP increasing from US$423 billion in 2000 to US$1,803.3 billion in 2019.[1] After a sharp decline in 2020, the total GDP in 2021 jumped to US$2,716.1 billion, and continued to increase by US$267.2 billion in 2022[2]. However, Africa's economic growth speed has slowed down. Affected by the COVID-19 pandemic, the GDP growth rate in 2020 in Africa saw a negative growth for the first time in the past two decades, from 2.56% in 2019 to -2.07%. According to the latest data of the World Bank, the economic growth of Sub-Saharan Africa slowed down from 4.1% in 2021 to 3.6% in 2022. The global economic downturn, declining growth and high inflation rate, the severe global and domestic financial situation, and the high debt in Africa have led to the downward adjustment of economic growth in Sub-Saharan Africa. It is estimated that the economic growth rate in 2024 and 2025 will rebound to 3.7% and 3.9%, respectively, which indicates that this year's growth slowdown should bottom out. However, in the medium and long term, the growth conditions are still insufficient to reduce extreme poverty and promote common prosperity.

Given the pressure of low urbanization rate and high population growth, slow economic growth can hardly exert its poverty reduction benefits. The urbanization rate in Africa is lower than other regions and the world average level. In Sub-Saharan Africa, the regional urbanization rate increased from 38.63% in 2015 to 41.83% in 2021. In the same period, the global urbanization rate increased from 53.83% to 56.47%, and the urbanization rate of African population is less than 75% of the world average. Against the backdrop of the low urbanization rate, the population of Africa has been increasing steadily year

---

1   Calculation based on World Bank data (2023 current US$), see:https://data.worldbank.org.cn/indicator/NY.GDP.MKTP.CD?locations=ZG, accessed on June 1, 2023.

2   Based on data of GDP of African countries from *Macro Poverty Outlook 2023*, calculated in 2023 current US$.

by year. Table 3-1 shows that, from 2015 to 2022, the average annual population growth rate in Sub-Saharan Africa exceeded 2.6%, while the population growth rate in other parts of the world dropped significantly during the same period. The global population growth rate dropped from 1.19% to 0.80%, and the population growth rate in Sub-Saharan Africa was more than three times the world average. In terms of GDP, on the contrary, compared with other parts of the world, the growth rate of GDP in Africa was relatively slow, rising in fluctuation from 2.87% in 2015 to 3.57% in 2022. In there eight years, the economic growth rate was slightly higher than the world average only in 2022. The per capita GDP growth closely related to population and GDP is also very difficult. From 2016 to 2020, the per capita GDP growth in Sub-Saharan Africa was negative for five consecutive years, and the growth rate in 2022 only hit 1%. The slow growth of per capita GDP fully reflects the fact that Africa's economic growth rate is far lower than the stable population growth rate, and the benefits of economic growth are offset by population growth, making it difficult for economic growth to accelerate the process of poverty reduction.

Table 3-1　Comparison of Population Growth and Economic Growth in Different Regions of the World (%)

	Region	2015	2016	2017	2018	2019	2020	2021	2022
Population growth rate	East Asia and the Pacific	0.71	0.71	0.71	0.61	0.53	0.43	0.26	0.21
	Latin America and the Caribbean	1.03	1.01	0.98	0.92	0.89	0.81	0.68	0.66
	South Asia	1.23	1.21	1.22	1.19	1.14	1.12	1.03	0.92
	Sub-Saharan Africa	2.77	2.72	2.68	2.68	2.67	2.65	2.59	2.54
	World	1.19	1.17	1.15	1.10	1.06	1.01	0.86	0.80
GDP growth rate	East Asia and the Pacific	4.72	4.67	5.05	4.76	3.96	-0.12	6.10	2.85
	Latin America and the Caribbean	0.52	-0.16	1.88	1.62	0.74	-6.45	6.73	3.75
	South Asia	7.34	7.68	6.53	6.33	3.94	-4.66	8.27	6.47
	Sub-Saharan Africa	2.87	1.27	2.44	2.65	2.59	-2.00	4.17	3.57
	World	3.08	2.81	3.39	3.29	2.59	-3.07	6.02	3.08

Continued

	Region	2015	2016	2017	2018	2019	2020	2021	2022
Per capita GDP growth rate	East Asia and the Pacific	3.97	3.94	4.31	4.12	3.41	-0.54	5.82	2.63
	Latin America and the Caribbean	-0.51	-1.16	0.89	0.70	-0.15	-7.20	6.01	3.07
	South Asia	6.04	6.39	5.25	5.09	2.76	-5.72	7.16	5.50
	Sub-Saharan Africa	0.10	-1.41	-0.23	-0.03	-0.07	-4.54	1.54	1.00
	World	1.87	1.62	2.22	2.16	1.52	-4.04	5.12	2.26

Source: Based on the data from the World Bank.

The heavy debt burden and low level of foreign investment also lead to sluggish economic growth momentum in Africa. In terms of debt, a series of overseas impacts since the turn of the century have caused the debt in Africa to rise rapidly, containing the growth potential of the African region. In 2000, Africa's public debt amounted to US$413 billion, and by 2022, it had soared to US$1.8 trillion, which was the highest in more than a decade (see Figure 3-1). Between 2010 and 2022, in particular, Africa's public debt increased by 183%, almost four times the growth rate of its GDP;the debt-to-GDP ratio in many countries was extremely high. In 2019, the public debt of 18 countries in Africa exceeded 60% of GDP; by 2022, the debt of 24 countries was higher than this threshold (see Figure 3-2). Compared with other developing countries, African countries are slow in reducing their debt. Meanwhile, data from IMF show that public debt in Africa is relatively concentrated. In 2022, the public debt of Egypt, South Africa, Nigeria, Algeria and Morocco reached US$108.7 billion, accounting for almost 60% of the debt of Africa. The rapid increase in debt has limited economic growth and the capability of many African countries to cope with future crises or invest in development.

Figure 3-1   Total Government Debt in Africa

Note: Figures represent the nominal value in current US dollars. Public debt refers to general government domestic and foreign debts. The general government consists of central, state and local governments and social security funds controlled by these organizations.

Source: Based on the IMF's World Economic Outlook Database (April 2023).

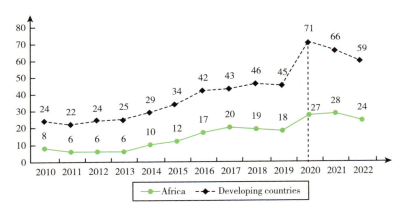

Figure 3-2   Number of Countries with High Debt Level (public debt exceeds 60% of GDP)

Source: Global Crisis Response Group, based on IMF's World Economic Outlook Database (April 2023).

In terms of foreign direct investment (FDI), the per capita and regional foreign direct investment received by Africa is extremely low, which can hardly boost economic growth. In terms of region, Africa is the region receiving the least amount of foreign direct investment in the world, and its global proportion is on the decline, decreasing from 1.61% in 2015 to 0.39% in 2022 (see Table 3-2), making it the only region with a declining proportion of foreign direct investment. In terms of per capita investment, the per capita foreign direct investment quota in Sub-Saharan Africa fell from US$44.04/person (12% of the world average) in 2015 to US$5.91/person (only 2.6% of the world average) in 2022, making it the region that saw the largest decline in the world (see Table 3-3).

Table 3-2   Proportion of FDI Obtained by Different Regions in the World to Global FDI (%)

Region	2015	2016	2017	2018	2019	2020	2021	2022
East Asia and the Pacific	22.35	19.41	25.53	63.55	31.20	46.06	38.49	35.21
Latin America and the Caribbean	11.66	8.08	9.27	22.22	11.58	11.60	9.88	11.74
South Asia	1.80	1.87	2.11	5.16	3.33	5.40	2.39	2.93
Sub-Saharan Africa	1.61	1.12	1.27	3.08	1.61	1.86	3.52	0.39

Source: Based on the data from the World Bank.

Table 3-3   Per capita FDI in Some Parts of the World (US$/person)

Region	2015	2016	2017	2018	2019	2020	2021	2022
East Asia and the Pacific	269.05	229.02	240.63	255.86	225.44	249.02	340.64	271.43
Latin America and the Caribbean	518.46	350.74	320.69	327.55	305.29	227.88	316.53	326.13
South Asia	28.00	28.34	25.47	26.44	30.45	36.63	26.32	27.93
Sub-Saharan Africa	44.03	29.53	26.1	26.62	24.47	20.67	62.59	5.91
World	373.05	363.83	289.47	123.04	219.7	163.41	265.93	230.3

Source: Based on the data from the World Bank.

3.2 Agricultural Production Has Long Remained at A Low Level, with Inadequate Food Self-sufficiency

The forecast model of the World Bank shows that, according to the existing economic growth trend, by 2030, the number of poor in Sub-Saharan Africa will reach 87% of the total number of poor in the world. According to the current increasing trend of hungry people, by 2030, Africa will become the region with the largest number of long-term hungry people. In addition, due to the fragile agricultural production environment and insufficient investment in agricultural factors, the agricultural production level in Africa is low and the grain output can hardly meet the basic survival needs, making it more uncertain to achieve the goal of zero hunger by 2030.

3.2.1 Fragile agricultural production environment

The fragile agricultural production environment, frequent climate disasters and violent social conflicts have made it more difficult to develop grain production. On the one hand, the unique geographical location of the African continent renders the agricultural ecological environment in this region extremely fragile, and vulnerable to various meteorological disasters such as droughts and floods caused by extreme weather, resulting in large-scale crop failures and crop yield reductions. For example, in March and April of 2019, hurricanes "Idai" and "Kenneth" hit Mozambique, Zimbabwe, Malawi and other countries in Southern Africa, seriously damaging a large number of crops to be harvested and limited agricultural infrastructure. In addition, African countries are also plagued by the invasion of pests and diseases. In early 2020, countries in the Horn of Africa suffered a serious locust plague, putting about 5 million people in eight East African countries into a food crisis. On the other hand, various violent conflicts have worsened the agricultural production environment. Some regions and countries in Africa are high-risk areas afflicted by frequent armed conflicts and unstable political situation. Even in 2020 and 2021, shrouded by the COVID-19 pandemic, terrorist attacks in Africa persisted unabatedly. Extremist organizations stepped up their activities in Africa, making agricultural production in this area unsustainable.

3.2.2   Low grain production capacity and seriously insufficient input of agricultural production factors

The long-term failure to substantively improve the level of agricultural development is also an important reason of food security and hunger in Africa. According to the relevant data of the World Bank, the grain yield of Sub-Saharan African countries was 1,031.64 kg/ha in 1978, which only increased slowly to 1,588.77 kg/ha by 2021. That is to say, over the past 40 more years, the grain yield only increased by 54% (see Table 3-4). Compared with the 88.97% increase in the world from 2,198.13 kg/ha to 4,153.72 kg/ha during the same period, the grain yield in Africa was less than 40% of the world average.

Table 3-4　　**Grain Yield of Sub-Saharan Africa and the World (kg/ha)**

Region	1978	1980	2012	2013	2014	2015
World	2,198.13	2,175.11	3,615.04	3,817.84	3,890.07	3,926.47
Sub-Saharan Africa	1,031.64 (46.93%)	1,064.54 (48.94%)	1,410.22 (39.01%)	1,325.25 (34.71%)	1,435.87 (36.91%)	1,437.31 (36.61%)
Region	2016	2017	2018	2019	2020	2021
World	4,011.04	4,073.45	4,029.56	4,125.45	4,116.43	4,153.72
Sub-Saharan Africa	1,402.19 (34.96%)	1,518.13 (37.27%)	1,525.19 (37.85%)	1,521.67 (36.88%)	1,605.74 (39.01%)	1,588.77 (38.25%)

Note: ( ) = the proportion of Sub-Saharan Africa to the world.
Source: Based on the data from the World Bank.

The average output of major food crops in Africa is lower than the world average. The average yields of potato and corn – the most important food crops in Africa – are less than 40% of the world average, being 3,030kg/ha and 2,276kg/ha, respectively; the average yield of rice is less than 50% of the world average, being 2,276kg/ha; and the average yields of wheat and cassava are also low, which are 67.27% and 80.50% of the world average, being 2,349kg/ha and 8,546 kg/ha, respectively (see Table 3-5).

Table 3-5   Output and Proportion of Major Food Crops in Africa

Region	Cassava	Corn	Paddy	Wheat	Potato Crops(Yams)
World average(kg/ha)	10,616	5,878	4,764	3,492	8,651
Africa average(kg/ha)	8,546 (80.50%)	2,276 (38.72%)	2,276 (47.77%)	2,349 (67.27%)	3,030 (35.02%)

Note: ( ) = the proportion of Africa average to the world average.

Source: Based on the data from the World Bank.

Despite the limited growth of grain supply, the consumption demand in Africa continues to show a trend of solid growth, resulting in a prominent contradiction between grain supply and demand. The population growth rate in Africa has stayed high for a long time, about 2.5% per year (the world average is slightly lower than 1% per year)[1], and the demand for food consumption is growing solidly, which brings additional pressure to the food system and economy. Meanwhile, due to many problems in grain production in African countries, such as low utilization rate of improved varieties, agrochemical products and agricultural machinery and equipment, and lack of field management ability, the level of grain production in this region is backward, and the growth of grain supply can hardly meet the growth of domestic consumption demand, directly leading to continuous expansion of population size offsetting the positive effect of improving food supply. From the relationship between food supply and demand, the demand gap of rice, wheat and corn increased from 58.01 million tons in 2010 to 82.237 million tons in 2021, accounting for 36.5% and 35.6% of the total consumption of staple foods in the same year, respectively, demonstrating the weak food self-protection ability and low food security level of African countries.

3.3 Fragile Food Supply System and High Dependence on Staple Food Imports, Easily Affected by the Fluctuation of International Food Prices

The grain industry system is weak in resilience and low in risk

---

1   International Food Policy Research Institute. *Global Food Policy Report 2023*. See:https://ebrary.ifpri. org/digital/collection/p15738coll2/id/136641, accessed on June 1, 2023.

resistance. The resilience of the grain industry system includes many dimensions such as grain supply, grain availability, grain utilization rate and grain market stability, among which the stability and sustainability of grain access are quite important. In 2021, the self-sufficiency rate of rice, wheat and corn in North Africa was 34.1%, and that of Sub-Saharan Africa was 76.1%, lower than the United Nations security standard of 85% (see Table 3-6). Additionally, the grain system in most African countries is not sound, with insufficient capacity building of grain reserves. In 2021, the stock consumption ratio of rice and wheat in Sub-Saharan Africa was 9.8% and 11.8%, respectively, far from the level of 17%-18% proposed by the FAO.[1] According to the relevant data of the African Union, the annual grain loss of Sub-Saharan Africa accounts for about 13% of the total output, among which the grain loss rates are as high as 59%, 19% and 18%, respectively in the three links of grain storage, transportation and processing and packaging.[2] Therefore, the above situation has inhibited the ability of African countries to resist various risks and respond to emergencies, leading to an increase in the vulnerability of the food security system in Africa.

Table 3-6   Food Self-sufficiency Rate in Sub-Saharan Africa (%)

	Average			Growth rate	
	2010-12	2020-22	2032	2013-22	2023-32
Cereal	83.5	81.9	77.6	0.09	-0.24
Meats	87.4	83.4	77.5	-0.71	-0.47
Sugar material	73.7	64.3	53.1	-0.61	-1.10
Edible oil	58.6	58.5	49.7	1.21	-1.46

Source: Based on the data from the World Bank.

The Food Price Monitoring and Analysis Bulletin issued by FAO in February 2023 shows that, 87.8% of lower-middle income countries, 93.0% of upper-

---

1 USDA Foreign Agricultural Service, see: https://apps.fas.usda.gov/psdonline/app/index.

2 FAO, The State of Food and Agriculture 2019: Moving forward on Food Loss and Waste Reduction, see: https://www. fao.org/3/ca6030en/ca6030en.pdf.

middle income countries and many other countries are experiencing double-digit inflation. In addition, about 87.3% of high-income countries are experiencing high food price inflation. The countries most seriously affected by the inflation are in Africa, North America, Latin America, South Asia, Europe and Central Asia. The food price inflation data shows that, Zimbabwe, a country of Sub-Saharan Africa, ranks first (see Table 3-7).[1]

Table 3-7   **Top 10 Countries in Food Price Inflation**

Country	Nominal food inflation	Real food inflation
Zimbabwe	264	41
Venezuela	158	26
Lebanon	143	22
Argentina	98	21
Türkiye	70	18
Surinam	61	17
Ghana	61	15
Sri Lanka	60	13
Rwanda	57	13
Laos	49	13

Source: https://www.gafs.info/home/.

3.4 Climate Change Leads to High Incidence of Disasters and A Series of Impacts

Climate change stands as one of the key causes of poverty in Africa, as climate change has greatly intensified the pressure brought by climate variability and extreme conditions, which undermined the food stability of the entire African continent, threatened Africa's ability to eradicate hunger, and aggravated extreme

---

1   See: https://www.gafs.info/home/.

poverty in Africa. The number of people in Africa falling into poverty due to climate change ranges between 32 million and 132 million. By 2030, climate change alone may put 100 million people into poverty.[1] In vulnerable developing countries and low-income countries, especially Sub-Saharan African countries, the poor and marginalized groups will be hit hardest. About 60% of the African population has no early warning system to deal with extreme weather and climate change,[2] and all kinds of abnormal weather conditions and their impacts will persist and become more and more serious.

3.4.1   Climate change has led to substantial drop of agricultural production rate in Africa

The rising temperature and the ensuing sea-level rise have directly impacted the agricultural and industrial production in Africa. On the one hand, rising temperature will have a negative impact on agricultural productivity, agricultural land and agricultural output in Africa, thus aggravating the problems of hunger and poverty in this continent. The temperature in all sub-regions of Africa experiences a rising trend, while the long-term temperature in the whole African region is abnormally high, and the number of extreme high-temperature days is also on the rise (see Figure 3-3 and Figure 3-4). Long-term persistent global warming and abnormal temperature have led to a sharp decline in agricultural productivity in Africa. Since 1961, the agricultural productivity in Africa has decreased by 34% due to rising temperature, making it the region with the serious decline of agricultural productivity in the world, constantly aggravating the risk of food insecurity and malnutrition in Africa. According to the statistics of the World Metrological Organization (WMO), the output of rain-fed crops in African countries will decrease by 50% due to climate change, and the output of crops in Sub-Saharan Africa will also decrease by about 20%.

---

1   See: *Revised Estimates of the Impact of Climate Change on Extreme Poverty by 2030* released by the Climate Change Group & Global Facility for Disaster Reduction and Recovery of the World Bank.

2   See: *State of the Climate in Africa 2021* released by the WMO.

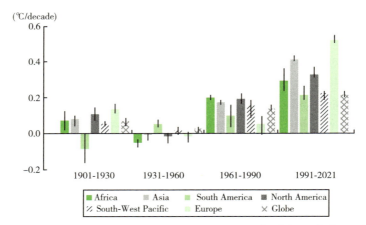

Figure 3-3   Trends of Average Temperature of African Sub-regions

Source: UK Meteorological Office.

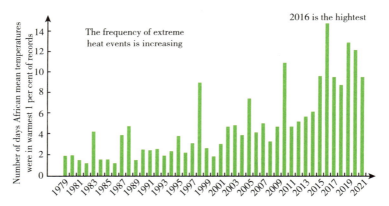

Figure 3-4   Annual Extreme High-temperature Weather in Africa, 1979-2021

Source: African Center of Meteorological Applications for Development (ACMAD), based on ERA5.

On the other hand, with the temperature rising, the relative sea-level rise in all parts of Africa may continue, which will lead to an increase in the frequency and severity of floods in low-lying areas and most sandy coastal areas. Low-lying coastal areas will also have to cope with the problems of decreasing land area, salinization of agricultural land, fish population reduction and migration caused by sea-level rise and climate change. By 2050, the losses related to sea-level rise in Sub-Saharan Africa countries may hit 2%-4% of GDP.[1]

---

1   See: *State of the Climate in Africa 2021* released by the WMO.

3.4.2   Extreme weather events have aggravated the vulnerability to food poverty and caused serious damage to infrastructure

Long-term drought is one of the major extreme weather events confronting Africa. One-third of Africans now live in drought-prone areas, most of which are concentrated in the Sahel, around the Horn of Africa and southern Africa.1 One-third of the global drought occurs in Sub-Saharan Africa, and long-term drought has led to long-term food poverty in these areas. Extreme weather events can significantly increase food security risks, especially for countries whose agricultural productivity is less than half of the global average.[2] Drought will also have a negative impact on the diversity of agricultural and animal husbandry production, and many countries in Sub-Saharan Africa will have to cope with semi-arid climate. In 2021, the climate in East Africa continued to deteriorate, and the equatorial and southern regions experienced the worst drought in the past 40 years, especially in southern Madagascar, where severe drought would last for at least two years.[3] Over the past 50 years, drought-related disasters have claimed more than 500,000 lives and caused more than US$ 70 billion in economic losses in Africa,[4] which aggravated Africa's vulnerability and led to serious food shortages. The Intergovernmental Panel on Climate Change (IPCC) estimates that by 2080, the arid and semi-arid areas in Africa will increase by 5%-8%, and the drought in the Horn of Africa will become more common.

Insufficient emergency response capacity and incomplete measures in Africa make it difficult to effectively address the problems caused by extreme weather such as tropical cyclones and large-scale floods. For example, in 2021, southern Africa was hit by tropical cyclone "Eloise" again, and more than 467,000 people in Mozambique and Madagascar were affected[5]. In Mozambique, in

1   See: *Climate Change and Poverty in Africa: Challenges and Initiatives* released by the United Nations Center for Regional Development (UNCRD).

2   See: Fuglie et al. (2020), Ritchie (2022).

3   See: *State of the Climate in Africa 2021* released by the WMO.

4   WMO, State of Climate Services report: Water. World Meteorological Organization, 2021, WMO-No.1278.

5   OCHA, 2021, Southern Africa Humanitarian Snapshot.

particular, over 60 resettlement sites and over 8,700 shelters were destroyed[1], over 43,000 people were displaced within the country and 34,500 people were evacuated. In addition, large-scale floods have had a wide impact on many African countries, such as extreme floods in South Sudan for the third consecutive year, affecting at least 835,000 people[2]. The rainstorm in Niger and the floods caused by it affected about 230,000 people, more than 12,000 houses were destroyed, nearly 6,000 hectares of arable land were flooded, and more than 10,000 livestock were lost.[3] A series of floods in Tanganyika, the Democratic Republic of the Congo affected more than 280,000 people (accounting for over 8% of the total population), causing 16 deaths and damaging more than 26,000 houses, 116 schools, 50 medical centers and 5,000 hectares of crops.[4]

3.4.3 Lack of water resources

Africa has experienced a high level of water resources pressure and climate change pressure, including changes in rainfall and temperature, leading to a significant decline in the availability of water resources. Water shortage has become a major problem faced by the poor all around the world . According to IPCC's estimates, the high pressure of water resources will affect about 250 million people in Africa.[5] In the fast-growing African economies, the demand for fresh water supply to maintain population growth is increasing, the demand for water in agriculture and industry is also increasing and increasingly frequent droughts and high temperature events exert additional pressure on the already scarce water resources. In 2021, 66 regions and more than 3.2 million people in Africa lacked water resources. Especially in Somalia, about 90% of the areas have limited access to water resources, and the southern and central areas have the most serious problems. Water resources are extremely scarce[6], and many wells, boreholes and berkads[7] have dried up. In 2021, southern Madagascar also

1   IOM, 2021, Mozambique Cyclone Eloise Response Plan.
2   OCHA, 2022, South Sudan Humanitarian Needs Overview 2022.
3   CHA, 2021, West and Central Africa: Weekly Regional Humanitarian Snapshot.
4   See: https://reliefweb.int/sites/reliefweb.int/files/resources/20210705_rdc_tanganyika_inondations.pdf.
5   IPCC, 2022, Climate Change 2022, Impacts, Adaptation and Vulnerability, Summary for Policymakers.
6   FAO/SWALIM, 2021, Somalia Drought Update.
7   A berkad is a water reservoir used in arid areas to collect water during the wet season for use in the dry season.

experienced the events of rivers drying up and water prices soaring. By the end of 2021, more than 70% people in southern Madagascar had no access to basic drinking water, and 50% people in this area were in bad need of water, sanitation and personal hygiene assistance.[1]

3.5   Regional Conflicts and Insecurity

Regional conflicts and insecurity and the ensuing large number of refugees have disrupted economic production activities and markets, damaged rural livelihoods and infrastructure, and aggravated poverty in African countries. Regional wars, conflicts and insecurity are the main reasons for the extreme poverty of the refugee population in Africa. In particular, the nine coups in seven countries in Central and West Africa in three years since 2020 have seriously aggravated poverty in various countries, such as Mali, Burkina Faso, Sudan and Chad (see Table 3-8). The number of extremely poor during the coup exceeded 10 million. The long-lasting conflicts and insecurity have disrupted economic production activities and markets in these countries and undermined rural livelihoods and infrastructure, and with untimely and insufficient assistance, it is difficult to alleviate and address the problem of poverty in these areas. In addition, resource competition is also an important cause of regional conflicts. For example, conflicts arising from resource competition in the northwest and southwest of Cameroon have also seriously disrupted the development of agriculture, animal husbandry, markets and trade, exerting a more serious impact on the rural poor.

Table 3-8   Coups and Poverty (US$2.15) in Seven West African Countries in the Past Three Years

Country	Time of coup	Number of the poor (thousands)	Poverty rate (%)
Gabon	August 2023	–	2.5
Mali	August 2020	–	14.8
	May 2021	348.21	
Burkina Faso	January and September 2022	691.14	30.5

---

1   See: *State of the Climate in Africa 2021* released by the WMO.

Continued

Country	Time of coup	Number of the poor (thousands)	Poverty rate (%)
Niger	July 2023	–	50.6
Guinea	September 2021	204.3	13.8
Sudan	October 2021	1,397.2	15.3
Chad	April 2021	623.63	30.9

Source: Based on the data from OECD's *Africa's Development Dynamics 2023: Investing in Sustainable Development,* and information about coups in relevant African countries.

Given regional conflicts and insecurity, the problem of internal and cross-border displacement in African countries is becoming increasingly prominent, while social instability is increasing. As far as Sub-Saharan Africa is concerned, the number of regional refugees has risen rapidly since 2010. By 2021, the number of refugees reached 7.06 million, the highest level since statistics were available (see Figure 3-5). In addition to refugees, the number of other people forcibly displaced in African countries, including asylum seekers, internally displaced persons, repatriates and others in need of international protection, is also increasing rapidly, especially in countries with serious food crisis.

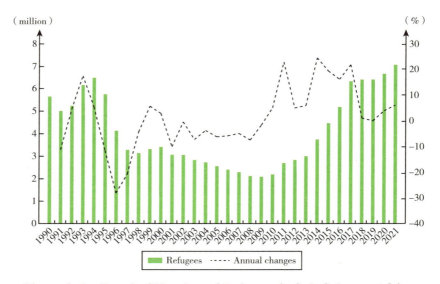

Figure 3-5 Trend of Number of Refugees in Sub-Saharan Africa

Source: Based on the World Development Indicators (WDI) data, updated, on May 10, 2023.

According to the statistical data of *Global Food Policy Report 2023*, the social instability in East Africa is the highest, with about 16.27 million forcibly displaced persons and 11.7 million internally displaced persons in eight countries with food crisis, mainly concentrated in Sudan (3.71 million), Somalia (2.97 million), Ethiopia (2.73 million), South Sudan (2.23 million) and Malawi (950,000). Following East Africa are Central Africa and Southern Africa, where more than 8.3 million people have been forcibly displaced due to conflicts in the Democratic Republic of the Congo and Mozambique, and political violence in the Central African Republic. Among them, the social instability in the Democratic Republic of the Congo is the most severe, with 5.7 million internally displaced persons and more than 520,000 refugees. There are about 1.03 million internally displaced persons in Mozambique. West Africa is also facing an increasingly serious displacement crisis. There are 7.23 million internally displaced persons in six food-crisis countries, with an obvious increase in Nigeria. At the end of 2022, the number of internally displaced persons reached 3.56 million, followed by Burkina Faso (1.88 million) and Cameroon (1.01 million). Due to the serious shortage of funds, food rations and other basic services in camps and settlements have been cut, aggravating the difficulties of forcibly displaced people and social instability in Africa.

3.6   Weak Infrastructure Can Hardly Support Socioeconomic Development

The basic conditions for Africa's development are still very weak, with the serious lag of infrastructure becoming a bottleneck holding back economic growth. Electricity access, Internet access and basic transportation are important indicators to measure development. Despite improvement of infrastructure construction in Sub-Saharan Africa in recent years, weak infrastructure is still an important factor restricting its economic development and poverty reduction progress.

In terms of electricity access, in 2021, less than 10% of the world's population had no access to electricity, but in Sub-Saharan Africa, the proportion amounted to nearly 50%, meaning that the current global population without electricity access was mainly concentrated in Sub-Saharan Africa countries (see Table 3-9). In 2022, the proportion of people with access to electricity in Africa was only 56%, and the proportion in urban areas was higher, reaching 82%, but the proportion in rural areas was only 36%, far less than half of that in urban areas (see Table 3-10). Regional and national differences between urban and rural areas are also very prominent. Among the 54 countries with available data, the proportion of people with access to electricity in rural areas in 47 countries is lower than the world average, among which the proportion in 14 countries is lower than 10%, that in 8 countries is lower than 20%, and that in 15 countries is lower than 40% (see Table 3-11). In many African countries, even where electricity can be used, the stability and reliability of power supply are relatively low due to unstable power supply and aging power facilities. Due to the absence or insufficiency of basic electricity supply, the industrialization progress in most African countries is very slow, especially in rural areas.

Table 3-9　　Proportion of Population with Access to Electricity (%)

Region	2012	2013	2014	2015	2016	2017	2018	2019	2020	2021
Sub-Saharan Africa	36.69	37.92	38.26	39.11	43.73	43.68	46.34	47.13	48.48	50.58
World	85.06	85.82	86.31	87.03	88.19	89.02	89.89	90.19	90.48	91.41

Source: Based on the data from the World Bank.

Table 3-10　Proportion of Urban and Rural Population with Access to Electricity by Region, 2022 (%)

Region	Proportion of total population with access to electricity	Proportion of urban population with access to electricity	Proportion of rural population with access to electricity
Southern Africa	54	81	27
Central Africa	28	56	5
East Africa	49	80	37
North Africa	98	99	97

Continued

Region	Proportion of total population with access to electricity	Proportion of urban population with access to electricity	Proportion of rural population with access to electricity
West Africa	53	84	26
Africa	56	82	36
World	90	97	82

Source: Based on the data from OECD's *Africa's Development Dynamics 2023: Investing in Sustainable Development*, see: https://www.oecd.org/dev/africa/development-dynamics/.

Table 3-11   Proportion of Urban and Rural Population with Access to Electricity by Country in Africa, 2022 (%)

No.	Country	Proportion of total population	Proportion of urban population	Proportion of rural population
Rural population with access to electricity accounts for less than 10% (14 countries)				
1	Burkina Faso	19	62	0
2	Equatorial Guinea	67	91	1
3	Congo, Dem.Rep.	19	41	1
4	Chad	11	41	2
5	Central African Republic	15	34	2
6	Burundi	12	64	3
7	Mauritania	51	88	4
8	Mozambique	31	75	4
9	sierra leone	26	55	5
10	South Sudan	7	14	6
11	Malawi	15	54	7
12	Angola	52	74	7
13	Libya	70	85	8
14	Liberia	28	45	8
Rural population with access to electricity accounts for 10%-20%(8 countries)				
15	Madagascar	34	70	11
16	Niger	19	48	13
17	Zambia	45	82	14
18	Congo,Rep.	50	66	15

Continued

No.	Country	Proportion of total population	Proportion of urban population	Proportion of rural population
Rural population with access to electricity accounts for 10%-20%(8 countries)				
19	Guinea-Bissau	33	56	15
20	Mali	51	94	16
21	Benin	41	66	18
22	Guinea	45	88	19
Rural population with access to electricity accounts for 20%-40%(15 countries)				
23	Tanzania	40	73	22
24	Togo	54	94	24
25	Nigeria	55	84	25
26	Djibouti	62	72	25
27	Cameroon	65	94	25
28	Botswana	72	91	26
29	Gabon	92	99	28
30	Gambia	62	81	32
31	Somalia	50	70	32
32	Uganda	42	70	33
33	Lesotho	47	78	35
34	Namibia	56	75	36
35	Zimbabwe	53	86	37
36	Rwanda	47	86	38
37	Eritrea	54	76	39
38	Ethiopia	51	93	39
Rural population with access to electricity accounts for 40%-80%(8 countries)				
39	Sudan	55	82	41
40	Côte d' Ivoire	70	94	43
41	Senegal	70	95	47
42	Kenya	71	94	63
43	Sao Tome and Principe	77	78	71
44	Ghana	86	95	74
45	South Africa	84	89	75
46	Eswatini	80	92	76

Continued

No.	Country	Proportion of total population	Proportion of urban population	Proportion of rural population
	Rural population with access to electricity accounts for more than 80% (8 countries)			
47	Comoros	87	100	81
48	Cabo Verde	94	94	94
49	Algeria	100	100	100
50	Mauritius	100	99	100
51	Seychelles	100	100	100
52	Morocco	100	100	100
53	Egypt	100	100	100
54	Tunisia	100	100	100

Source: Based on the data from OECD's *Africa's Development Dynamics 2023: Investing in Sustainable Development*, see: https://www.oecd.org/dev/africa/development-dynamics/.

In terms of Internet access, the rate in Africa is low, making it difficult for African countries to effectively use Internet platforms and technologies to create economic and social benefits, and enjoy the benefits of the Internet economy. With the constant development of the Internet era, the mobile Internet has changed the mode and method of economic development, becoming an important platform for participating in economic and social development. In 2019, only 33.2% of people in Africa had access to the Internet, far lower than the world average (53.6%). In Central Africa and East Africa, in particular, only 18.8% and 17.2% of the population has access to the Internet (see Table 3-12). At the same time, less than 10% of the population has access to the Internet in seven countries, namely Burkina Faso, Eritrea, Chad, Central African Republic, Uganda, South Sudan, and Burundi. This means that, Africa has not yet participated in the trend of global digitalization, digitalization development is slow on this continent, and it has not benefited from digital economic development.

Table 3-12   Proportion of Population with Access to the Internet by Region, 2019 (%)

Region	Proportion of population with Internet access
Southern Africa	38.2
Central Africa	18.8

Continued

Region	Proportion of population with Internet access
East Africa	17.2
North Africa	62.7
West Africa	36.3
Africa	33.2
World	53.6

Source: Based on the data from OECD's *Africa's Development Dynamics 2023: Investing in Sustainable Development*, see: https://www.oecd.org/dev/africa/development-dynamics/.

In terms of transportation, there isn't a complete transportation system covering the whole African continent. In Africa, transportation is mainly dependent on road network, leading the high transportation cost. On the one hand, the total route of African roads that contribute 85% of cargo transportation is 2.64 million kilometers, and the road density is only 1/2 of that of Latin America and 1/3 of that of Asia. The road network construction in many African countries is not sound. Highways are only between cities, and there are almost no direct highways between urban and rural areas. For example, paved roads in Malawi only account for 26.36%, major highways has not been all paved, and there are almost no paved regional roads (see Table 3-13). On the other hand, African railways are not popular, only carrying 1%-2% of the world's passenger and freight volumes. The total length of rail lines is 90,000 kilometers, accounting for 6% of the world, and 26% of them are not connected with neighboring countries. No railway networks between countries and regions have been formed. For example, 15 countries such as Central Africa Republic and Somalia have no railways, and the total length of rail lines of many countries is low (see Table 3-14). In addition, Africa's aviation and shipping are also seriously lagging behind. There is no big port in Africa, and most airports are non-civilian with few routes. The insufficiency of all kinds of basic transportation leads to extremely high transportation costs in Africa. For example, the cost of transporting a container from Mombasa to Uganda by land is as high as US$3,000-US$4,000, while the cost of shipping a container from China to Mombasa is only over US$1,000.

Table 3-13　　　　　　　　　**Road Network in Malawi**

Road grades	Paved roads (km)	Unpaved roads (km)	Total (km)	Ratio of paved roads of various grades to all roads (%)
Primary highway	2,809	548	3,357	83.68
Secondary highway	442	2,683	3,125	14.14
Tertiary highway	44	4,077	4,121	1.07
Regional roads	8	3,492	3,500	0.22
City roads	770	578	1,348	57.12
Total	4,073	11,378	15,451	26.36

Source: Based on the data of the Malawi Roads Authority (2011).

Table 3-14　　**Total Railway Mileage in Some African Countries (km)**

Country	Total railway kilometrage	Country	Total railway kilometers
Burkina Faso	518	Madagascar	673
Algeria	4,000.5	Mauritania	728
Botswana	886	Zimbabwe	3,120
Côte d' Ivoire	639	Congo, Dem.Rep.	3,684
Cameroon	884	Tunisia	1,777
Morocco	2,295	Zambia	1,248
Gabon	648	Sudan	2,747
South Africa	20,953		

Source: Based on the data from the World Bank.

3.7　Underemployment, Informal Employment and Agricultural Employment Lead to Limited Income Increase

Underemployment is the root cause of poverty in Africa. High unemployment of the labor force as a result of the low-level overall economic development is an important challenge facing Sub-Saharan Africa, and the main reason for the existence of a large number of extremely poor. According to the moderate statistics of the International Labour Organization (ILO), the unemployment rate of the labor force in Sub-Saharan Africa is on the rise. Especially since the COVID-19 pandemic, the employment situation in this region has become more severe, with its unemployment rate reaching 12.65% in

2020. Despite some decline in 2021 and 2022, the rate still exceeded 12%, standing at more than twice the global average (see Table 3-15). In addition, most of the employed labor force in Sub-Saharan Africa is in informal employment and agricultural employment, which are extremely unstable.

Table 3-15   Unemployment Rate of Labor Force, 2012-2022(%)

Region	2012	2013	2014	2015	2016	2017	2018	2019	2020	2021	2022
Sub-Saharan Africa	11.49	11.12	11.19	11.28	11.29	11.30	11.30	11.57	12.56	12.42	12.35
World	6.14	6.12	5.98	6.01	6.00	5.87	5.70	5.54	6.90	6.20	5.77

Source: Based on the data from the World Bank.

According to the relevant data of the World Bank, although the proportion of agricultural employees in Sub-Saharan Africa has declined, the rate of decline is very slow. In 2000, the proportion of agricultural employees was 61.91%, and in 2021, the proportion only dropped to 51.57%, a drop of only 10 percentage points. At present, the world average proportion of agricultural employees is only 26.42% (see Table 3-16). It can be therefore concluded that promoting the development of non-agricultural industries in Africa and creating more non-agricultural employment opportunities are important paths for poverty reduction in Africa in the future.

Table 3-16   Proportion of Agricultural Employment, 2000-2021(%)

Region	2000	2001	2002	2003	2004	2005	2006	2007	2008	2009	2010
Sub-Saharan Africa	61.91	61.67	61.35	60.99	60.55	60.27	59.60	58.90	58.35	57.82	57.04
World average	39.73	39.34	39.02	38.52	37.36	36.43	35.38	34.44	33.88	33.38	32.74
Region	2011	2012	2013	2014	2015	2016	2017	2018	2019	2020	2021
Sub-Saharan Africa	56.24	55.58	55.32	54.21	53.39	53.10	52.61	52.02	51.58	51.96	51.57
World average	31.80	30.93	30.07	29.15	28.53	28.01	27.50	26.87	26.39	26.95	26.42

Source: Based on the data from the World Bank.

The second typical feature of employment in Africa is the high proportion of informal employment. In many African countries, 80%-90% of employment is informal employment, for example, 93% in Mali, 91.7% in Côte d'Ivoire, 90.2% in Senegal, 88.2% in Zimbabwe, 87.8% in Rwanda, 84.8% in Zambia, and 80.9% in Lesotho. Informal employment includes domestic helpers, street vendors, garbage collectors and vendors, among others. Without any formal contracts or social security from employers, informal employees are very likely to lose their jobs in case of risks or emergencies. For example, during the COVID-19 pandemic, 5 million people were unemployed in Nigeria, 2 million people were unemployed in the Democratic Republic of the Congo, and 150,000 people were unemployed in Ethiopia in the gardening sector alone in the first half of 2020.

There are two main reasons for the low proportion of formal employment in Africa. First, there is a shortage of highly skilled labor in Africa. Second, the secondary and tertiary industries are backward, and unable to offer sufficient employment opportunities.

These two problems were very prominent in the process of the author's field research.

The authors did researches with some Chinese-funded enterprises in Malawi. Heads of the enterprises all noted that, it was easier to hire unskilled workers in Africa with relatively low labor employment cost, but it was very difficult to hire skilled workers. A hotel management company noted that skilled employees could be retained only by paying wages higher than the local average level. For example, the minimum wage in the local hotel industry then was only 15,000 kwachas per month, while the average wage paid by the company to local employees amounted to 60,000 kwachas per month. The authors also interviewed local employees during the research, who generally said that, the high salary paid by the hotel was the main reason for staying in the hotel for a long time. The person in charge of another construction enterprise also said that, it was easy to find unskilled laborers locally, whose wage was around 700 kwachas per day. However, the wage of local skilled workers, such as operators and drivers of various machinery, was 1,500 kwachas per day, in addition to special travel subsidies.

During the authors' field research tour in Malawi, it is found that, two doormen in the hotel where he stayed graduated from a local university of science and technology, majoring in computer and communication technology. As they failed to find a job of their specialty half a year after graduation, they came to this hotel to serve as doormen, providing guidance services for tourists. They had been working in this hotel for two years, and their monthly salary was 40,000 kwachas. Over the past two years, they had been looking for professional jobs but in vain.

Due to the lack of employment opportunities and the low level of agricultural production, many people, to meet the basic survival needs, operate non-agricultural small businesses in the countryside, which leads to the high competition of small businesses in villages, each only maintaining the lowest profit level. When the authors did researches in rural areas of Tanzania, the small-scale business mainly in the tertiary industry was an important way for local farmers to make a living. According to a field survey in Africa, the authors found that, more than 20 small shops were in Wasmba village with only over 100 households in Tanzania. This low-cost and low-return business format is a very common way of informal economy in Tanzania.

3.8 The Overall Improvement of the Quality of African Population Still Faces Many Challenges

Clean drinking water is an important prerequisite for public hygiene and health. During the fight against poverty, China has also taken drinking water for the poor as an important indicator to eradicate poverty. Also highly concerned about the safety of drinking water in Africa, the international community has carried out many assistance projects on improving drinking water. However, judging from the current situation, the population of Sub-Saharan Africa has made relatively slow progress in drinking water safety. By 2020, only 64.41% of the population in Sub-Saharan Africa, including urban population, could enjoy basic drinking water (see Table 3-17). Therefore, the proportion of rural population who could enjoy basic drinking water should be even lower, far below the world average.

Table 3-17   Proportion of Population with Basic Drinking Water,2012-2020(%)

Region	2012	2013	2014	2015	2016	2017	2018	2019	2020
Sub-Saharan Africa	56.48	57.51	58.55	59.60	60.62	61.63	62.60	63.57	64.41
World		76.69	77.33	77.97	78.61	79.23	79.87	80.48	81.09	81.67

Source: Based on the data from the World Bank.

The overall improvement of the quality of the African population is still facing severe challenges. Education, especially basic education, has always been a focus of international assistance to Africa. Although the basic education in Africa have been significantly improved, and the enrollment rate of primary education has basically reached 100%, the enrollment rate of secondary education in Africa is still relatively low. Over the past decade, in particular, the enrollment rate of secondary education in Sub-Saharan Africa countries has not improved significantly, which is more than 20 percentage points lower than the world average. In 2020, the secondary education enrollment rate in Africa only reached 43.91%, which means that a large number of African laborers have not mastered good skills (see Table 3-18). This can also be seen from the adult literacy rate. In 2020, the adult literacy rate in Sub-Saharan Africa was only 67.27%, nearly 20 percentage points lower than the world average (see Table 3-19). In 2022, the literacy rate of young people aged 15-24 in Africa was only 78.6%, 11.6 percentage points lower than the world average, and the literacy rates of all kinds of young people in various sub-regions in Africa were also lower than the world average (see Table 3-20).

Table 3-18   Enrollment Rate at Different Stages of Education,2012-2020 (%)

		2012	2013	2014	2015	2016	2017	2018	2019	2020
Enrollment rate in primary education	Sub-Saharan Africa	99.59	99.84	99.35	97.90	98.09	98.53	99.15	99.05	98.75
	World	103.68	103.93	102.69	102.35	103.80	103.65	101.22	101.43	101.85
Enrollment rate in secondary education	Sub-Saharan Africa	42.00	44.63	43.37	43.86	43.20	43.40	43.57	43.73	43.91
	World	63.79	64.90	65.65	65.71	65.83	66.20	66.27	–	–

Source: Based on the data from the World Bank.

Table 3-19   **Adult Literacy Rate, 2012-2020 (%)**

Region	2012	2013	2014	2015	2016	2017	2018	2019	2020
Sub-Saharan Africa	61.49	62.35	63.00	63.60	64.31	64.69	66.14	67.06	67.27
World	84.76	84.95	85.40	85.56	86.01	86.25	86.28	86.66	86.81

Source: Based on the data from the World Bank.

Table 3-20   **Literacy Rate of Young People in Different Regions, 2022 (%)**

Region	Literacy rate of population aged 15-24	Literacy rate of female population aged 15-24	Literacy rate of male population aged 15-24
Southern Africa	87.7	87.9	87.7
Central Africa	74.6	70.9	78.7
East Africa	82.7	82.8	82.7
North Africa	88.7	86.8	90.5
West Africa	68.0	62.0	74.6
Africa	78.6	76.1	81.4
World	90.2	89.2	91.4

Source: Based on the data from OECD's *Africa's Development Dynamics 2023: Investing in Sustainable Development*, see: https://www.oecd.org/dev/africa/development-dynamics/.

3.9 Summary

From the external environment, unfavorable economic environment and extreme weather events have constrained Africa's economic growth. On the one hand, the unbalanced macroeconomic conditions such as persistent inflation and tight monetary policy around the world confront African countries with the highest level of public debt in decades, which, coupled with the long-term decline of aid budget and the increase of debt interest burden, leads to the lack of stamina for economic recovery in Africa. On the other hand, the impact of global climate change, especially large-scale extreme weather events such as drought and flood, has greatly intensified the pressure brought by climate variability and extreme conditions, causing disastrous damage to agricultural production, food security and infrastructure in Africa, threatening Africa's ability to end hunger, and aggravating extreme poverty in Africa.

From the internal environment of Africa, slow economic growth and stable population growth, aggravating food crisis, persistent regional conflicts and weak development conditions are multiple internal factors not conducive to development, making it difficult to promote poverty reduction and development in Africa. First of all, given Africa's slow economic growth, it is difficult to effectively drive poverty reduction. Under the pressure of low urbanization rate and high population growth, it is difficult for slow economic growth to deliver its poverty reduction benefits, while the heavy debt burden and low-level foreign investment also lead to weak economic growth momentum in Africa. Secondly, the fragile agricultural production environment, low grain production capacity and low self-sufficiency rate in Africa have greatly increased the market fragility and risk of African countries, resulting in a significant decline in food accessibility in Africa. Furthermore, regional conflicts and insecurity and the resulting large number of refugees have disrupted economic production activities and markets, damaged rural livelihoods and infrastructure, and aggravated poverty in African countries. Finally, the basic conditions for development in Africa are still very weak, with insufficient employment and low population quality significantly hindering the process of poverty reduction.

On the whole, the short-term prospects of African countries are extremely uncertain, because the prospects of the region are closely related to the development of the global economy and the pressing socio-political and security situation faced by some countries. The shortage of funds in Africa will also affect the long-term prospects of the region, because such shortage may force countries to reduce resources in key development sectors such as health, education and infrastructure, thus weakening the growth potential of African countries.[1] How to effectively promote the process of poverty reduction in Africa requires the joint efforts of African countries and regional organizations.

---

1   IMF, *Regional Economic Outlook for Africa*, see: https://www.imf.org/en/publications/reo?sortby=Date&series=Sub-Saharan%20Africa, accessed on June 1, 2023.

Chapter 4　Major Issues on Poverty Reduction in Africa

African countries suffering from serious poverty problems have to rely on external investment and assistance to address poverty, but they are also constantly strengthening their own capability of independent development. In terms of politics, African countries have been strengthening the development of political democracy and the reform of economic system, and initiating various African revival plans. After the establishment of the African Union (AU), they also put forward the African Peer Review Mechanism (APRM) to promote the development among member States. In terms of economy, African leaders have formulated the New Partnership for Africa's Development (NEPAD) and won the support of Western countries. The African Union has formulated the *2050 Africa's Integrated Maritime Strategy* to develop the blue economy, and African countries have formulated appropriate financial strategies to promote local economic development and provide financial support to poor families. In terms of regional cooperation, the Economic Community of West African States (ECOWAS), the East African Community (EAC), the Common Market for Eastern and Southern Africa (COMESA) and the Southern African Development Community (SADC) have been effectively promoting the development of poverty reduction in an extensive range of fields, such as infrastructure, finance, education, health and security.

4.1 Poverty Reduction Strategy and Progress of the African Union (AU)

The African Union (AU), consisting of 55 African countries, is an all-African political entity with political, economic and military integration, aiming to help Africa develop its economy, promote the process of political, social and economic integration; promote pan-African cooperation on various fields and improve people's living standards. The AU and international institutions should strengthen their partnership and cooperate to promote the construction of free trade zones on the African continent and the implementation of infrastructure development plans in Africa. China has maintained long-term friendly cooperation with the AU, providing assistance to Africa, and maintaining communication with the AU on key international issues such as climate change and the 2030 Agenda for Sustainable Development. Other countries also support the policies put forward by the AU, and the process of poverty reduction in the AU has also been supported by international institutions. Poverty eradication has always been an important issue in the development of African countries. To achieve this goal, in 2015, the AU adopted a long-term master plan called *Agenda 2063*, aiming at building a new Africa with regional integration and peace and prosperity in the next 50 years.

4.1.1 New Partnership for Africa's Development (NEPAD)

The New Partnership for Africa's Development (NEPAD)[1] covers a series of strategies for reducing poverty and boosting sustainable development, including improving access to education and health care, promoting private sector investment and economic growth, advocating good governance and democracy, and addressing environmental and climate change issues. Africa's unique challenge lies mainly in its long-term failure to achieve economic growth. It is particularly important to note that agriculture occupies a major position in the vast majority of poor communities. Therefore, efforts to eradicate extreme poverty must be focused on improving agricultural production and productivity.

---

1   See: https://au.int/en/nepad.

Additionally, commodities in Africa are weak and inefficient in marketing, which causes farmers to fall into poverty, who are faced with such problems as damaged harvest and low commodity prices, and are also exploited by middlemen, affecting their profits and income.

4.1.2 African Continental Free Trade Area (AfCFTA)

The exchange rate systems vary among African countries. At present, about half of the economies have adopted a pegged exchange rate system, while the other half have chosen a more flexible exchange rate arrangement. The African Continental Free Trade Area (AfCFTA), launched in January 2021, is an important milestone in Africa's economic integration. The agreement cancels 90% tariffs among member countries, realizing the barrier-free flow of services, capital and personnel, which will enhance the convenience and freedom of trade, stimulate the vitality of intra-African trade, promote the development of regional supply chains, and further enhance the cohesion and competitiveness of the market. However, at the 36th Summit of the African Union, African Union Commission (AUC) Chairperson emphasized the uncertainty of the international situation, the intensification of geopolitical conflicts and the challenges faced by the global economic governance system, which had a far-reaching impact on Africa.

4.1.3 Strategy to deal with food security

Judging from the planning of agricultural development in the AU's *Agenda 2063*, the future agricultural development in Africa will focus on introducing external agricultural technology and experience to promote agricultural modernization, paying attention to social and ecological benefits, including improving food safety and environmental protection. According to the Comprehensive Africa Agricultural Development Programme (CAADP), African countries plan to invest 10% of their financial budget in agriculture every year to address food security by relying on internal forces. However, only 13 countries, including Burundi, Burkina Faso, the Republic of Congo, Ethiopia, Ghana, Guinea, Madagascar, Malawi, Mali, Niger, Senegal, Zambia and Zimbabwe, once reached the target of 10% investment, and only 7 countries have been able to maintain a relatively stable 10% investment in agriculture. On average, the investment in agriculture only accounts for about 4% of public expenditure in African countries.

4.1.4　Infrastructure construction strategy

According to the implementation of the first ten-year plan (2014-2023) of the African Union's *Agenda 2063*, Africa has made remarkable progress in accelerating the construction of a free trade zone on the African continent and promoting sustainable socio-economic development. At present, 54 AU member states have signed the African Continental Free Trade Area (AfCFTA). As of November, 2022, 44 member countries had submitted their ratification documents, making this agreement the FTA with the largest number of member States since the establishment of the World Trade Organization (WTO). In practice, positive progress has been made in trade integration.

In 2021, African countries adopted 71 priority projects in the second priority action plan of the Programme for Infrastructure Development in Africa (PIDA) for 2021-2030 through the AU summit. These projects cover transportation, communication, energy, water conservancy, agriculture and other sectors, covering more than 40 African Union countries. The implementation of these projects will help improve the infrastructure level of the African continent and promote economic development and sustainable growth.

4.1.5　Education strategy for the African continent

With a full hearing to the voices of the people on the African continent, the African Union's *Agenda 2063* has identified seven major themes for Africa's development, among which the realization of the third aspiration (an Africa of good governance, democracy, respect for human rights, justice and the rule of law) and the sixth aspiration (an Africa whose development is people-driven, relying on the potential of African people, especially its women and youth, and caring for children) is inseparable from the gender equality in girls' education. UNESCO's assistance to girls' education in Sub-Saharan Africa has synergy with the AU, and UNESCO's vision of gender equality in girls' education is completely consistent with the AU.

The Continental Education Strategy for Africa (CESA 2016-25) has identified 12 strategic objectives and their action areas, the fifth of which is "accelerate processes leading to gender parity and equity", and the action areas include "ensure successful progression from one level to another throughout the system and mobilize communities to become partners". In addition, the strategy emphasizes stimulating teachers' enthusiasm, using information technology to guarantee the right to education, and launching comprehensive and effective literacy campaigns. UNESCO's educational assistance for girls in Sub-Saharan Africa is in line with the education strategy of the region.

4.1.6 Strategy for encouraging employment and entrepreneurship

(1) Policies to encourage women and youth

The African Union's *Agenda 2063* encourages African women and youth to actively participate in agricultural production, and provide policy support in means of production and finance. This includes developing and implementing affirmative policies and advocacy to ensure women's increased access to land and inputs, and ensuring that at least 30% of agricultural financing are accessed by women. The agenda is also dedicated to promoting women's and young people's access to financial resources for investment to improve their economic rights and interests.

(2) AU-FAO develops agricultural opportunities with African youth

In 2022, the FAO and the AU jointly published *Investment Guidelines for Youth in* Agrifood *Systems in Africa* and *Youth-sensitive value chain analysis and development*. These two documents are the results of a joint program jointly implemented by FAO, UNIDO and African Union Commission (AUC). Through value chain skills development training, capacity-building activities and workshops on financing and market access, the program have supported more than 700 young entrepreneurs. This move has raised people's awareness of the importance of youth employment and entrepreneurship, and created a more favorable environment for young people to participate in the agrifood system.

However, despite these positive efforts, Africa are still confronted with some challenges. Low income and insufficient research funds are one of the main reasons leading to brain drain in Africa. The funds for scientific and technological development and attracting talents are very limited, since the primary task of the absolute majority of African countries is to address the basic survival issues of their citizens. In Africa, except South Africa, the investment in science and technology only accounts for 0.2% of the gross national product. Therefore, despite some progress, Africa still faces constraints in the support for education and employment.

4.1.7   Financial support strategy

The AU has formulated the *2050 Africa's Integrated Maritime Strategy* to support and encourage the development of dynamic, environmentally friendly and sustainable blue economy. In 2022, during the 27th Conference of the Parties to the *United Nations Framework Convention on Climate Change*, the World Bank also announced the Blue Economy for Resilient Africa Program (BE4RAP), which further emphasized the importance of the blue economy to Africa's sustainable development.

Over a long time, Africa is confronted with severe challenges in poverty reduction. As the only regional organization representing the African continent, the AU regards ensuring poverty reduction in Africa as an important goal, and regards the implementation of the UN poverty reduction strategy as the key way to achieve this goal. Nevertheless, a certain gap is found between the AU's policy design and implementation judging from the actual results, because the financial and educational environments have exerted a negative impact on the AU's agenda of economic development and poverty reduction.

4.2   Poverty Reduction Strategies of Regional Organizations in Africa

In Africa, regional organizations promote the process of poverty reduction. The Economic Community of West African States (ECOWAS), the East African Community (EAC), and the Southern African Development Community (SADC) have developed a series of poverty reduction strategies for the goal of eradicating poverty, including *Vision 2050 of ECOWAS*, *Vision 2050* and *Regional Indicative Strategic Development Plan (RISDP) 2020-2030* developed by the ECOWAS and the SADC, and *Somalia's Ninth National Development Plan 2020-2024* developed by the EAC in 2021 (see Table 4-1).

Table 4-1   **Poverty Reduction Strategies of Some Regional Organizations in Africa**

Country	Policy documents	Goal of poverty reduction	Specific measures
Economic Community of West African States (ECOWAS)	*Vision 2050 of Economic Community of West African States (ECOWAS)*	Improve the living standard of citizens in the region, and reduce poverty	Specific measures in this regard include making the best use of demographic dividend to improve people's living conditions and education level, creating good employment opportunities for young people and women, and strengthening the resilience of the public health system
Southern African Development Community (SADC)	*Vision 2050 and Regional Indicative Strategic Development Plan (2020-2030) (RISDP2020-2030)*	Realize such goals as sustainable economic growth, socio-economic development and eradication of poverty	RISDP 2020-2030 operationalizes the SADC Vision 2050, which is a long-term ambition by SADC that sets out the aspirations of the Region until 2050. It will also ensure the coordination of policies, strategies and initiatives to support cross-border infrastructure and services; It identifies diversified regional infrastructure and services to promote the development of goods, services and skills and regional energy markets, including renewable energy; information and communication technology, water and transportation

Continued

Country	Policy documents	Goal of poverty reduction	Specific measures
East African Community (EAC)	*National Development Plan 2020-2024*	Effectively promote the development of **poverty reduction**; In the future, the cooperation mechanism will continue to play itsrole in reducing and alleviating debts and guiding African countries to deploy poverty reduction work	The objectives of poverty reduction strategy involve an extensive range of sectors such as education, health and security. Poverty reduction and growth strategies are developed. Relevant government departments timely release information on poverty diagnosis and policy objectives, actively seek national and local participation, and consult civil society and the private sector
	EAC Agenda 2050	Reduce poverty through the strategy of structural development and reconstruct countries	Poverty reduction measures of countries in Agenda 2050 of the East African Community (EAC): Rwanda's 2020 development plan aims at developing human resources and promoting regional and global economic development through structural economic transformation; Tanzania's 2025 plan is to encourage work, creativity and reform, create a learning society, improve infrastructure and promote investment; Kenya's 2030 development plan is to achieve the regional development goals of the EAC and abide by regional and global development commitments; Uganda's 2040 development plan aims to strengthen the economic foundation and gain more opportunities for cooperation. It is estimated that by 2050, the per capita income of the member countries of the EAC will increase tenfold, bringing the region to the middle and high income level

Source:Based on the information released by different organizations.

4.3 Poverty Reduction Strategies and Specific Actions of African Countries

4.3.1 African countries' poverty reduction and agricultural development plans

Influenced by the above strategies, African countries have also been actively adjusting their agricultural policies, which, to a certain extent, have effectively addressed the food security problem, leading to a positive trend of decline in the poverty level of rural areas. It should be noted, however, that although agricultural policies in various countries have achieved results to some extent, only a few farmers, not the vast rural population, have benefited from such policies.

(1) Tanzania: Agricultural Support Policy

In 2015, Tanzania launched a micro, small and medium-sized enterprise plan to promote the livelihood of small farmers and fishermen. The implementation of the plan has led to employment growth and food security improvement, while helping reduce rural poverty. In Tanzania, the policies include agriculture and animal husbandry policies, development plans for the agricultural sector, and micro, small and medium-sized enterprise plans.

(2) Sierra Leone: Agricultural Poverty Reduction Strategy

Sierra Leone's poverty reduction strategy is a national multi-sectoral strategy from 2008 to 2012, mainly aiming to provide stable power supply, improve the quantity and added-value production capacity of agriculture and fisheries, develop the national transportation network, and ensure sustainable human development by providing better social services, with a focus on addressing the problems of food insecurity and malnutrition.

(3) Zambia: The Farmer Input Support Programme (FISP) and the Farm Support Programme (FSP)

The Farmer Input Support Programme (FISP) aims to resolve the problem of crop output reduction after continuous drought and flood seasons, especially corn output, as these disasters have weakened the assets foundation of many small farmers. The FSP has not only made important contributions to the success of small-scale farmers, but also promoted rural development and poverty alleviation by increasing household income. The beneficiaries of the FSP are vulnerable groups, while the FISP mainly supports small-scale farmers.

4.3.2   Infrastructure construction plans of some African countries

In Sub-Saharan Africa, the government's support for infrastructure construction is limited. Most countries in this region are facing the problem of poverty and weakness, and it is difficult to attract investment in infrastructure projects. Due to limited funds, many African countries mainly rely on the support of international organizations such as the United Nations, the World Bank, the International Monetary Fund and the African Development Bank to develop infrastructure projects.

(1) Digital Village Initiative (DVI) for Sustainable Agriculture

At present, nine countries in Africa are participating in the pilot phase of Digital Village Initiative (DVI), namely Ghana, Kenya, Liberia, Malawi, Niger, Nigeria, Senegal (a Sub-Saharan African country), Somalia and Zimbabwe. In Senegal (a Sub-Saharan African country), more than 300,000 farmers have registered on the local digital platform SAIDA. The main obstacles of the program include lack of entrepreneurship and technical education or skills, insufficient investment, weak infrastructure and imperfect supervision and taxation institutions.

(2) Ethiopia: United Nations Sustainable Development Cooperation Framework (UNSDCF) 2020-2026

According to the cooperation framework, during the period from 2020 to 2026, in order to support Ethiopia to realize the *2030 Agenda for Sustainable Development*, the total budget of the work planned and implemented by United Nations agencies in Ethiopia is about US$ 7.1 billion. This cooperation framework is signed to help Ethiopia achieve sustainable development goals in various sectors through the concerted action of United Nations agencies, in efforts to promote the country's sustainable economic, social and environmental growth.[1]

(3) Mauritania: Receiving financial assistance from financial organizations

Faced with limited financial resources, the Mauritanian government usually needs to seek financial support from international financial institutions such as the World Bank, the International Monetary Fund and the African Development Bank, as well as financial institutions in Arab states such as the Arab Fund for Economic and Social Development and the Islamic Development Bank. Over the recent five years, the Mauritanian government has received about US$5 billion in foreign aid, of which the loan is about US$3 billion, and the rest is aid and aid loans. Most of these funds are invested in infrastructure construction, mainly in electricity (about US$900 million, accounting for 17%), water conservancy and water supply and drainage (about US$900 million, accounting for 17%), highways (about US$560 million, accounting for 12%), and ports (about US$340 million, accounting for 7%), and funds invested in agriculture, medical care, education, food security and other sectors each account for about 5%.[2]

(4) Mali: Strategic Framework for Growth and Poverty Reduction

The Strategic Framework for Growth and Poverty Reduction (SFGPR) is Mali's poverty reduction strategy, covering a series of policies and plans aimed at reducing poverty, including improving agricultural productivity, promoting rural development, improving the availability of basic services such as health care and education, promoting private sector investment and economic growth, and strengthening governance and promoting democracy. [3]

4.3.3 Policies related to education development in some African countries

African countries also attach great importance to education development,

---

1 Center for African Union Studies, see: https://caus.tute.edu.cn/info/1085/1607.htm.

2 Based on Mauritainia statistics of the World Bank.

3 See: https://www.worldbank.ora/en/countrv/mali/brief/stratedic-framework-for-arowth-and-poverty-reduction.

such as Tanzania and Zambia, but there are still gender inequality, educational inequality and backwardness in education. On the whole, Africa's education level is low.

(1) Tanzania

In Tanzania, the education sector pays attention to different stages to ensure that all groups have equal access to education, including preschool education, secondary education, special education and higher education. These measures are aimed at ensuring that all people can benefit from education, regardless of their group. Tanzania's efforts in the field of education are aimed at ensuring that people can get equal and high-quality education, thus enhancing their personal abilities and promoting the overall development of society.

(2) Zambia

The Gender Equity and Women's Empowerment Project (GEWEL) aims to support the government of Zambia to increase women's access to livelihood support. The focus of the project is to provide loans to support women to engage in income-generating activities, thus improving their livelihood. In addition, the project also pays attention to disadvantaged girls in extremely poor families and provides them with access to secondary education, thus breaking the cycle of poverty.

4.3.4　Employment policies in some African countries

Some African countries have also developed a series of employment strategies for specific groups, vigorously supporting the employment of young people in rural areas. Due to limited funds, however, most projects need the support of international financial organizations.

(1) Tanzania: Youth Agribusiness Initiative

Tanzania has developed the strategy of Building a Better Tomorrow: Youth Agribusiness Initiative (BBT-YIA) for the period 2022-2030, which aims to strengthen youth participation in the agricultural sector in order to achieve sustainable livelihood improvement. This agenda aims to increase youth employment by 1 million by 2030 and increase the growth rate of the agricultural sector to 10%. However, due to Tanzania's cultural norms and prejudice against women and people with disabilities, the dependence rate and poverty rate of young people remain high. As a result, their participation in governance and political processes is low, and their access to employment, education and economic opportunities is limited.

(2) Mali: Skills Development and Youth Employment Project

Mali implements the Skills Development and Youth Employment Project, a project to promote the skills development of young people, especially those in rural areas, and provide employment opportunities in agriculture and other sectors. The project is supported by the African Development Bank.

4.3.5 Financial strategies adopted by some African countries

(1) Nigeria: Central bank digital currency policy

The financial development in Sub-Saharan Africa mainly depends on external forces. For example, some countries in Africa are exploring the possibility of adopting a central bank digital currency (CBDC). For example, eNaira has been launched in Nigeria. CBDC can deliver a number of benefits, such as improving financial inclusion, reducing remittance costs and reducing dependence on private cryptocurrencies that may hinder currency transmission and facilitate illegal capital flows.

(2) Tanzania: Development fund policies

The government has launched the Women Development Fund (WDF) and the Youth Development Fund (YDE), through which soft loans are provided to women and young people to support their development.[1] The allocation of these funds is managed by community departments and decided by their board of directors, of which women are allocated 5% and 5% for youth. These arrangements are made to help economically disadvantaged women and young people with difficulty in obtaining loans from financial institutions because of the lack of collateral. These loans are interest-free (CAG, 2022).[2]

1,2　Rogers Rugeiyam. Impromptu Decisions: Tanzania's Local Government Authorities' challenge in Establishing and Managing the Women, Youth, and People with Disabilities Fund. Local Administration Journal, 2022,15(4): 345-361.

However, Tanzania's preferential financial loan policies for youth, women and people with disabilities have helped young entrepreneurs to some extent, but they also face some challenges. First of all, due to the low acceptance of this policy by young people, some beneficiaries may disappear before repaying loans, affecting the effectiveness of the policy. Secondly, the target groups' lack of entrepreneurial skills may bring difficulties to their business pioneering process. In addition, the overall poor business environment has also affected the implementation of the policy. For example, between 2018 and 2019, 16,252 enterprises in Tanzania closed down. In addition, local governments have insufficient revenue mobilization and limited sources of funds, which may lead local councils to think that these donations have weakened other plans, thus affecting the contribution of loan funds and hindering the efforts of prospective beneficiaries.[1]

(3) Rwanda: Poverty Reduction Plan

Rwanda has implemented the Vision 2020 Umurenge Program (VUP) to provide financial support to poor families. The plan faces some challenges in practice, including delayed payment, weak monitoring and evaluation skills, and insufficient understanding of the plan implementers.

Social assistance funds also face a series of problems, such as unstable government policies, ineffective medical facilities, unexpected strikes, threats from Boko Haram and Fulani herders, kidnappings and lack of necessary infrastructure, which all affect women and youth empowerment projects. In this context, the implementation of the livelihood empowerment and anti-poverty plan also faces some difficulties, including administrative problems, the instability of capital inflows and the perception of political intervention by the outside world. At the same time, because decision-making is mainly made at the central level, local participation is inadequate, obstructing the implementation of poverty reduction plans.[2]

1,2   Rogers Rugeiyam. Impromptu Decisions: Tanzania's Local Government Authorities' challenge in Establishing and Managing the Women, Youth, and People with Disabilities Fund. Local Administration Journal, 2022,15(4): 345-361.

4.3.6 Major poverty reduction strategy documents in Sub-Saharan Africa

To reduce rural poverty, African countries have taken a wide range of actions, such as cash transfer, food aid, affordable medical expenses, child protection services and responding to life-threatening emergencies, in efforts to strengthen the coping mechanisms of disadvantaged groups. To make agrifood systems more inclusive and efficient, all countries seek to improve agricultural productivity. Table 4-2 provides the poverty reduction plans of African countries.

Table 4-2   Details of Poverty Reduction Plans of some African Countries

Country	Policy document	Poverty reduction objective	Specific measures
Burundi	National Development Plan (2018-2027)	The plan has been developed in accordance with the UN 2030 Sustainable Development Goals, the AU's *Agenda 2063* and Burundi's resource endowments, for the purpose of solving economic difficulties and reducing poverty by 2027	The long-term goal of this plan is to improve food self-sufficiency, increase the export proportion of agriculture, industry, commerce and mining industry, realize the diversification of export structure, develop energy and art industries, stimulate growth with infrastructure construction and maintenance projects, increase the access to basic social services such as education, medical care and social security, strengthen environmental protection and rational land planning, improve the governance and decentralization of financial industry, and develop regional and international partnerships to achieve coordinated economic development in Burundi
Ethiopia	Productive Safety Net Program (PSNP 2019)	Address the chronic food insecurity in rural areas	The method is to provide predictable cash or food to poor households every month during the six-month off-season in exchange for their labor contribution to building community assets. A few households benefit from "direct support", which lasts for 12 months and is provided to households without able-bodied adults
Madagascar	Initiative Emergence Madagascar (IEM 2019-2023)	Stimulate growth and reduce poverty	Develop animal husbandry and agroindustry to ensure food security and conquer export markets; develop health and hygiene. (Madagascar has made community health a priority); improve water, environmental sanitation and personal hygiene, Analanjirofo has been selected as the pilot area of Madio Plan in Madagascar in 2020 to promote the popularization of drinking water, sanitation facilities and personal hygiene

Continued

Country	Policy document	Poverty reduction objective	Specific measures
Somalia	The ninth National Develop-ment Plan (NDP-9)	Present three national priorities: political stability, improved security and economic growth	Reduce insecurity in all parts of Somalia and strengthen the effective governance capacity of Somali institutions, thereby improving inclusiveness and reducing violent conflicts; strengthen institutional capacity to enable Somali citizens to have better access to health care, education and other basic services when they are in dire need, and implement strategies to empower women; strengthen the commitment and capacity of Somali institutions to effective political and environmental governance, and accelerate economic growth and development that creates employment, with special emphasis on creating opportunities for young people
Angola	Long-Term Development Strategy Angola 2025	By 2025, the poverty index will be lowered by 75%, extreme poverty will be eradicated, and relative poverty and hunger will be substantially reduced (2/3)	Increase and expand social welfare of family nature for the whole population; develop appropriate incentives, such as access to land and means of production, settlement of floating population, especially displaced persons, demobilized persons or refugees; support the expansion of productive and fair-paying employment to eliminate poverty and distribute income fairly
Cameroon	National Development Strategy (2020-2030)	Substantially reduce poverty, with the national poverty rate falling below 25% by 2030	Improve people's living conditions and access to basic social services by ensuring a substantial reduction in poverty and underemployment. Improve productivity by strengthening agricultural and industrial activities and modernizing farms, thus significantly reducing rural poverty
Congo, Dem.Rep.	Country Strategic Plan (2021-2024)	Reduce poverty, food insecurity and malnutrition	Promote sustainable and inclusive economic growth and meet food demand by promoting agricultural transformation, open and innovative economic diversification and boosting youth and women's entrepreneurship
Namibia	The fifth National Development Plan (NDP5 2017/18-2021/22)	Reduce poverty and inequality, achieve inclusive, sustainable and fair economic growth, and train capable and healthy human resources. By 2022, the proportion of people living in extreme poverty will be reduced to 5.00%, the Gini coefficient will be reduced to 0.5, and the human development index (HDI) will increase to 0.695	Improve agricultural productivity and sustainability and help eradicate hunger, food insecurity and malnutrition. Bring marginalized communities into the mainstream economy; invest the investment of all stakeholders in activities to stimulate economic growth, create jobs and reduce poverty; strengthen skills training and establish competent and healthy human resources. Strengthen social security, strengthen the social security system, and improve the coordination of departmental actions

Continued

Country	Policy document	Poverty reduction objective	Specific measures
Benin	Programme d'Actions du Gouvernement (PAG) 2021-2026	Reduce the monetary poverty rate to 36.5% by 2026	Government departments will promote quality education and vocational and technical education and training to promote high-quality education; fully implement the social capital insurance plan, strengthen the health system to achieve effective health coverage, and improve people's access to basic social services and social welfare
Liberia	Pro-Poor Agenda for Prosperity and Development (PAPD)	To provide greater income security to an additional one million Liberians, and reduce absolute poverty by 23 percent across 5 out of 6 regions – through sustained and inclusive economic growth driven by scaled-up investments in agriculture, in infrastructure, in human resource development, and in social protection	To realize the goals of PAPD and *Vision 2030* in the next five years, the strategy and intervention measures are carried out around four pillars, which will constitute the approaches for the next five years
Mauritania	Strategy for Acelerated Growth and Shared Prosperity (SCAPP)	The economic growth rate will exceed 12%, the productive capital will be further accumulated, the share of informal economy will be reduced, and economic development will be more competitive, inclusive and resilient	Two volumes have by far been compiled for the SCAPP: the first volume is social, economic, institutional and environmental assessment, and the second volume is SCAPP's strategic direction and action plan for 2016-2020. The first five-year plan has been completed, which mainly involves maintaining macroeconomic stability, improving the ability to transform natural resources and improving the business environment. The SCAPP 2021-2025 plan is still being developed, and the first and second volumes involve some specific measures such as employment, business development and education

Source: Based on the information released by the World Bank, the United Nations and governments of different countries.

4.4 Summary

The problem of poverty in African countries is prominent. From the perspective of the whole world, the government revenue in 2021 totaled US$30,913.366 billion, while the total government revenue in Africa only accounted for about 1.7% of the world. To get rid of poverty, African countries have developed and implemented a series of poverty reduction strategies. From the Lagos Action Plan to *Agenda 2063*, Africa's overall development strategies are becoming more and more comprehensive and perfect, ranging from strategies focusing on economic and social development to strategies encompassing economy, society, politics, culture, science and technology, foreign relations and many other aspects. However, compared with other regions such as East Asia and South Asia, the poverty reduction work in African countries has been facing the dilemma of much investment with meager results.

An important reason for the difficulties of African countries in poverty reduction is the low degree of national autonomy and the lack of national financial capacity. In 2021, the government revenue in Africa totaled US$527.57 billion, but the total government expenditure amounted to as high as US$670.881 billion (see Table 4-3). Given a population of about 1.4 billion in Africa, the proportion of fiscal revenue, expenditure and population was unbalanced, and Africa relied heavily on international aid and investment in the process of poverty reduction.

Table 4-3　　Public Fiscal Situations in Africa and the World, 2021

Region	Population (100 million)	Government fiscal revenue (US$100 million)	Government fiscal expenditure (US$100 million)	Per capita fiscal revenue (US$)	Per capita fiscal expenditure (US$)
Africa	14.25 (17.97%)	5,275.70 (1.71%)	6,708.81 (1.80%)	370.22 (9.49%)	470.79 (10.03%)
World	79.28	309,133.66	372,118.88	3,899.26	4,693.73

Note: ( )=Proportion of Africa to the world's total.

Source: The Statistical Annex to the annual Africa's Development Dynamics (AFDD) report, see:https://oe.cd/AFDD-2023.

From the perspective inside Africa, the national financial capacity is low, and the effect of implementing poverty reduction strategies and policies is poor. Due to the low level of economic development, inadequate institutional development and serious corruption, most African countries have weak financial absorption capacity, resulting in the loss of a large number of tax resources, and making it impossible to raise huge funds necessary for providing public services and implementing poverty alleviation projects. Meanwhile, African countries, with insufficient financial capacity and poor management and utilization of funds, see very little funds really invested in infrastructure construction and poverty alleviation projects. Most of the poverty reduction documents in Africa are strategic documents designated by the African Union or regional alliances, not considering the poverty control status of local governments in Africa or involving education, people's livelihood and infrastructure projects that people really need, hence delivering meagre benefits. Whether the poverty reduction policies developed by the African Union and others can be effectively implemented is related to whether the poverty reduction goal can be achieved and whether the interests of the poor can be guaranteed. However, in most African countries, the bureaucratic capacity is inadequate, work efficiency is low, the sense of responsibility is lacking, and the working ability and quality of government staff are relatively low, making it impossible to effectively implement poverty reduction strategies, and leading to limited results of many poverty reduction policies.

From Africa's external perspective, African countries are highly dependent on the international community's aid and funds, and most African countries are burdened with heavy foreign debts. Moreover, the conditions attached to Western aid weaken the autonomy of African countries in developing their own poverty reduction strategies and hinder the improvement of their government's governance capacity. As the financial expenditure of African countries is highly dependent on the development assistance provided by the international community, African countries pay more attention to the requirements of donor countries than to the real needs of domestic people when developing policies in order to obtain aid funds, giving rise to the irresponsibility of governments to citizens. More importantly, the aid given by Western countries to Africa has not really helped it address the poverty problem. Too much intervention and guidance by donor countries in the policy-making and other government processes of recipient countries has encouraged African governments to be dependent, reduced their willingness to explore their own poverty reduction policies, and damaged their governance capacity. In short, excessive dependence on external funds has led to the loss of autonomy of African countries in poverty reduction, making it difficult to deliver real results.

In summary, in the future practices of poverty reduction, African countries should, under the prerequisite of maintaining autonomy, make rational use of external assistance, constantly improve their national capabilities, independently develop and implement effective poverty reduction strategies and policies, and take a path to poverty reduction that suits their own countries.

Chapter 5   International Assistance to Africa

Poverty reduction and development in Africa are among the key concerns of the international community. Different poverty reduction effects have resulted from different scales, ideas and approaches of assistance to Africa by different types of donors in the international community. This chapter, from a comparative perspective, reviews the scales, fields and characteristics among traditional donors, emerging economies and China in their assistance to Africa, for a deeper understanding of Africa's poverty reduction and development in the international social structure.

5.1   Traditional donors' Assistance to Africa's Development

5.1.1   In scale: Africa is the key region of Western development assistance, but the assistance has been decreasing in recent years

Africa is a key region of international official development assistance (ODA), which is one of the important sources of funds for solving development problems on the African continent. However, since 2020, the scale of Africa's access to international ODA has shown a downward trend.

First, in terms of the share of ODA received by Sub-Saharan Africa in the global ODA, since the 1990s, the total amount of ODA received by Africa has been about 30% of the total amount of global ODA. Since 2018, Sub-Saharan Africa has received over US$50 billion in ODA every year, reaching US$66.9

billion in 2020, the highest level in recent years. However, by 2021, the total amount of ODA received by Sub-Saharan Africa dropped to US$62.3 billion (see Figure 5-1).

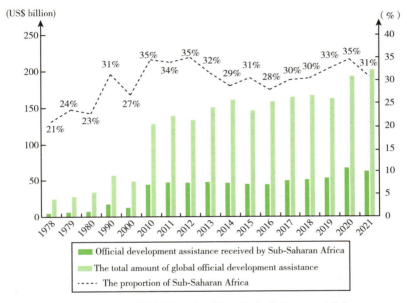

Figure 5-1   ODA Received by Sub-Saharan Africa

Source: World Bank.

Second, in terms of the scale of per capita ODA, the amount of ODA received per capita in Sub-Saharan Africa was always higher than the world average in 1978-2021, and far higher than South Asia, Latin America and the Caribbean, East Asia and the Pacific. Since 2012, the amount has stabilized at around US$50 per capita, while in other regions it has always been below US$20. In terms of growth rate, the per capita ODA received by Sub-Saharan Africa had been rapidly increasing from the beginning of this century, rising from US$19.45 in 2000 to US$58.1 in 2020, while the highest increase in the other regions was less than US$10. However, from the perspective of increase in this region, the per capita ODA of Sub-Saharan Africa in 2021 decreased to US$52.73, US$5.37 lower than that in 2020 (see Figure 5-2).

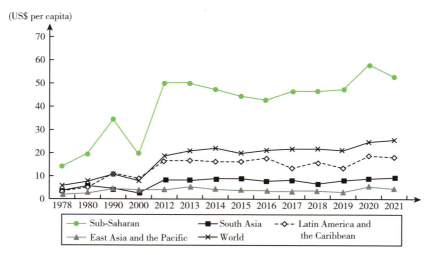

Figure 5-2   Scale of ODA Received Per Capita by Region in the World
Source: https://data.oecd.org.

Third, judging from the scale of international multilateral institutions'
assistance to Africa, the total amount of assistance received by Sub-Saharan
Africa has accounted for over 40% of the total amount of international
multilateral institutions' assistance since 2012, and it accounted for more than
50% in 2019, reaching the largest scale in the decade – US$32.855 billion in
2020. However, from 2020, the share of Sub-Saharan Africa's assistance from
international multilateral institutions in the total assistance from international
multilateral institutions began to decline, from 51.88% in 2019 to 45.79% in
2021, and from 2021, the aid scale also decreased from US$32.855 billion in
2020 to US$26.036 billion in 2021 (see Table 5-1).

Table 5-1   Scale and Share of International Multilateral Institutions'
Assistance to Sub-Saharan Africa, 2012-2021 (US$100 million)

	2012	2013	2014	2015	2016	2017	2018	2019	2020	2021
Total amount of assistance	403.23	426.64	436.49	418.29	415.18	439.54	433.54	447.44	661.11	568.57
Sub-Saharan Africa	176.32 (43.73%)	188.95 (44.29%)	184.48 (42.27%)	179.96 (43.02%)	173.1 (41.69%)	200.48 (45.61%)	205.18 (47.33%)	232.15 (51.88%)	328.55 (49.70%)	260.36 (45.79%)

Source: https://data.oecd.org.

Fourth, judging from the scale of ODA to Africa by the Development Assistance Committee (DAC), the scale of ODA to Africa by DAC countries basically progressed steadily from 2019 to 2021, maintained at around US$25 billion, but an "inverted U-shaped" development trend was still found, with the aid amount increasing first and then decreasing, reaching US$23.14 billion, US$24.95 billion and US$24.58 billion respectively. In addition, more ODA flows to Sub-Saharan Africa countries. In 2021, US$19.72 billion was used for assistance to Sub-Saharan Africa countries, accounting for 80% of the aid to Africa in that year (see Table 5-2).

Table 5-2   **Regional Distribution of African Assistance of DAC, 2019-2021 (US$100 million)**

Region	2019	2020	2021
Africa	231.40	249.50	245.80
North Africa	30.60	31.50	35.40
Sub-Saharan Africa	185.10	205.00	197.20

Source: https://stats-1.oecd.org/index.aspx?DatasetCode=CPA.

Fifth, the scale of Western countries' bilateral aid to Africa has also declined in recent years. For example, Japan's bilateral ODA to Sub-Saharan Africa generally presents a trend of increasing first and then decreasing,[1] that is, it increased rapidly from US$8 million in 1970 to US$1.835 billion in 2010, and then slowly decreased to US$1.338 billion in 2020 (see Figure 5-3). For another example, although Africa is the largest recipient of the UK's bilateral ODA in specific areas, accounting for 50.5% of the total UK development assistance in 2021, it also shows a decreasing trend with the decline of total ODA expenditure[2].

---

1   See: https://www.jica.go.jp/english/publications/reports/annual/2022/fh2q4d000001doiv-att/2022_all. pdf.

2   According to *Statistics on International Development: Final UK Aid Spend 2021*, the final ratio of ODA to GNI in the UK was 0.50% in 2021, and the ODA expenditure was 11.423 billion pounds, a decrease of 3.054 billion pounds (21.1%) from 2020.

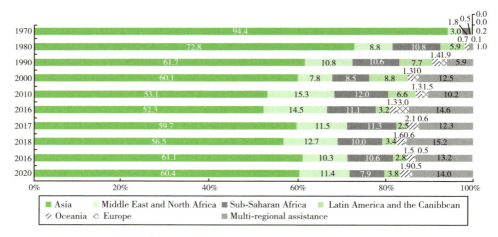

Figure 5-3　Japan's Bilateral ODA Trend by Region

Source: JICA, *2022 Japan International Cooperation Agency Annual Report.*

5.1.2　In sectors: the sectors covered by ODA differ from what Africa wants, and Africa's own development needs are ignored

First, Western development assistance focuses on social development, but rarely supports large-scale public infrastructure construction and industrial development in underdeveloped countries. Western development assistance pays special attention to the improvement of education, health, population and public health, water supply and governance capacity (including government and non-governmental organizations) in African countries and regions. According to OECD-DAC statistics, more than one third of aid funds flow to these sectors of social development every year.[1] In 2021, investment in the sectors of social development such as education, health and drinking water safety accounted for 40.35% of the total aid, indicating that the focus of Western development assistance was still on improving the living environment and poverty alleviation conditions of the poor. However, the aid to transportation, communication, electricity and agro-economic infrastructure accounted for only 13%, even lower

---

1　Tang Lixia, Li Xiaoyun. Review on the Management and Practice of Western Development Assistance [J]. *Fudan International Relations Review*, 2016 (2):153-167.

than emergency humanitarian aid, which accounted for 16.43%. This shows that Western development aid still rarely supports the public infrastructure construction and industrial development of underdeveloped countries. This is a salient difference between Western development assistance and Chinese assistance.[1] From the aid sectors of IDA, aid resources in 2022 were used in social services (education, health, and social protection), infrastructure (energy, information and communication technology, transportation, water supply, and nuclear waste management), public administration, agriculture, industry and trade, finance and other fields, accounting for 30%, 33%, 16%, 11%, 6% and 3%, respectively,[2] while agriculture, as the most important socio-economic sector in Africa, received only 11% of the aid.

Second, Western development assistance, involving many sectors, usually focuses on soft capacity building, but rarely directly provides means of production in assistance measures. On the one hand, this way of assistance promotes the growth and development of local institutions, local NGOs and farmers' organizations through various kinds of training. On the other hand, however, due to limited aid resources and poor aid management, aid resources are embezzled, poverty reduction experience can hardly be spread and disseminated outside, the scope of poverty reduction is limited, and a wider range of disadvantaged groups can hardly benefit from aid. Africa's special development stage and needs are thus ignored.

Case 5-1   Typical assistance projects of Western countries in Africa

France: France put forward the "Choose Africa" initiative in 2018, aiming to provide various types of financial and technical support for start-ups and micro, small and medium-sized enterprises in Africa. In cooperation with 250 local partners throughout the African continent, France has allocated 3.5 billion euros to over 40,000 micro, small and medium-sized enterprises and hundreds of thousands of micro-entrepreneurs, and provided technical assistance to 8,700 start-ups and micro, small and medium-sized enterprises, which will create 2 million direct and indirect employment opportunities in the next five years.

---

1 OECD (2023), ODA by sector (indicator). doi: 10.1787/a5a1f674-en (Accessed on 08 July 2023).

2 See: https://ida.worldbank.org/en/ida-financing.

In addition, at the beginning of 2022, France established the French Bureau of Experts as an inter-ministerial agency responsible for France's technical cooperation, employing about 1,000 experts in 380 projects, 65% of which came from Africa.

Germany: The German Agency for International Cooperation (GIZ) cooperates with the African Union (AU) to help its member countries define the colonial-era borders on the African continent, which is more than 6,000 kilometers long, which will help reduce natural resource conflicts and crimes. In order to benefit from the opportunity of economic integration on the African continent provided by the African Continental Free Trade Area (AfCFTA), GIZ helps to promote countries to ratify the AU *Protocol on Free Movement of Persons*, so as to realize visa-free travel and engage in cross-border work and trade.

Japan: In August, 2022, the Japan International Cooperation Agency (JICA) held the Eighth Tokyo International Conference on African Development (TICAD 8). JICA put forward the direction of establishing a resilient society and economic cooperation on Africa under the slogan of "striving for a flexible, inclusive and prosperous Africa" . For example, JICA provides bilateral cooperation to Kenya, Ethiopia, Nigeria and Rwanda, which aims at establishing industrial ecosystems, and establishes a platform for young entrepreneurs to connect with various stakeholders such as investors, educational institutions and functional departments.

5.1.3 In results: Western aid to Africa is attached with conditions and tend to make Africa dependent on aid

First, although no consensus has been reached on the relationship between development assistance and economic development and poverty reduction in recipient countries, yet the international development assistance over 70-plus years, especially aid to Africa, while promoting local development to a certain extent, also brings about serious aid dependence, making Africa the region with the highest dependence on aid in the world. In essence, Western official development assistance (ODA) has continuously shaped the unequal power relationship between the North and the South, under which no matter how the narrative changes or how the policies are revised, it would be difficult to break free from the result that the dependence on aid is strengthened and the effectiveness is reduced if the core motivation of developing countries are required to remain unchanged according to Western developed countries' pursuit of modernization.

In terms of supporting data, on the one hand, the ratio of ODA to GNI in Sub-Saharan Africa is stable at about 3%, much higher than the world average and other regions, and the difference is widening. By 2020, the ratio of ODA to GNI in Sub-Saharan Africa (4.02%) was 3.97 percentage points higher than that in East Asia and the Pacific (0.05), which undoubtedly demonstrated that this region was heavily dependent on ODA (see Figure 5-4).

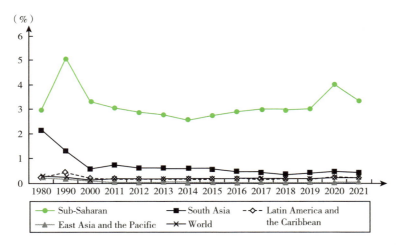

Figure 5-4　Ratio of official development assistance to national income in different regions of the world

Source: Based on the data from the World Bank.

On the other hand, a total of 75 countries in the world are eligible for assistance resources from the International Development Association (IDA), of which 39 are African countries. From the concept of "countries that have graduated from the IDA", eleven African countries have won the title of graduate countries in history, of which only 6 are African countries (Angola FY14, Egypt FY81 and FY99, Equatorial Guinea FY99, Eswatini FY75 in Morocco FY75, Tunisia FY79). Five countries, Cameroon, the Republic of Congo, Côte d'Ivoire, Nigeria and Zimbabwe, have once again become countries that can obtain IDA resources after graduation, and their poverty reduction effect is not stable[1]. In fiscal year 2022, among the top ten IDA recipients, except Bangladesh (with a loan of US$2.161 billion), the other nine countries are all from Africa, namely Nigeria, Democratic Republic of the Congo, Ethiopia, Kenya, Niger, Uganda, Tanzania, Mozambique and Cameroon, with loans of US$2.4 billion, US$2.125 billion, US$1.904 billion, US$1.8 billion, US$1.728 billion, US$1.715 billion, US$1.65 billion, US$1.287 billion, and US$1.12 billion respectively.[2]

Second, aid conditions are the core of international development assistance. Many aid subjects begin to implement conditional aid for different purposes. A country's fiscal policy, trade liberalization, privatization of public enterprises and privatization of agriculture have become the focal consideration of aid conditions for policy loans. Due to various additional conditions, the cost of obtaining development assistance for developing countries is getting higher and higher. From the perspective of international multilateral institutions, taking the World Bank as an example, the aid conditions for recipient countries have changed in recent years, the importance of trade policy is declining, and the management capacity of public sector, public financial management, public expenditure and public sector reform have become more and more important aid conditions. At the same time, the implementation of some aid programs requires the recipient countries to develop specific action strategies, which must be reviewed and evaluated by aid agencies before the countries can be supported by aid funds. With the Debt Relief Plan for Heavily Indebted Poor Countries (HIPC) and the Multilateral Debt Relief Initiative, for example, these two most important debt relief plans require the recipient countries to formulate a Poverty Reduction Strategy Paper (PRSP), which will be reviewed by the World Bank system in two stages. Only when the decision point is reached can the HIPC Plan be launched, and only when the completion point is reached can the Multilateral Debt Relief Initiative be launched.

From the perspective of bilateral aid subjects, on the one hand, the political

---

1 See: https://ida.worldbank.org/en/about/borrowing-countries/ida-graduates.
2 See: https://ida.worldbank.org/en/ida-financing.

conditions of the recipient countries directly affect the aid provided by aid agencies. In the event of "ethnic cleansing", military coup or termination of democratization process and human rights issues in the recipient countries, aid agencies will institute four different levels of aid sanctions: suspending all aid projects, suspending the renewal of new aid projects, suspending some aid projects and comprehensively reducing aid rationing. For example, the United States provides aid to Africa according to the *Foreign Assistance Act* promulgated in 1961, and most of its aid projects are implemented by American entities[1]. In its aid to Africa, the United States follows the traditional mode of attaching the political reform of the recipient country as a condition to aid. For example, while supporting the improvement of local public health conditions, requirements such as "promoting regional peace and stability and political system reform" are attached.[2] On the other hand, bilateral aid is obviously selective and directional, instead of being based on poverty alleviation. For example, in 2021, six of the top ten recipients of bilateral country official development assistance from the United Kingdom were African countries, namely Nigeria (140 million pounds), Ethiopia (120 million pounds), South Africa (102 million pounds), Somalia (101 million pounds), South Sudan (96 million pounds), and Sudan (94 million pounds). In 2022, the development aid expenditure budget of the United States was US$38 billion, of which nearly 25% was only used in ten countries, six of which were African countries, namely Ethiopia (US$1.13 billion), South Sudan (US$821 million), the Republic of Congo (US$814 million), Nigeria (US$803 million), Sudan (US$488 million) and Somalia (US$475 million). Among the top ten countries in France's international development assistance in 2022, five were African countries, namely Morocco (597 million euros), Côte d'Ivoire (361 million euros), South Africa (301 million euros), Tunisia (286 million euros) and Egypt (284 million euros). In the Japanese International Cooperation Agency (JICA) projects of Japan, Tanzania is the African country receiving the most support from China, amounting to 39.245 billion yen, and the aid

---

1   Joint Strategic Plan, see: https://www.usaid.gov/results-and-data/planning/joint-strategic-plan/fy-2022-2026.

2   Zhou Shangsi, Xu Zhiming. Comparative Analysis of Official Development Assistance Models of China and the United States to Africa [J]. Shandong Social Sciences, 2021, 316(12):160-166.

received Ghana, Kenya, Malawi and Djibouti all reached more than 4 billion yen (see Table 5-3).

Table 5-3　　Total Amount of JICA Projects by Country, 2022
(100 million yen)

Country	Amount
Tanzania	392.45
Ghana	63.06
Kenya	56.20
Malawi	49.45
Djibouti	40.95
Senegal	34.77
Mozambique	23.90
Rwanda	22.03
Uganda	20.56
Madagascar	18.48
South Africa	17.66
Ethiopia	17.07
Zambia	16.86
Congo,Dem.Rep.	16.84
Sudan	12.82
Côte d'Ivoire	12.71
Nigeria	9.33
Cameroon	8.86
Burkina Faso	8.30
South Africa	6.36
Angola	2.86
Other 28 countries	149.64

Note: The table only lists the countries where JICA's overseas offices are located. Totals may not add up due to rounding.

Source: Based on the data from the World Bank.

5.2   Development Assistance from Emerging Economies to Africa

5.2.1   Overview of development assistance from emerging economies to Africa

(1) Scale and type of assistance funds

Judging from the scale of aid funds, the total amount of aid from emerging economies to Africa is on the rise, becoming an important supplementary force for international aid to Africa. Vertically, the amount of aid from emerging economies to Africa rose from US$340 million in 2011 to US$520 million in 2017[1], and there was a substantial increase in 2018, from US$934 million to US$1.656 billion, up by 77.27% year-on-year.[2] However, the proportion of aid from some countries shows a downward trend. For example, in Türkiye's aid to Africa from 2015 to 2020, the proportion of Southern Africa dropped from 9.66% to 0.71%, and the proportion of North Africa dropped to 0.001% after 2017.[3] Horizontally, all countries attach importance to aid to Africa. With the average aid to Sub-Saharan Africa from 2019 to 2020, for example, Türkiye's aid was US$75.77 million, Thailand's aid was US$1.52 million, UAE's aid was US$1,074.47 million, and Saudi Arabia's aid was US$419.46 million.[4]

In terms of the types of aid funds, aid from emerging economies is different from that from traditional countries in that emerging economies use more forms of aid such as grants and loans. In terms of direct grants, the UAE's total grant to Africa reached US$575.8 million[5], and India provided US$500 million for capacity building and human resources development.[6] In terms of preferential

---

1   See: http://world.people.com.cn/n1/2019/1018/c1002-31407967.html.

2   See: International Assistance to Africa-Institute of West Asia and Africa, Chinese Academy of Social Sciences.

3   Assessing Türkiye-Africa Engagements.

4   OECD-DAC, see: http://www.oecd.org/dac/financing-sustainable-development/development-finance-data/aid:at-a-glance.htm.

5   United Arab Emirates Foreign Aid 2021.

6   Wen Cuiping. Comparative Study of Chinese and Indian Aid to Africa in the 21st Century [D]. Beijing:China Foreign Affairs University, 2014.

loans, on the one hand, it is used to develop important projects and priority development projects in the field of people's livelihood in Africa; on the other hand, it is used to buy machinery, equipment or products from donor countries.[1] For example, more than 50% of the credit lines provided by the Export-Import Bank of India are for development projects in Africa, which are used in key areas such as agricultural production, food processing, infrastructure, information technology, energy and pharmaceuticals.[2] Brazil's Foreign Trade Bureau provided loans of US$95 million to Ghana,and US$98 million to Zimbabwe to import Brazilian agricultural products.[3]

(2) Regional flow of aid

In the choice of aid recipients, emerging economies focus on regions with geographical proximity, similar socio-economic development, rich resources and similar cultural traditions as the basis for determining key aid regions. UAE's aid to Africa is mainly concentrated in West Africa, North Africa and East Africa, accounting for 63.3%, 58.4% and 47.3%, respectively.[4] India's aid is concentrated in Southeast African countries with traditional friendly relations and resource-rich African countries.[5] Brazil's aid to Africa was concentrated in Portuguese-speaking areas from the beginning, and then extended to the whole African continent[6]. Saudi Arabia's aid to Africa is mainly aimed at Islamic countries.[7] Türkiye's investment in Africa is mainly concentrated in Sub-Saharan areas.[8]

(3) Aid mechanisms and forms

In terms of aid mechanisms to Africa, emerging economies actively construct

---

1 Tang Lixia, Li Xiaoyun. Review of India's foreign aid [J]. *South Asian Studies Quarterly* 2013, 154 (3):7-12,32,1.

2 India's Development Cooperation in Africa: The Case of "Solar Mamas" Who Bring Light.

3 See: http://iwaas.cass.cn/xslt/fzlt/201508/t20150831_2609374.shtml.

4 See: United Arab Emirates Foreign Aid 2021.

5 Devex Emerging Donors Report.

6 See: http://iwaas.cssn.cn/xslt/fzlt/201508/t20150831_2609356.shtml.

7 Chen Mo. Characteristics, Motives and Effects of Saudi Arabia's Foreign Aid [J]. *West Asia and Africa*, 2021, 278(3):113-136.

8 Zhang Chun. Türkiye's Economic and Trade Cooperation with Africa [J]. *Arab World Studies*, 2012, 139 (2): 86-99.

tripartite cooperation mechanisms and keep enriching methods and approaches of international development cooperation. India teamed up with Japan to establish an "Asian-African Growth Corridor" with African countries; Türkiye and Japan held a conference on "Türkiye -Japan-Africa Partnership"; Brazil participated in the "South America-Africa Summit" and the "India-Brazil-South Africa Forum", carried out tropical grassland development projects with Japanese development aid agencies, strengthened Mozambique's research capacity projects with American international development agencies, and carried out grain purchase projects for family farms in five African countries with FAO and WFP.[1] In the form of aid, emerging economies are vying to hold summits with Africa to promote the development of bilateral cooperation on an all-round, multi-level and high-quality direction. In order to further strengthen the political, economic and cultural relations with African countries, summit diplomacy seems to be a standard activity for various countries' diplomacy with Africa (see Table 5-4).

Table 5-4   Summit Diplomacy of Selected Countries with Africa

Country	Year	Conference	Core contents
India	2008	The First India-Africa Forum Summit (IAFS)	Make science and technology a key area of India-Africa cooperation, provide US$ 5.4 billion of credit to support the development of African countries in the fields of information technology, communication and energy, and biomedicine, and strengthen the training of non-technical talents
	2011	The Second India-Africa Forum Summit (IAFS)	India-Africa partnership is based on three pillars: capacity building, technology transfer, trade and infrastructure development
	2015	The First India-Africa Forum Summit (IAFS)	Deepen cooperation on clean energy, public transport and agriculture adapted to climate change, and provide Africa with US$10 billion as preferential loans and US$600 million as free aid in the next five years

---

1   Tang Luping. Foreign Aid from Developing Countries and Its Development Direction [D]. Xiamen: Xiamen University, 2014.

Continued

Country	Year	Conference	Core contents
Türkiye	2008	The first Türkiye-Africa Summit	With the theme of strengthening partnership to promote common development and prosperity, the *Istanbul Declaration* and the *African Partnership Cooperation Framework* were adopted
	2014	The second Türkiye-Africa Summit	A new partnership model with the theme of strengthening sustainable development and integration and the *Declaration and Joint Implementation Plan for 2015-2019* were adopted, and seven principles of Africa policy were put forward
	2021	The third Türkiye-Africa Summit	Strengthen partnership and cooperation on various fields, including establishing a peaceful and secure environment and increasing investment in improving infrastructure in Africa
Russia	2019	The first Russia-Africa Summit	Provide political and diplomatic support, national defense and security assistance, economic assistance, disease control advice, humanitarian relief assistance, education and vocational training to Africa
	2023	The second Russia-Africa Summit	Three documents were adopted on the prevention of an arms race in space, cooperation on the field of international information security, and strengthening anti-terrorism cooperation, as well as the *Russia-Africa Partnership Forum Action Plan 2023-2026*

Source: Based on the information collected from India, Türkiye, Russia and African countries, and some organizations.

5.2.2 Characteristics of emerging economies' aid to Africa

(1) New assistance ideas

With the improvement of economic strength of emerging markets and developing countries, emerging economies are playing an increasingly important role in international development assistance. Unlike traditional official development assistance, however, emerging economies follow the concepts of South-South cooperation such as equality and mutual benefit and non-interference in each other's internal affairs, pursue mutually beneficial economic growth and long-term trade development, and help recipient countries improve their development and governance capabilities through economic and trade cooperation, knowledge exchange, experience sharing and talent training. For example, China pays attention to human resources training and sharing of experience in poverty reduction; India attaches importance to education and training, information technology, etc.; Brazil mainly provides technical assistance in the fields of agriculture and food safety.[1] The emergence of such new aid concepts not only promotes the innovation in the field of international development assistance, and makes international development assistance more sustainable, but also further urges all parties to deeply reflect on the Western-led development assistance system.

(2) Extensive range of assistance

Emerging economies' aid to Africa involves various sectors such as medical care, education and security. In terms of medical assistance, the first is to provide medical services. As a "world pharmacy", India sells a large number of drugs to Africa, and the Vision Foundation of India provides free surgery for African eye patients. Turkey provides health checks for Africans and provides treatment for African patients without access to treatment at home.[2] During the COVID-19 pandemic, India, Türkiye, Brazil, the United Arab Emirates and other countries provided medical equipment, vaccines and other materials fighting the pandemic to African countries, and India also held an online COVID-19 seminar to support Africa in fighting the spread of the pandemic.[3] The second is to train medical professionals. India employs telemedicine technology for professional training,[4] the Ministry of Health of Türkiye provides vocational training to African countries,[5] and Brazil sends experts to help Africa develop plans for the

---

1   See: http://world.people.com.cn/n1/2019/1018/c1002-31407967.html.

2, 4   Wei Min. A Review on Türkiye's Foreign Policy towards Africa after the Justice and Development Party Took Power [J]. *Middle East Studies*, 2020, 11(1):112-132,278.

3   See: https://user.guancha.cn/main/content?id=322649.

5   Zhang Yonghong, Zhao Mengqing. India's Science and Technology Cooperation with Africa: Main Foci, Mechanism and Strategical Orientation [J]. *South Asian Studies Quarterly*, 2015, 163(4):47-55,5.

prevention and treatment of AIDS.[1]

In terms of educational assistance, the first is to establish training institutions. India has provided more than 300 training programs for African countries, covering many sectors and effectively promoting employment improvement.[2] Brazil has established rural economic research institutes, environmental and agricultural research institutes, agricultural research institutes and agricultural scientific research centers in Mali, Burkina Faso, Chad and Benin, respectively, which has effectively improved the productivity and competitiveness of cotton supply chain.[3] Türkiye has established 175 schools in 26 African countries[4], and more than 11,000 young Africans have been trained in Turkish universities.[5] The second is to support African students. In 2011-2015, India provided scholarships to 25,000 African students, and in 2012-2021, Türkiye provided scholarships to 12,600 students from 54 African countries.[6]

In terms of security assistance, the first is to train military personnel.[7] Türkiye helps to restore security in Somalia and fight terrorism. India provides anti-terrorism training to Africa, assists countries along the Indian Ocean in eastern and southern Africa in anti-piracy and exclusive economic zone investigation, and helps Africa enhance its maritime security capabilities. The second is to participate in peacekeeping operations. Türkiye has participated in four of the seven peacekeeping operations led by the UN and contributed to peacekeeping operations on the African continent. India promised to continue to support UN peacekeeping operations in Africa and train African officers in the UN Peacekeeping Center in India.

---

1   See: http://www.holine.com/July/171902.htm.

2   75 years of development cooperation, see: https://www.researchgate.net/publication/362790779_75_years_of_development_cooperation.

3   See: https://www.fx361.cc/page/2022/0916/11559757.shtml.

4   The Rise of Turkey in Africa.

5   Türkiye's Partnership with Africa: A Development-oriented Approach, see: https://www.sohu.com/a/366732488_120073528#google_vignette.

6   Visualizing Turkey's Activism in Africa.

7   Chen Yang. *The Performance, Reasons and Influence of Türkiye's Intervention in the Horn of Africa* [D]. Jinhua: Zhejiang Normal University, 2021.

(3) Prioritizing key assistance projects

Despite extensive coverage, emerging economies' aid to Africa mainly focuses on infrastructure assistance, technical assistance and humanitarian assistance. In terms of infrastructure assistance, India has built basic life-related facilities such as hospitals, gymnasiums and schools for African countries.[1] Brazil undertakes construction projects such as roads and bridges.[2] Saudi Arabia and the United Arab Emirates have increased their investment in infrastructure such as real estate, hotels and transportation in the Horn of Africa.[3] Türkiye is known as "infrastructure mania" in Africa. In 2021, the projects undertaken by Turkish builders in Sub-Saharan Africa accounted for 17% of all overseas construction projects of Türkiye, up from 0.3% before 2008.[4] To facilitate the travel and logistics between Türkiye and Africa, Turkish Airlines has even opened flights to 61 destinations on the African continent.

In terms of technical assistance, Brazil's aid to Africa is provided mainly in the form of technical cooperation, which primarily involves four major sectors, namely tropical agriculture, tropical medicine, vocational and technical education, and social policy promotion. Türkiye transfers technology to Africa by subsidizing agricultural infrastructure and agricultural research in African countries. India has promoted the "Pan-African Telecommunication Network" plan in the field of information technology, built industrial parks, optical fiber cables, network data processing centers and other facilities in Africa, and provided remote education, telemedicine, e-government, information and entertainment, resource mapping and meteorological services to 53 countries in Africa. [5] India also shares the experience of "green revolution" in the field of agricultural technology, transfers farming technology to African countries for

---

1　Wen Cuiping. *Comparative Study of Chinese and Indian Aid to Africa in the 21st Century* [D]. Beijing: China Foreign Affairs University, 2014.

2　See: http://iwaas.cssn.cn/xslt/fzlt/201508/t20150831_2609356.shtml.

3　Wang Lei. Frequent Moves of Middle East Countries in the "Horn of Africa" [J]. 2018, 1726(11):52-53.

4　Dipama, S., & Parlar, E. (2023). Assessing Turkey-Africa Engagements (APRI Policy Brief 2/2023). Berlin: APRI.

5　Feng Libing, Guo Dongyan, India-Africa Summit and the Construction and Influence of India-Africa Cooperation Mechanism.

agricultural production[1], and implements cotton technical assistance programs in four cotton countries to help these countries improve their cotton planting capacity.

In terms of humanitarian assistance, India mainly provides disaster relief assistance after natural disasters[2]. The Turkish Red Crescent Society provides services to thousands of vulnerable communities by building public facilities such as houses, schools and prayer houses.[3] The United Arab Emirates established Sharjah Charity International to support students, help orphans and poor families, build schools, clinics and mosques, provide emergency relief for victims, dig wells and provide food and medicine.[4]

5.3 Summary

From the aspect of contents of aid, international aid to Africa initially consisted of simple economic, military and humanitarian aid including education and health, which helped and promoted the economic development of African countries to some extent. Since the 1990s, international aid to Africa has gradually emphasized good governance and capacity-building, and at the same time, assistance in the field of scientific and technological innovation has also been enhanced, mainly with a focus on technology, health, poverty alleviation and sustainable development. For example, in international assistance and cooperation, the skills and income of local residents are upgraded by strengthening employment training, the development of education is promoted by the construction of cultural and sports facilities, the living conditions are improved by giving care to vulnerable groups, and the living habits are bettered by drawing attention to nutrition and health. Judging from the aid effect, these aid measures are of great significance to alleviating poverty and promoting

---

1 Wen Cuiping. *Comparative Study of Chinese and Indian Aid to Africa in the 21st Century* [D]. Beijing:China Foreign Affairs University, 2014.

2 Tang Lixia, Li Xiaoyun. A Review of India's Foreign Aid [J]. *South Asian Studies Quarterly*, 2013, 154 (3): 7-12,32,1.

3 Chen Yang. *The Performance, Reasons and Influence of Turkey's Intervention in the Horn of Africa* [D]. Jinhua: Zhejiang Normal University, 2021.

4 Yu Guangling. *A Study on UAE Foreign Aid*, 2010-2016[D]. Shanghai: Shanghai International Studies University, 2018.

sustainable development to some extent. Without international aid, many African countries would not be able to achieve sustained economic growth. The remark that "development depends on aid" vividly reflects the relationship between African countries and foreign aid countries. However, over the past 50 years, even though Africa has received the largest amount of international development assistance, no obvious progress has been registered in economic growth and poverty reduction, and African countries are still in the "aid trap" over a long time.[1]

From a macro point of view, the modern international development assistance system led by the West is facing the pressure of transformation. On the one hand, the system suffers from the poor actual effect of assistance; on the other hand, it is constrained by the overall economic situation, and the "aid fatigue" of Western developed countries is also intensifying. From the microscopic point of view, there are still doubts about the effectiveness of aid. Some traditional donors still attach conditions in the process of aid, such as requiring the recipients to agree to a series of economic and political policies developed by the donors, requiring the services and products provided to developing countries through aid to be purchased and selected from specific countries, requiring the purchase of the donors' products and the projects to be implemented by designated companies or institutions, etc., which increase the cost of project implementation to a certain extent, while aid, in turn, has become a channel and way to promote the export of the donors' products. In addition, international aid to poverty reduction in Africa is also constrained by many conditions, such as the colonial history of recipient countries, the political and strategic relationship between donor countries and recipient countries, the economic level and poverty level of recipient countries, the consistency between recipient countries' political policies and donor countries, and the classification of different countries (heavily indebted poor countries, fragile countries), which has impaired the effect of aid to poverty reduction to some extent in Africa.

More and more active in providing assistance to Africa, emerging economies such as India and Brazil have begun to become new forces in

---

1　See: http://jer.whu.edu.cn/jjgc/5/2016-01-07/2119.html。

providing international development assistance. Unlike the traditional "donor-recipient" master-slave relationship, emerging donors regard themselves as development partners rather than donors, and new development assistance is a parallel process based on experience sharing and knowledge co-creation. The rapid rise of emerging economies in the field of international aid to Africa is of great significance, which challenges the "aid:recipient" paradigm centered on the traditional Western aid concept having lasted for a long time, promotes the change of the concept of international development assistance, makes the international community pay more and more attention to building a new international development cooperation idea of equal development partnership, and then fundamentally changes the structure of international development cooperation.[1]

---

1   Hu Yong. Transformation of International Development Assistance and India's Development Cooperation with Africa [J]. *Foreign Affairs Review* (Journal of China Foreign Affairs University), 2016, 33(6): 131-156.

Chapter 6   New Development and Future of China-Africa Cooperation on Poverty Reduction under the FOCAC Framework

Africa is the region with the most severe poverty issues globally, and is the main area for poverty alleviation efforts worldwide, facing significant challenges in development. China has eradicated extreme poverty, achieving the poverty reduction goals of the United Nations 2030 Agenda for Sustainable Development ten years ahead of schedule, significantly reducing the global poverty population. Within the framework of the Forum on China-Africa Cooperation, China's poverty reduction concepts and approaches have been profoundly recognized by African countries. China and Africa have continuously strengthened their cooperation in poverty reduction, achieving a series of major outcomes. Summarizing and promoting the experiences of China-Africa poverty reduction cooperation will further deepen this collaboration and is of great significance and far-reaching impact for the internationalization of China's poverty reduction experience, the poverty alleviation efforts in Africa, and the global poverty reduction.

6.1   The Foundation of China-Africa Cooperation on Poverty Reduction: China's Great Achievements in Poverty Reduction

China's great achievements in poverty reduction form the basis for China-Africa cooperation on poverty reduction. By the end of 2020, China had achieved the goal of eliminating extreme poverty as scheduled. All of the 98.99 million rural residents,832 counties,and 128,000 villages that fell below the current poverty line have been lifted out of poverty. Regional poverty has been eliminated on the whole. China has achieved the poverty reduction target of the UN's 2030 Agenda for Sustainable Development ten years ahead of schedule. UN Secretary-General António Guterres has acclaimed China as the country making the greatest contribution to global poverty reduction. With such remarkable achievements in poverty reduction, China has not only lifted hundreds of millions of poor out of poverty, but also provided a new approach to global poverty reduction.

6.1.1 China's experience in poverty reduction I: Targeted Poverty Alleviation and Eradication

China has achieved significant success in poverty alleviation through small-scale relief, institutional reform-driven poverty alleviation, large-scale development-oriented poverty alleviation, and village-wide poverty alleviation initiatives. However, it also faces numerous new challenges. On the one hand, the increase in poverty line has led to an increase in the number of poor, while the decline in economic growth has weakened its contribution to reducing poverty. On the other hand, there are still issues such as "blanket coverage", "leakage of poverty alleviation funds", and "significant room for improvement in poverty alleviation efficiency" in the process of poverty alleviation.

Addressing these problems and deficiencies, General Secretary Xi Jinping proposed the concept of targeted poverty alleviation in 2013, and made a series of new decisions and deployments. China's poverty alleviation and development path began to transition from "blanket coverage" to "precision drip irrigation". In 2015, General Secretary Xi issued a general order to win the battle against poverty alleviation. In 2017, at the 19th National Congress of the Communist Party of China, a comprehensively plan was made to targeted poverty alleviation as one of the three critical battles, aiming to decisively win the battle against poverty alleviation. The Chinese government adheres to the strategy of "targeted poverty alleviation and eradication", and has organized and implemented the largest-scale poverty alleviation campaign in human history, [1]achieving comprehensive victory.

The precision poverty alleviation ideology proposed by General Secretary Xi guides the top-level design of precise poverty alleviation and precise poverty eradication strategies. At the macro level, it seeks to optimize the allocation of regional development resources to achieve the practical goal of "helping those in need and delivering genuine assistance" and accelerating the modernization of poverty governance systems and governance capabilities. From the perspective of the main content, the core of precision poverty alleviation lies in achieving "Six precisions", implementing "Five key measure", and solving "Four key issues" in poverty alleviation. Among them, "Six precisions" are the basic requirements of targeted poverty alleviation, which means that to ensure precision in six areas, namely identifying target groups, carefully planning projects, making good use of funds, following through with measures on a household-by-household basis, assigning first secretaries in consideration of local needs, and setting clear objectives. "Five key measures" were launched through which people would be lifted out of poverty, namely increased production, relocation, ecological compensation, education, and social assistance for basic needs. "Four key issues" in poverty alleviation are how to identify the people that need help (who needs help), who should do the work of poverty alleviation (who provides help), how this work should be carried out (how to help), and what standards and procedures should be adopted for exiting poverty (how to be removed from the poverty list). The establishment of a national registration system of the poor and the stationing village work teams are the two main pillars of implementing the macro top-level design and promoting targeted poverty alleviation practices, while tailored policies are the core of targeted poverty alleviation.

On the one hand, to improve the directionality, pertinence, and effectiveness of poverty alleviation, setting up a national registration system to identify poor villages and households, and continuously improving identification work through follow-up work and reevaluation, effectively addressing the issue of "who needs

---

1   Tang Lixia. Development Demonstration and Resource Provision: The Significance of China to the "Global South" [J]. People's Forum: Academic Frontier, 2023 (23): 70-79.

help." At the same time, more than 3 million officials from county-level and above government agencies and state-owned enterprises have been selected and sent to poor village, of which, 206,000 were served as first secretaries of Party committees and 700,000 were served as village officials in 2020. Along with 1.974 million township officials and millions of village officials, they enhanced frontline poverty alleviation forces and effectively solved the issue of "who provides help."

On the other hand, tailored policy is the core of targeted poverty alleviation, as well as a realistic requirement for the relatively underdeveloped areas. China insists on implementing tailored policies based on individuals, regions, poverty causes, and poverty types. Through the implementation of the "Five key measures" and tailored measures, it effectively solves the issue of "how to help". In terms of promoting poverty reduction, the targeted poverty alleviation has also clearly defined standards and procedures for the exiting poverty of poor counties, villages, and populations, guiding localities to scientifically and reasonably formulate rolling poverty alleviation plans and annual plans, organizing third-party evaluations for proposed exit counties, and maintaining stability in relevant policies, effectively solving the issues of "how to be removed from the poverty list." China, with development-oriented poverty alleviation and targeted poverty alleviation as its core, has explored a poverty governance system tested by practice, which can provide effective experience and theoretical references for poverty reduction practices in other developing countries and contribute a Chinese solution to global poverty governance.

6.1.2 China's experience in poverty reduction Ⅱ: Joint work of pro-poor macroeconomic growth and sector-specific poverty alleviation

A consensus has been reached through a large number of studies on China's poverty reduction factors that the most important driver for China's poverty reduction is long-term high-speed economic growth. Over the three decades from 1978 to 2008, China's economy grew at an average annual rate of 9.8%, while the poverty rate dropped from 63% to less than 10%. China's economic growth is pro-poor mainly because rapid economic growth has created a large number of non-agricultural employment opportunities, and a large number of rural people have moved to cities to engage in non-agricultural work. In the background of long-term high-speed economic growth, two major transformations have occurred in the socio-economic structure: a large number of rural people move to non-agricultural sectors, and with the rapid decline of the number and ratio of agricultural working population, the urbanization rate continues to increase; the income structure of rural population has been transformed, featuring the rise of the ratio of wage income and the drop of the ratio of household operating income. These two transformations form the main driving forces for poverty reduction in China.

While maintaining rapid economic growth, the Chinese government has long implemented a supportive policy system targeting poor areas and poor people, so that the fruits of economic growth can benefit more people. In 1980, it set up a fund to support the development of economically underdeveloped areas. Since the establishment of the special fund for poverty alleviation, the scale of poverty alleviation funds provided by the central finance to local governments increased year by year from the initial RMB500 million to RMB139.6 billion in 2020. In 1986, the Chinese government established a special poverty alleviation agency, the leading group for economic development in poor areas under the State Council. Since then, poverty alleviation has become an important function of the Chinese government, marking China's formal entry into the stage of large-scale government-led development-oriented poverty alleviation. The establishment of special poverty alleviation institutions, the arrangement of special financial funds for poverty alleviation and the adoption of special actions for the poor constitute a development-oriented poverty alleviation action system with Chinese characteristics.

6.1.3　China's experience in poverty reduction Ⅲ: The long-term, continuous and phased poverty reduction policy in China

The achievement of poverty reduction in China benefits from the long-term, continuous and phased poverty reduction policy. Since 1980, the Chinese Government has, every few years, issued an overall poverty reduction policy based on the level of socio-economic development then and the characteristics of poverty, determining the key points, objectives, paths and resource guarantees of poverty reduction at the current stage.

In 1984, to address the issue of problem in mountainous areas, areas inhabited by ethnic minorities, old revolutionary areas and remote areas, the Central Committee of the Communist Party of China and the State Council issued the *Circular on Helping Poverty-Stricken Areas*, putting forward the poverty alleviation concept that poverty relief efforts alone are not as good as economic development, and clarifying the development idea of fostering strengths, avoiding weaknesses and focusing on investment, which marks a change in poverty alleviation from simply injecting help to poverty-stricken areas to enabling them to help themselves in China. In 1987, the *Circular on Strengthening Economic Development in Poverty-Stricken Areas* put forward the goal of solving the problem of food and clothing for most people in poverty-stricken areas during the period of the Seventh Five-Year Plan. In 1994, the *National Plan for Poverty Alleviation in the Eighth Seven-Year Plan (1994-2000)*, the first programmatic document on poverty alleviation in China's history with clear objectives, targets, measures and deadlines, was issued, which clearly stated that it should mobilize all kinds of resources and all sectors in efforts to basically solve the problem of food and clothing for the 80 million poor people in rural areas in about seven years (by the end of 2000). In 1996, the *Decision of the Central Committee of the Communist Party of China and the State Council on Solving the Problem of Food and Clothing for the Poor in Rural Areas* stated that,it should continue to increase support for poverty alleviation and ensure the successful completion of the Eighth Seven-Year Priority Poverty Alleviation Program by 2000. In the *China Rural Poverty Alleviation and Development Program (2001-2010)* promulgated in 2001, consolidating the achievements of ensuring proper food and clothing was set to be one of the important goals. The focus of poverty alleviation work was thus shifted from centering on fighting poverty to the combination of fighting and maintaining achievements, and the targeted objectives for poverty alleviation were extended from poor counties to poor villages and poor households. In 2011, to achieve the goal of building a well-off society in an all-round way, the

Outline of Development-driven Poverty Alleviation in Rural Areas (2011-2020) was issued, putting forward the goal of ensuring adequate food and clothing, access to compulsory education, basic medical services and safe housing for poor rural residents ("The Two Assurances and Three Guarantees"). The *Decision on Winning the Battle against Poverty* issued in 2015 further clarified the goal of eradicating absolute poverty under the current poverty line by 2020, and realizing the goal of "The Two Assurances and Three Guarantees." After winning the battle against poverty in 2020, the Chinese Government did not stop supporting the underdeveloped areas and low-income population. In the background of comprehensively promoting the rural revitalization strategy, the government set up a five-year transition period to consolidate the achievements of the fight against poverty.

6.1.4 China's experience in poverty reduction Ⅳ: Targeted and inclusive poverty reduction tools

In China's poverty reduction actions, great importance has always been attached to the effectiveness of resources, with both inclusive and targeted policy arrangements in the use of poverty reduction instruments. Since 2000, with the improvement of economic development level and the enhancement of financial capacity, more and more inclusive policies have been implemented, including agricultural subsidies, basic endowment insurance for urban and rural residents, basic medical insurance for urban and rural residents, and free compulsory education. Illness and school dropout used to be the important reasons causing the poverty of rural households. The implementation of these policies has reduced rural residents' medical and educational burdens. The coverage of inclusive endowment insurance policy for residents, the agricultural subsidy policy based on land distribution and the minimum living security system achieving nearly 100%, among others, have increased rural residents' transfer income, which has become the main source of income for many rural poor people unable to work, playing an important role in ensuring basic security.

Targeted policy is also an important factor for the effectiveness of China's poverty reduction policy. There are two main mechanisms for targeted policy arrangements in China. One is regional targeting, which is employed to allocate central financial resources for poverty alleviation; the other is group targeting to identify the poor and provide them with targeted poverty alleviation measures. Regional targeting mainly identifies poor counties, which is a key endeavor for allocating various poverty alleviation resources. China's county-level targeted policy began in 1986, when 331 state-level poverty-stricken counties were identified. Since then, three major adjustments have been made, and the number of state-level poverty-stricken counties has changed accordingly. China has also implemented strict group targeting. Registration of poverty-stricken populations was the method of targeting adopted by China at the stage of targeted poverty alleviation. To accurately identify the rural poor, the Chinese Government took rural residents' per capita net income in 2013 as the poverty line, and at the same time takes clothing, food, housing, education and medical care which are easy to identify as indicators to comprehensively evaluate the poor. By the end of 2014, 29.48 million poor households and 89.62 million poor people had been identified.[1] Since 2015, measures has been taken to see if anyone is not covered every year, and a total of 98.99 million poor people have been identified and registered. In addition to the inclusive support of the registered poor, additional support in housing security, employment, education and medical care, and industrial development are offered to them.

6.1.5 China's experience in poverty reduction Ⅴ: Development-driven and protection-oriented poverty reduction actions

Development-driven poverty alleviation is an important feature of poverty reduction in China, which is mainly manifested in three aspects. First, improve the industrial development capacity of poverty-stricken areas and promote their regional overall economic development by upgrading the infrastructure conditions in these areas; second, the self-development ability of poor rural residents can be improved by enhancing their ability to participate in employment and industrial development, including skills training and offering industrial development support; third, cultivate poor rural residents' financial awareness

---

1 The State Council's Report on Poverty Alleviation[EB/OL]. (2017-08-29)[2023-07-19].http://www.npc.gov.cn/zgrdw/npc/xinwen/2017-08/29/content_2027584.htm.

and provide financial support for them to develop their businesses by introducing the micro-credit model, cultivating and developing community mutual funds. In recent years, the poverty alleviation models, such as e-commerce, tourism, photovoltaic and assets poverty alleviation, are all promoted by the Chinese government in the hope of transforming the limited resources in the hands of poor rural residents into assets through the power of the market, so that they can also become main players of the market. A considerable proportion of the poor is unable to work, so subsistence allowances are provided for those unable to shake off poverty through their own efforts alone. China has also taken protection-oriented measures, including various subsidy policies and the minimum living security system, which are mainly based on cash transfer payment and social security network construction.

6.1.6　China's experience in poverty reduction Ⅵ: Government-led and social participation of poverty reduction

Poverty reduction in China is led by the government, while social participation is also encouraged. The Chinese government, which is able to powerfully mobilize the whole society, has assembled a large amount of social resources to build a mechanism of social participation in poverty alleviation with Chinese characteristics. The cooperation between eastern and western regions, which began in 1996, has helped to establish a formal mechanism for the eastern developed region to support the development of the western underdeveloped region. Poverty alleviation assistance directed to designated targets, which officially began in 2012, has involved the Party, the government, the military, large and medium-sized state-owned enterprises, other political parties, and colleges and universities in poverty alleviation. The campaign of "Ten Thousand Enterprises Helping Ten Thousand Villages", which started in 2015, has established a relationship between private enterprises and poor villages. To create a good social environment for the whole society to participate in poverty alleviation, the General Office of the State Council issued the *Opinions on Further Mobilizing All Social Forces to Participate in Poverty Alleviation and Development* in 2014. Voluntary activities and public welfare actions for poverty alleviation have gradually become important forces in poverty alleviation.

6.2 China's Aid to Africa

Africa has always been a key region for China's foreign assistance. According to the White Paper *China and Africa in the New Era: A Partnership of Equals*, China's foreign aid from 2013 to 2018 totaled RMB270.2 billion, 44.65% of which flowed to African countries in the form of grants, interest-free loans and concessional loans (see Figure 6-1). Compared with other regions, Africa has received the largest scale and amount of aid from China. China's aid to Africa, involving all aspects of economic and social life, is widely welcomed and supported by African governments and people. China has announced to exempt certain African countries from outstanding debts incurred in the form of interest-free Chinese government loans due by the end of 2018. The exemption were granted to Africa's least developed countries, heavily indebted and poor countries, landlocked and small island developing countries that have diplomatic relations with China. During the COVID-19 pandemic, China cancelled the outstanding debts of 15 African countries in the form of interest-free Chinese government loans due by the end of 2020. In terms of content and methods, China's aid to Africa mainly has three characteristics.

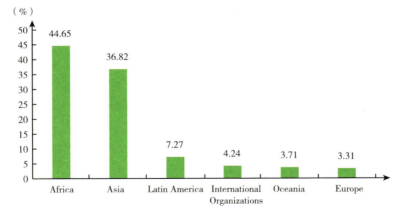

Figure 6-1   Distribution of China's Foreign Aid Funds by Region and International Organization, 2013-2018

Source: (White Paper) *China and Africa in the New Era: A Partnership of Equals.*

First, China's aid to Africa is an important source of funds for infrastructure construction in Africa. China attaches great importance to the role of infrastructure development in poverty reduction in Africa. a) Fully considering the fact that most African countries are developing countries with poor infrastructure conditions and lack of advanced production technology and equipment in infrastructure construction, China's aid to Africa focuses on infrastructure, which accounts for about 68.64% of the total aid.[1] China is currently involved in infrastructure projects of 35 African countries, involving power generation (especially hydropower), transportation (especially railways), information and communication technology (mainly equipment supply) , and other fields. From 2000 to 2020, China helped African countries build more than 13,000 km of roads and railway and more than 80 large-scale power facilities, and funded over 130 medical facilities, 45 sports venues and over 170 schools. It also trained more than 160,000 talents for Africa, and built a series of flagship projects including the AU Conference Center.[2] b) China's aid to Africa focuses on the role of infrastructure in poverty reduction. Helping African countries to improve their infrastructure by providing them with funds, technology, equipment and talents has a positive effect on promoting African countries' economic growth, thus improving the poverty reduction effect.

Second, China attaches great importance to assistance with people's livelihood, and plays an active role in agriculture, health, education and other sectors. By providing assistance and sharing social development experience, China helps African countries to improve their comprehensive social development and create internal driving forces for economic development in Africa. In the field of food security, China not only attaches importance to enhancing the agricultural production capacity of African countries in aid, but

---

1　Hu Jianmei, Shan Lei. China's Aid to Africa, Infrastructure and Economic Growth of Recipient Countries: An Empirical Analysis Based on the Mediation Effect Model [J]. *International Economic Cooperation*, 2022(5):53-68,95.

2　*China and Africa in the New Era: A Partnership of Equals*, see: http://www.scio.gov.cn/zfbps/ ndhf/2021n_2242/202207/t20220704_130719.html.

also continuously cultivates agricultural research and technical personnel. By the end of 2019, 81 agricultural technical expert teams had been sent to 37 Asian and African countries with a total of 808 persons, and 22 agricultural technology demonstration centers had been built in African countries to test and popularize high-yield new varieties for relevant countries, guide farmers to improve their productivity and enhance their confidence in development. In the sector of health, following the African epidemic, China launched the most extensive and difficult humanitarian aid operation since the founding of the People's Republic of China in 1949, providing 120 batches of emergency anti-epidemic materials such as testing reagents, protective clothing and ventilators to 53 African countries and the African Union. In the sector of education, from 1999 to 2018, the total number of African students studying in China maintained a high-speed growth trend. By 2018, African students had amounted to 81,562.[1] Among them, the number of international students from East Africa, West Africa and South Africa significantly surpasses that in North Africa and Central Africa.[2] Additionally, China has increased its assistance to non-vocational education and established the China-UN Trust Fund for Statistical Capacity Development to provide training for nearly 900 government statisticians for 59 developing countries.

Third, China's aid to Africa not only depends on bilateral channels, but also stresses multilateral cooperation and strengthens cooperation with the FAO, trust funds, the AU and other organizations. a) China has stepped up its donations, increasing the amount of donations to such institutions as the International Development Association of the World Bank, the Asian Development Fund and the Global Environment Facility. By the end of 2018, China had donated US$939 million and RMB800 million to the African Development Bank Group to support the development of poverty

---

1   See: http://www.moe.gov.cn/jyb_xwfb/gzdt_gzdt/s5987/201904/t20190412_377692.html.

2   Li Bing, Huang Wenjie. A Study on the Developmental Trend and of African Students Studying in China: Statistical Analysis Based on the Data from 1999 to 2018 [J]. *Journal of Yunnan Normal University* (Teaching and Research Edition of Chinese as a Foreign Language), 2021,19(6):82-89.

reduction, food security, trade, medical care, disaster management, education and environmental protection in Africa. b) China attaches importance to strengthening exchanges and cooperation with the World Bank, the African Development Bank and other bilateral and multilateral financial institutions to jointly provide financial support to the countries concerned. For example, China has invested US$2 billion to set up the Africa Common Growth Fund with the African Development Bank, covering water supply and sanitation, transportation, agricultural development, youth employment and other sectors.[1]

With the in-depth development of the Belt & Road Initiative and the Global Development Initiative, China has been fulfilling its commitment to continuously increase its aid to Africa, expand its investment and financing cooperation with Africa, and strengthen mutually beneficial cooperation with African countries in agriculture, manufacturing and other sectors, helping African countries to turn their resource advantages into development advantages and realize independent and sustainable development.

6.3   Policy Framework and Evolution of China-Africa Cooperation on Poverty Reduction

The policy framework for promoting and guiding China-Africa cooperation on poverty reduction mainly involves two levels. The first level is the goal of global development cooperation, the most important of which is the United Nations framework for sustainable development. The second level is the cooperation strategy and framework reached between China and Africa, which mainly includes the Forum on China-Africa Cooperation and its follow-up action plan, *China's Africa Policy Paper*, and the *Program for Strengthening China-Africa Cooperation on Poverty Reduction*, among others.

---

1   *China's International Development Cooperation in the New Era*, see:http://www.scio.gov.cn/zfbps/ndhf/2021n_2242/202207/t20220704_130669.html.

6.3.1 The United Nations framework for sustainable development and China's response plan

In September 2010, at the United Nations Millennium Development Goals Summit, many countries advocated the start of discussions on the post-2015 development agenda. After several years of discussions and consultations, the 2015 United Nations General Assembly put forward a framework for sustainable development. The United Nations Framework for Sustainable Development consists of 17 sustainable development goals and 169 targets. It is worth noting that, poverty and hunger are presented as a goal in the Millennium Development Goals, but the sustainable development framework separates poverty and hunger into two sustainable development goals, namely Goal 1"End poverty in all its forms everywhere" and Goal 2 "Eradicate hunger, achieve food security, improve nutrition and promote sustainable agriculture".

The United Nations framework for sustainable development has become a universal policy framework and goal orientation to guide countries' domestic development and international development cooperation. China has successively issued *China's Position Paper on Implementing the 2030 Agenda for Sustainable Development*, *China's National Plan on Implementation of the 2030 Agenda for Sustainable Development*, and *China's Progress Report on Implementing the 2030 Agenda for Sustainable Development*, clearly stating that China will continue to deepen South-South cooperation and help other developing countries to implement the 2030 Agenda for Sustainable Development. In the *China's National Plan on Implementing the 2030 Agenda for Sustainable Development*, in particular, the Chinese government has put forward corresponding commitments and plans for the targets with international significance for poverty reduction in Goals 1, 2, 3, 4, 9, 10, 11, 14 and 17. The National Plan has become an important guiding plan for China to promote global international development cooperation and realization of sustainable development goals, which is also of guiding significance to China-Africa cooperation on poverty reduction (see Table 6-1).

Table 6-1   Some Chinese Approaches for Implementing the Sustainable Development Agenda

Goals	Targets	Chinese approaches
Goal 1. End poverty in all its forms everywhere	1.a Ensure significant mobilization of resources from a variety of sources, including through enhanced development cooperation, in order to provide adequate and predictable means for developing countries, in particular least developed countries, to implement programmes and policies to end poverty in all its dimensions	Implement the South-South Cooperation Assistance Fund and the "Six 100 Projects" announced by President Xi Jinping during his attendance at the United Nations Sustainable Development Summit in September 2015, to help other developing countries develop their economies, improve people's livelihood and eradicate poverty. Promote international cooperation on poverty reduction on a larger scale, at a higher level and at a deeper level under the framework of foreign aid
	1.b Create sound policy frameworks at the national, regional and international levels, based on pro-poor and gender-sensitive development strategies, to support accelerated investment in poverty eradication actions	Employ such platforms as "High-level Forum on Poverty Reduction and Development", "China-ASEAN Forum on Social Development and Poverty Reduction" and "Forum on China-Africa Cooperation – Sub-forum on Poverty Reduction and Development" to share China's ideas, experiences and practices in poverty reduction and explore ways to introduce more investment into poverty reduction
Goal 2. Eradicate hunger, achieve food security, improve nutrition and promote sustainable agriculture	2.a Increase investment, including through enhanced international cooperation, in rural infrastructure, agricultural research and extension services, technology development and plant and livestock gene banks in order to enhance agricultural productive capacity in developing countries, in particular least developed countries	China had planned to cooperate with the FAO to implement about 10 national South-South cooperation projects by 2022, and cooperate with countries and regions of the Belt and Road Initiative in the fields of crop breeding, animal husbandry, fishery, agricultural product processing and trade under the Framework of Jointly Promoting Agricultural Cooperation
Goal 3. Ensure healthy lives and promote the well-being for all at all ages	3.c Substantially increase health financing and the recruitment, development, training and retention of the health workforce in developing countries, especially in least developed countries and small island developing States	Increase assistance to other developing countries, especially the least developed countries and small island developing countries, in health care facilities, professional and technical training, and help other developing countries to strengthen financing in the health sector

Continued

Goals	Targets	Chinese approaches
Goal 4. Ensure inclusive and equitable quality education and promote lifelong learning opportunities for all	4.b By 2020, substantially expand globally the number of scholarships available to developing countries, in particular least developed countries, small island developing States and African countries, for enrolment in higher education, including vocational training and information and communication technology, technical, engineering and scientific programmes, in developed countries and other developing countries	Implement President Xi Jinping's initiative of "providing 120,000 training and 150,000 scholarships to developing countries and training 500,000 professional technicians for developing countries by 2020" announced during his attendance at the United Nations Sustainable Development Summit in September 2015. For other developing countries, especially the least developed countries, small island countries and African countries, it should provide more consulting and training in human resources, development planning and economic policies, and strengthen cooperation and assistance in science, technology and education
	4.c By 2030, substantially increase the supply of qualified teachers, including through international cooperation for teacher training in developing countries, especially least developed countries and small island developing States	Provide short-term education program and training for other developing countries, and actively consider the needs of the least developed countries and small island countries for teachers in training course planning and enrollment
Goal 9. Build resilient infrastructure, promote inclusive and sustainable industrialization and foster innovation	9.2　Promote inclusive and sustainable industrialization and, by 2030, significantly raise industry's share of employment and gross domestic product, in line with national circumstances, and double its share in least developed countries	Promote Belt and Road Initiative cooperation and promote the industrialization development of other developing countries, especially the least developed countries, through international cooperation in production capacity and equipment manufacturing. Jointly promote the development of small- and medium-sized enterprises by building international cooperation parks (zones) for small- and medium-sized enterprises
	9.a Facilitate sustainable and resilient infrastructure development in developing countries through enhanced financial, technological and technical support to African countries, least developed countries, landlocked developing countries and small island developing States	Under the framework of South-South Cooperation, increase technical support and assistance to other developing countries to help them strengthen sustainable infrastructure construction and improve disaster resistance and other related capacity building

Continued

Goals	Targets	Chinese approaches
Goal 10. Reduce inequalities within and among countries	10.b Encourage official development assistance and financial flows, including foreign direct investment, to States where the need is greatest, in particular least developed countries, African countries, small island developing States and landlocked developing countries, in accordance with their national plans and programmes	Urge developed countries to fulfill their official development assistance commitments and provide more financial, technical and capacity-building support to developing countries. Enrich foreign aid models and provide more consulting and training for other developing countries in human resources, development planning and economic policies
Goal 11. Make cities and human settlements inclusive, safe, resilient and sustainable	11.c Support least developed countries, including through financial and technical assistance, in building sustainable and resilient buildings utilizing local materials	Support the least developed countries to build sustainable infrastructure, promote technical cooperation with relevant countries in the field of energy-saving buildings, and help the least developed countries train local skilled workers
Goal 13. Take urgent action to combat climate change and its impacts	13.b Promote mechanisms for raising capacity for effective climate change-related planning and management in least developed countries and small island developing States, including focusing on women, youth and local and marginalized communities	Through the South-South Cooperation Fund on Climate Change established in China, help the least developed countries and small island developing States to strengthen their capacity building to cope with climate change, including the overall planning and management of the response work. Pay attention to the special difficulties of women, youth, local communities and marginalized communities in the above-mentioned countries in combating climate change, and provide assistance within their capacity
Goal 14. Conserve and sustainably use the oceans, seas and marine resources	14.7 By 2030, increase the economic benefits to small island developing States and least developed countries from the sustainable use of marine resources, including through sustainable management of fisheries, aquaculture and tourism	Provide aquaculture technical support to the least developed countries and small island countries through South-South Cooperation, including promoting aquaculture energy saving and emission reduction, circulating aquaculture techno-logy, cage aquaculture emission reduc-tion technology, etc. Promote South-South Cooperation in sustainable fishe-ries management and tourism

Continued

Goals	Targets	Chinese approaches
Goal 17. Strengthen the means of implementation and revitalize the global partnership for sustainable development	17.2　Developed countries to implement fully their official development assistance commitments, including the commitment by many developed countries to achieve the target of 0.7% of ODA/GNI to developing countries and 0.15% to 0.20% of ODA/GNI to least developed countries; ODA providers are encouraged to consider setting a target to provide at least 0.20% of ODA/GNI to least developed countries	Promote countries to implement the *Addis Ababa Action Agenda*, urge developed countries to fully fulfill their official development assistance commitments, and set a timetable and road map to help developing countries in terms of funds, technology and capacity building
	17.3　Mobilize additional financial resources for developing countries from multiple sources	Actively participate in South-South Cooperation, raise the South-South Cooperation assistance fund, and promote the China-United Nations Peace and Development Fund to play an active role. Promote the construction of the AIIB and the New Development Bank, give play to the role of the Silk Road Fund, and attract international funds to build an open, diversified and win-win financial cooperation platform
	17.16　Enhance the Global Partnership for Sustainable Development, complemented by multi-stakeholder partnerships that mobilize and share knowledge, expertise, technology and financial resources, to support the achievement of the Sustainable Development Goals in all countries, in particular developing countries	Actively participate in global development cooperation, and promote the establishment of a more equal and balanced global development partnership. Maintain the main channel position of North-South cooperation, call for South-South cooperation and tripartite cooperation to play a greater role, and welcome international organizations, the private sector and civil society to participate in the implementation of sustainable development goals

Source: Based on the *National Plan of China for Implementing the 2030 Agenda for Sustainable Development* and other related plans.

6.3.2　Evolution of China-Africa Cooperation on Poverty Reduction under the Framework of the Forum on China-Africa Cooperation (FOCAC)

China-Africa cooperation on poverty reduction is mainly carried out under the Framework of the Forum on China-Africa Cooperation (FOCAC). The FOCAC, a collective dialogue mechanism between China and Africa within the scope of South-South cooperation founded in 2000, has become an important institutionalized framework and an important communication platform for China-Africa cooperation. Since the first Forum on China-Africa Cooperation in 2000, all the ministerial meetings of the forum have taken poverty reduction as an important discussion content, issuing a series of follow-up action plans. Under the Framework of the FOCAC, China and Africa have carried out various types of cooperation on poverty reduction, achieving gratifying results. China-Africa cooperation on poverty reduction under the Framework of the FOCAC has experienced three stages of development:

At the stage of reaching consensus, from the first to the third FOCAC, China and Africa began to reach a consensus on poverty reduction, but no special cooperation mechanism had yet been formed. The *Program of China-Africa Cooperation on Economic and Social Development* issued by the first FOCAC clearly focused on areas related to poverty reduction, such as debt relief, agricultural cooperation, medical and health care, and human resources development. The *Declaration of the Beijing Summit of the Forum on China-Africa Cooperation* issued by the third Forum emphasized the need to strengthen China-Africa cooperation in the field of poverty reduction and deepen China-Africa cooperation on poverty reduction. Its follow-up action plan, the *FOCAC Beijing Action Plan (2007-2009)*, put forward that both sides believe that strengthening agricultural cooperation will play a positive role in eradicating poverty, promoting development and ensuring food security.[1] The two sides gradually deepened their understanding and attention to "poverty reduction", and many fields related to poverty reduction have been listed as priorities of cooperation, but "cooperation on poverty reduction" was never been discussed as an independent topic, and the exchange and cooperation mechanism was yet to be established.

At the stage of experience exchange, the fourth to sixth FOCAC began to focus on the exchange and sharing of poverty reduction experience, and China-Africa cooperation on poverty reduction also began to become institutionalized.

---

1   The FOCAC, the FOCAC Beijing Action Plan (2007-2009). See: http://www.focac.org.cn/zywx/zywj/200909/t20090917_8044399.htm.

In the *FOCAC* Sharm *el-Sheikh Action Plan (2010-2012)* issued by the 4th Forum, the cooperation on poverty reduction appeared as a separate section in the plan for the first time, and both sides realized that "eradicating poverty is an arduous task for both sides" and "will step up cooperation and exchanges in the field of poverty reduction".[1] In 2010, the first China-Africa Conference on Poverty Reduction and Development was held, and the two sides conducted in-depth discussions on a wide range of topics, such as the Millennium Development Goals, China's poverty reduction experience, Africa's new poverty alleviation strategy, and South-South cooperation. Since then, cooperation on poverty reduction has officially become one of the important topics of China-Africa cooperation, and the China-Africa Conference on Poverty Reduction and Development, an intergovernmental dialogue and exchange mechanism, has also been initially established. In 2015, the *FOCAC Johannesburg Action Plan (2016-2018)* released by the 6th Forum on China-Africa Cooperation listed "experience exchange on poverty reduction" as one of the important plans. The China-Africa Conference on Poverty Reduction and Development was formally incorporated into the overall FOCAC to become a supporting mechanism of the Forum. The establishment of the China-Africa poverty reduction exchange and cooperation mechanism has played a significant role in ensuring the implementation of the cooperation plan between the two sides.

At the stage of deeping cooperation, since the Sixth Forum on China-Africa Cooperation, China-Africa cooperation on poverty reduction has entered the stage of deeping cooperation, with poverty reduction demonstration projects and projects implemented, and the cooperation mechanism improved and the partnership further deepened. The *FOCAC Beijing Action Plan (2019-2021)* issued by the Sixth Forum proposed to "rally extensive participation of Chinese and African enterprises, social organizations, research institutes and other parties in China-Africa poverty-reduction cooperation, and work to gradually establish multi-tiered dialogue mechanisms between the government and the society of the two sides", promote the exchange of poverty reduction experience, and

---

1 The FOCAC. The FOCAC Sharm el-Sheikh Action Plan (2010-2012). See: http://et.china-embassy. gov.cn/chn/zgxx/policy/200911/t20091112_7213871.htm.

implement poverty reduction demonstration projects and pilot projects. At the Eighth FOCAC Ministerial Conference, "Nine Programs" were put forward, with "the poverty reduction and agricultural development program" as one of the key programs, which, with a focus on agricultural cooperation, aimed to promote poverty reduction by implementing agricultural cooperation projects, conducting technical exchanges, building demonstration villages for agricultural development and poverty reduction in China and Africa, and supporting Chinese enterprises in Africa to assume social responsibilities. The forms of cooperation thus became more diversified.

In addition, with the constant advancement of global poverty reduction and development, global poverty reduction goals and issues related to China-Africa cooperation on poverty reduction have moved from "poverty reduction" to "poverty reduction and rural development". The theme of the 2023 International Forum on Poverty Governance and Global Development (Nujiang) and the 2021 China-Africa Conference on Poverty Reduction and Development both focused on rural development. In the *FOCAC Dakar Action Plan (2022-2024)*, the theme of cooperation on poverty reduction has also changed from "exchange of poverty reduction experience" to "cooperation and exchange of poverty reduction and rural development", indicating that "rural development" and "rural revitalization" have become the new blueprint for global poverty reduction.

China's Africa Policy Paper issued in 2015 clearly regards "sharing and popularizing poverty reduction experience" as one of the main contents of China-Africa cooperation, which is consistent with the focus of cooperation on poverty reduction put forward in the above-mentioned FOCAC.

6.4   Ways of China-Africa Cooperation on Poverty Reduction and Development

6.4.1   Cooperation and exchange mechanisms become more mature

With the deepening of China-Africa cooperation on poverty reduction and development, multi-tiered dialogue mechanisms between the government and the society of the two sides on poverty reduction and rural development under the overall FOCAC framework has been gradually established, which has become an important platform for cooperation on poverty reduction and experience exchange.

In terms of **intergovernmental dialogue**, the FOCAC and its supporting mechanism, the China-Africa Conference on Poverty Reduction and Development, have become a stable intergovernmental collective dialogue mechanism and an important platform for China-Africa cooperation on poverty reduction and development, providing important support for China-Africa official cooperation. The Conference gives counsel for China-Africa cooperation on poverty reduction and deepens China-Africa exchanges and cooperation in the field of poverty reduction and development by inviting government officials, representatives of international organizations, experts and scholars, representatives of enterprises, representatives of civil society and other groups to attend the Conference. At the 12th China-Africa Conference on Poverty Reduction and Development in 2022, the China-Africa Alliance for Poverty Alleviation was formally inaugurated, further deepening the China-Africa partnership.

As an important mechanism for the exchange of experience in poverty reduction between China and Africa, academic seminars such as the **China-Africa Advanced Seminar on Sharing Development Experience** also provide an important platform for the exchange and promotion of experience in poverty reduction between China and Africa.

A multi-tiered and multi-field dialogue mechanism for poverty reduction consisting of non-governmental organizations, entrepreneurs and think tanks has been gradually established, and **non-governmental dialogues have become increasingly frequent**. The China-Africa People's Forum has made significant contributions to promoting pragmatic cooperation between China and Africa. The China-Africa Think Tanks Forum provides support for the wisdom of China and Africa to help the governance of the two sides. The China-Africa People's Forum and the China-Africa Think Tanks Forum have become institutionalized supporting events for the FOCAC. In 2021, the Alliance of Chinese Business in Africa for Social Responsibilities (ACBASR) was formally established; in 2022, the China-Africa Vocational Education Federation was established and a China-Africa Vocational Education Forum will be held.

It can thus be concluded that a multi-tiered dialogue mechanism between China and Africa on poverty reduction and rural development is becoming more and more mature, which provides a good foundation for China and Africa to strengthen cooperation on poverty reduction and development, promote the exchange of experience in poverty reduction, and actively address global challenges in poverty reduction and development.

6.4.2 The content and form of cooperation has become diversified

The content of China-Africa cooperation on poverty reduction has gradually extended to specific and multi-sector cooperation projects. According to the main documents issued by the FOCAC, the third to Sixth FOCAC mainly proposed to carry out the exchange and dialogue on China-Africa poverty reduction experience by holding seminars, training courses and forums, with the main purpose of letting African countries know and understand China's poverty reduction experience. The Seventh and Eighth FOCAC successively proposed to implement the "Cooperation Plan for Poverty Alleviation and Agricultural Development" and the "Program for Poverty Alleviation and Agricultural Development". It can be therefore concluded that China and Africa started to gradually implement some specific cooperation on poverty reduction projects. The "Cooperation Plan for Poverty Alleviation and Agricultural Development" focuses on people's livelihood projects such as infrastructure construction, and implements the "Happy Life Project" and poverty reduction projects with women and children as the main beneficiaries in Africa. The Program for Poverty Alleviation and Agricultural Development, with a focus on agricultural cooperation, promotes poverty reduction by implementing agricultural cooperation projects, sending agricultural experts, conducting technical exchanges, building demonstration villages for agricultural development and poverty reduction, and launching "Hundred Enterprises and Thousands of Villages" activities for Chinese enterprises in Africa. The forms of cooperation have become more diversified. The first batch of four China-Africa joint centers for modern agricultural technology exchange, demonstration and training had been established[1]; the Demonstration Village of Agricultural Development and Poverty Alleviation in Central Africa in Matanjitisa Village, Nakuru County, Kenya was established, and the project of the Nigerian agricultural technology demonstration center supported by China was put into operation.

The two sides also continue to promote cooperation in traditional areas such as infrastructure construction. During the COVID-19 pandemic, China provided 189 million doses of COVID-19 vaccine to 27 African countries[2]. The Government of China is also committed to improving the level of human resources in Africa through vocational education cooperation, sending experts, holding training courses, and coming to China for exchanges. In recent years, China-Africa vocational education cooperation has become an important way of human resources cooperation between China and Africa. Since the proposal of "Future of Africa: a project for China-Africa cooperation on vocational education", China and Africa have formed 15 pairs of partnerships, jointly trained more than 200 African students, provided training and practical training for more than 300 African principals and backbone teachers,[3] and trained local talents with high technical skills for Africa.

China-Africa cooperation on poverty reduction has been expanding. In addition to traditional areas such as infrastructure construction, agricultural cooperation and human resources upgrading, the development cooperation between the two sides in capacity cooperation, clean energy, climate change, digital economy also plays a role in poverty reduction, which will help enhance Africa's capacity for sustainable development and thus promote poverty reduction. For example, the two sides held a seminar on the construction of the Great Green Wall in Africa, and organized officials from African countries

---

1　China-Africa Vocational Education Federation is Inaugurated. See: https://news.eol.cn/yaowen/202205/t20220512_2225019.shtml.

2　The FOCAC. The FOCAC-Beijing Action Plan (2019-2021). See: http://www.cidca.gov.cn/2018-09/07/c_129949203.htm.

3　China contributes to the construction of the Great Green Wall in Africa. See: http://www.focac.org.cn/chn/zfzs/202205/t20220512_10685226.htm.

to participate in the study of desertification prevention, drought relief and sustainable land management[1].

6.5   Future of China-Africa Cooperation on Poverty Reduction: Direction and Vision

At the end of November 2021, the Eighth FOCAC Ministerial Conference adopted China-Africa Cooperation Vision 2035 (hereinafter referred to as *Vision*), which put forward the main framework of China-Africa cooperation in the next 15 years and pointed out the direction for the future of China-Africa cooperation. According to the objectives and tasks set in the *Vision*, China-Africa cooperation will focus on supporting Africa to cultivate internal growth capacity, promote the transformation and upgrading of China-Africa cooperation, improve quality and efficiency, consolidate traditional cooperation, open up new fields, innovate cooperation models, and promote the high-quality development of China-Africa cooperation on promoting the Belt and Road Initiative.[2]

6.5.1   Continue to deeper China-Africa cooperation on poverty reduction

Africa's development is facing three bottlenecks: lagging infrastructure, lack of talents, and shortage of funds. In recent years, the relevant policy framework of China-Africa cooperation on poverty reduction has continuously defined the key points of cooperation between the two sides. In the future, China will deepen its economic and trade cooperation with Africa through a series of measures, such as boosting Africa's industrialization, helping Africa's agricultural modernization, fully participating in Africa's infrastructure construction and strengthening China-Africa financial cooperation, and strengthen China-Africa cooperation on poverty reduction and development through such measures as increasing development aid to Africa, supporting Africa to strengthen public health prevention and control system and capacity building, expanding cooperation in education and human

---

1   China helps build the "African Green Great Wall". See:http://www.focac.org.cn/chn/zfzs/202205/t20220512_10685226.htm.

2   See: the China-Africa Cooperation Vision 2035.

resources development, and sharing and popularizing experience in poverty reduction.

6.5.2 Actively support African countries in capacity building for poverty reduction and development

Over the past decades, the poverty problem in China could not have been solved without the leadership of government. By fully leveraging the advantages of the government in integrating social resources and formulating national development strategies, a series of policies have been introduced and economic and social development models have been selected to promote the national poverty reduction process and improve the effect. This capability is not only reflected in governance capacity, but also in financial capacity and resource mobilization capacity, that the Chinese government is able to arrange large-scale funds for targeted poverty alleviation actions. However, general government expenditures of African countries depend on international development assistance, making it even more difficult to invest in targeted poverty alleviation. In addition to the level of specific action plans, more attention should be paid to capacity building for poverty reduction and development. In the future, in China-Africa cooperation on poverty reduction, more consideration can be given to promote the capacity building regarding poverty reduction and development in African countries, and enhance the effect of Africa's local poverty reduction actions.

6.5.3 Strengthen cooperation on "small and beautiful" poverty reduction projects

Attention should be focused on village-based poverty reduction demonstration to expand support for the construction of poverty reduction demonstration villages, and build demonstration villages in Africa that successfully draw on China's poverty reduction experience. The form of villages in Africa is similar to that in China, so carrying out village-level poverty reduction demonstrations on the African continent and mobilizing Chinese enterprises to participate will help African countries to focus not only on the poor, but also on the areas where the poor live, taking regional development as a prerequisite for poverty reduction;

meanwhile, such efforts will also help African countries to understand that poverty reduction is not just the responsibility of the government or just seeking international development assistance, but enterprises and the private sector can also play an important role in poverty reduction, thus expanding the ability of African countries to mobilize social capital and solving the shortage of resources in poverty reduction.

6.5.4   Continue to carry out various forms of exchange activities on poverty reduction and expand the participants of exchange

Various exchange activities on poverty reduction between China and Africa have helped African countries to know and understand China's poverty reduction experience. More and more African countries come to recognize the effectiveness of China's poverty reduction experience and show a strong willingness to learn. It in needed to organize different forms of exchange activities for different groups, and expand the subjects participating in various exchange activities, meanwhile, letting more people know about China's experience in poverty reduction.